WHEN YOUR WORLD MAKES NO SENSE

BY
DR. HENRY CLOUD

A Division of Thomas Nelson Publishers
Nashville

Published in Nashville, Tennessee, by Oliver-Nelson Books, a division of Thomas Nelson, Inc., Publishers, and distributed in Canada by Lawson Falle, Ltd., Cambridge, Ontario.

Unless otherwise noted, the Bible version used in this publication is THE NEW KING JAMES VERSION. Copyright © 1979, 1980, 1982, Thomas Nelson, Inc., Publishers.

Scripture quotations noted NASB are from the New American Standard Bible, © 1960, 1962, 1963, 1968, 1971, 1972, 1973, 1975, 1977 by The Lockman Foundation. Used by permission.

Names and circumstances have been fictionalized to protect privacy.

Printed in the United States of America.
ISBN 0-8407-9017-1

Library of Congress Cataloging-in-Publication Data

Cloud, Henry.
    When your world makes no sense / Henry Cloud.
      p.   cm.
    ISBN 0-8407-9017-1
    1. Emotional maturity—Religious aspects—Christianity.
    2. Christianity—Psychology. I. Title.
    BV4509.5.C56 1990
    248.8'4'019—dc20   90-30554
                                        CIP

1 2 3 4 5 6 — 95 94 93 92 91 90

**To
Julie and Christi**

*My prayer is that the fruit of your grace
can be seen in these pages.*

Contents

——Acknowledgments——

I did not set out to write this book. It is the product of a lot of people, without whose input this book would not exist. The ideas presented here are composites of many experiences over the last fifteen years that involve faithful servants of Jesus Christ, and I would like to acknowledge some of the persons specifically.

Dr. John Townsend, my friend and associate, has been instrumental in the development of the model presented in this book. Through many hours of dialogue and team teaching, his input and thinking have added much to my understanding of Scripture and of emotional life. I am indebted to him for the loyalty of his friendship, the discipline of his professional life, and the example of his heart, which is attuned to the hurts of others. We have taught this material together for several years, and there has never been a single presentation where some idea of his has not influenced my thinking. I am grateful for his involvement in the concepts presented here.

Dr. John Carter deserves many thanks for introducing me to the understanding of what an incarnational gospel really means, and to the understanding of the value of relationship at the center of any true scholarship. He was a model instructor at Rosemead Graduate School, and his continuing input over the years has shown me that Jesus holds all understanding in His hand.

Dr. Phil Sutherland's model of a wisdom perspective on the Scriptures gave me new lenses through which to approach the Bible, and significantly helped me to discover "new wineskins" that could contain the true miracle of therapy. Everything that I think about the

ways that humans grow contains the seeds of his perspective. I am
thankful for his input into the early manuscript as well.

Dr. Bruce Narramore's thinking on the concepts of guilt and conscience, as well as on a process understanding of growth, were invaluable to me in my training. His commitment to training professionals
has borne fruit for the last twenty years.

I will be forever grateful to *Dr. Frank Minirth* and *Dr. Paul Meier,*
who fifteen years ago encouraged me to go into the field of helping. If
it were not for them, I would certainly be doing something else with
my life.

And I am grateful to *Dr. Althea Horner* for her supervision and
humanity. Her thinking about how people grow has been more than
helpful to me as I have developed my own thinking. She has shown
me that psychoanalysis must bow to love.

Dr. Doug Wilson deserves special thanks for giving me a place to
begin practice and for encouraging me to integrate that practice into
ministry, as do the rest of CORE: *Dr. Michele McCormick, Monte
Pries, Ann Huffman.*

Campus Crusade for Christ deserves special thanks for the development of this book. It was under their original request that this material was developed and envisioned. *Loren Lillistrand,* then U.S. field
director, put the original project together, and deserves much credit
for its coming to fruition. In addition, other Crusade staff members
have been very encouraging to the development of this work. Special
thanks go to *Mary Graham* for thinking that this could be used in
training, and *Melanie Alquist* for reading the manuscript.

The staff at the *Minirth-Meier Clinic West* have been superior
models with whom to work in recent years. Their continued commitment to healing in the lives of others has encouraged me profession-
ally as well as personally. I love seeing the fruits of their daily gifts to
others.

Also I'd like to thank *Dr. Anita Sorenson* for reading the manuscript and making some helpful observations.

Dr. Dave Stoop has been a constant encouragement in the writing
of this book, and his input as he taught the material with me was
invaluable. Thanks go to him for helping bring metaphor to life.

Thanks also go to the *Friday group* for their application of faith to
life.

Dr. Victor Oliver deserves special thanks for seeing the original outline and thinking that it could be published in this form. His help, as well as that of my editor, *Lila Empson*, have given this project legs.

I appreciate the support that *Jana Swanson* has offered personally and for interacting with the material.

If anything comes through in the message of this book, it is that the Body of Christ is the only place in which we grow. My community of friends has been the place where I have "grown into" the concepts presented here. They deserve special thanks: *Dr. Edward Atkinson* for being a true friend through the years and showing me the Lord when He was not easily found; *Bill and Julie Jemison* for taking a new Christian in and walking through the early days of faith—their love and support will never be forgotten; *Guy and Christi Owen* for their supreme ability to produce a safe harbor for me; *Toby Walker* for keeping theology practical and being a truly giving friend; and *my parents*, whose early and sustained commitment to me have imparted much toward my ability to see God as good.

CHAPTER ONE

Why Your World Makes No Sense

I stood in the foyer of the emergency room awaiting the ambulance. The call to the hospital from the police had given little information about the suicide attempt, and I really didn't know what to expect. I found myself wondering why a thirty-five-year-old woman would try to kill herself. What circumstances would have forced her to make such a drastic decision in the prime of her life? Maybe she didn't know the Lord . . . maybe her husband had left her or had died . . . maybe she had lost a child . . . maybe they were on the verge of financial ruin and she saw this as the only way out.

When the ambulance arrived, the woman was still conscious. We quickly wheeled her into the ER and attempted to stabilize her. I say "attempted" because we had a fight on our hands.

"Get away from me!" she screamed as the nurse tried to take her blood pressure. "You have no right to not let me die! It's my life, and I can do as I please. You can't do this to me! You can't do this to me! You can't . . ." She slipped into unconsciousness.

Later in the evening I learned from her family members that none of my speculations had been correct. She seemingly had everything going for her: she was a committed Christian leader in her church, her husband was a well-respected pastor, she was exceptionally attractive, she had four beautiful and successful children as well as an army of friends. "Why?" I continued to wonder.

The ER doctor did not take long to stabilize her, but it was apparent that I could not do a psychological evaluation until morning.

When I returned then, she looked pale. "How are you feeling?" I asked.

"Horrible, thanks to you people."

"Did someone here hurt you last night?"

"You kept me alive. That's hurt enough," she replied with a scowl. "All I wanted to do was die, and now I can't even do that."

I could tell that it would be quite a while before Joan would be willing to talk, but it eventually became clear why she desperately wanted to end her life. Her internal world was far different from her external one. Outside, she was a spiritual leader; she had the "model" Christian home, a phone that rang off the hook with invitations from friends, a theological education and knowledge that could have wooed Bible teachers, four loving children, and an accomplished husband.

Inside, however, she experienced vastly different pictures and feelings. Her days would begin, she described to me, with a blackness inside so deep that she could literally see it. When she finally forced herself to get out of bed, her chest would alternate between a dull ache and a weighty depression that made her feel hopeless and without meaning. The loss of meaning was the most difficult for her to deal with because she thought she had done everything possible in her faith, social life, and family life to have enough meaning for ten people. She could barely make it through the day, for it always involved interactions with people, and people terrified her. She was convinced that they despised her in spite of their nice words.

The afternoon would grow into a heavier evening, and she could find comfort only in the thought of sleep. However, over the last few months, even sleep offered no relief. She would awaken a few hours after falling asleep and stare at the ceiling. She would try to pray and read her Bible, but that didn't help.

What was wrong? Why could she have an accomplished life, try all of the formulas her Christian teaching had given her, and still be so depressed that she would try to kill herself? During her weeks in the hospital, the reason became evident. Despite the many people in her life, she was alone and isolated. In many ways she was in a place like that the Bible refers to as hell.

When Stephen started in the ministry, he was enthusiastic about serving God and others. He talked of "those days" as times of excitement and joy as the possibilities of giving to others filled his heart and mind. His wife shared his vision, and he felt that together they would have a wonderful marriage and ministry. He wasn't quite sure how it happened, but fifteen years later, he considered himself "burned out." He described symptoms of fatigue, mild depression, no motivation to do his work, surges of anxiety whenever he had to meet with his board of elders, and fantasies of "tossing it all" and running away.

He had difficulties in his work before the burnout set in, however, and he always wondered why. A very loving and compassionate person, Stephen was good at the "people" aspects of his job. In fact, he was almost too good. His "soft" heart could not allow a suffering person to go without help, and he responded to every crisis.

As a result, the "task" parts of his responsibilities were always a problem. Repeatedly behind schedule on meeting deadlines for budgets and preparing reports that the board needed, he frequently showed up late for meetings. The decision makers in the church had to weigh the value of having such a "nice" guy as a pastor against Stephen's irresponsibility. There were just too many times that he did not fulfill his promises, and that was disturbing to his boss and elders.

In addition, he felt that every minute of his time was accounted for and that he did not have any time for the things he enjoyed doing. He thought the church and the people were selfish to want so much of him, and he resented them for it. At the same time he felt unappreciated. He didn't know quite who to blame, though, because his compassion compelled him to answer every need.

Even more disturbing was his home life. He said that his wife was generally angry with him over some task that he had promised to do but then did not undertake. The yard went for weeks at a time without attention, and they often got notices from the bank that some payment was late or that their credit rating was suffering.

Whenever they went somewhere or did something, he "gladly" agreed to do what pleased his wife. He felt resentful of her and yet selfish if he disagreed with her wishes. He believed that he should do what she requested in the same way that he should do whatever his church requested. He suffered horrible guilt whenever he denied someone's wishes.

It was difficult for Stephen to seek counseling for his problems. As a people "helper," he thought he shouldn't be taking time out from work to be a "helpee." He wondered why, with all of his good intentions, he had ended up in such a mess. However, if he were sitting in my seat looking at him, he would have seen the problem: Stephen had no limits on others' control of him, no sense of personal boundaries and space, and very little of what the Bible calls will.

Ted had always been an "up" person. He succeeded in just about everything he ever tried. His youth was marked by successes academically and athletically; he was popular with all of his peers. After he was recruited to a major university on a basketball scholarship, his college life was more of the same. He seemed to be the "ideal" guy who had it all together.

By the age of thirty he had amassed an industrial manufacturing fortune in the millions of dollars. He had a great reputation in the community. He had married the "most beautiful girl in the world," and they had two "perfect" children. What could have stopped him?

The decline came as several lawsuits against his subsidiaries plagued him in the business world, and his popularity began to wane. Within a few short years, his fortune and family were virtually lost. Ted ended up in the hospital from an overdose, and all of his friends and fans were startled. He would go through the days in a stupor, unable to communicate with hardly anyone. He didn't want to see any of his old friends. In fact, he was most adamant about that. He didn't want anyone who idealized him to see him then.

As Ted began to open up about his pain, it became clear that any sort of failure or loss was totally unacceptable to him. Any threat to his ideal picture of himself would drive him to further accomplishment, thus covering any disappointment or pain. He had never been able to face a great deal of pain in his life that went all the way back to his youth in a broken home. His way of coping with anything bad about himself, his family, or his surroundings was to create more good. That very thing had made Ted a time bomb with a clock apparently set at age thirty-eight. He was unable to deal with a world that wasn't all good—a world that had badness and disappointment along with goodness and success. In short, he needed the ideal.

Sara came into therapy because of anxiety. She said she was "never able to relax," no matter how well things were going or how successful she was. She was always worried that something would go wrong with whatever project she was working on or that her kids would somehow make irreversible mistakes or that she just "hadn't done quite enough."

Her biggest worries had to do with what people thought of her. She was constantly on guard to make sure that her superiors approved of her work and that community leaders were pleased with the projects she led. Sara shared that she had been "hooked into" several women in her life. That is, from college age into her early forties, there was always an older woman she looked up to but could somehow never please. Those women were proper, sweet, and concerned, but without exception, they had a critical streak that would find some way in which Sara could be doing just a little bit better. When they would say that she "should" do anything—whether it was change the color of her drapes or discipline her kids differently—she would faithfully comply and await their approval. The problem was that if they didn't approve, she would feel enormously guilty, and if they did approve, she would get only short-lived satisfaction. It seemed that the performance did not really satisfy her; it only staved off the feeling of failure.

The pattern was apparent in her relationship with her husband. She would seek his approval and feel horrible if she didn't receive it. Her attitude particularly affected their sexual life. Over the years, she was losing interest, but she did not like his seeing her as cold.

As she began the arduous task of examining her life, one theme recurred. Sara was in a one-down relationship to everyone important to her. She was acting like a child seeking parental approval and therefore was not able to enjoy peer relationships with other adults. The freedoms that adults have—to make their own decisions without permission from others, to evaluate and judge their own performance, to choose their own values and opinions, disagreeing with others freely, and to enjoy sexual relations with an equal spouse, to name a few—somehow had escaped her.

These four issues—feeling isolated, having no sense of personal boundaries, needing the ideal, and achieving adulthood in relation to other adults—represent not only the struggles of Joan, Stephen, Ted, and Sara. They comprise the basic developmental issues that all of us must negotiate to function and grow emotionally and spiritually. If we fail to resolve these basic growth crises, meaning, purpose, satisfaction, and fulfillment will escape us, and our lives will not function in the way that God intended.

Across the land, people are increasingly seeking the answers to emotional and psychological struggles, and even Christians find that their "spiritual" answers sometimes leave them less than whole. The four people mentioned above sincerely sought to live as God would have them, but the maturity they longed for had escaped them in certain vital areas of life. As a result, they were losing hope and becoming disenchanted with their faith.

The Crisis

This problem—how committed evangelical Christians who have tried sincerely to resolve emotional struggles to little or no avail—has the church in a virtual split. People on one side of the issue say that if individuals struggle emotionally, they are "in sin," "don't have enough faith," "aren't obedient," "don't spend enough time in the Word," "aren't having enough quiet times," or are in some other way to blame for their pain. These Christians give answers that seem to fall into the categories of those offered by Job's friends. "To him who is afflicted, kindness should be shown by his friend, even though he forsakes the fear of the Almighty" (Job 6:14). The hurting persons may feel further away from God than when they sought help because they now have two problems instead of one: the original pain plus the guilt over not being able to "apply" the "answers" given. Such judgmental "help" has done untold damage and has led many to the conclusion that Job reached:

> But you forgers of lies;
> You are all worthless physicians.
> Oh, that you would be silent,
> And it would be your wisdom! (Job 13:4–5).

On the other side of the issue are the believers who reach out to hurting people in their pain. They try to find real answers that work and because of the limitations of the "theology" they have been trained in, they turn to psychology to find methods to cure the pains of the soul and spirit. Oftentimes they have results and their "helpees" find relief, but they aren't sure what cured them. They know at some level that the results must be from God, but as yet there seems to be no agreed-upon system by which to defend it. They just know that "it works."

As a Christian, a professional, and a fellow struggler, I have been on both sides of that fence. I tried the "standard" Christian answers for myself and others, and I came to the same conclusions that Job reached: they are worthless medicine. I also tried to "baptize" psychological insights so that they would somehow feel "Christian" enough to allow me to think that my "theological" answers and training were the real key to healing. Somehow that never worked, either. I found myself saying to God something like this: "I quit. I really don't know what helps, and God, if there is something that does, You will have to show me." Over a period of years, He has graciously answered that desperate prayer.

This book does not attempt to speak to the debate in the church regarding psychology and theology. I have a different goal in mind: I want to share with you that there are solutions to the struggles of persons walking the path of depression, anxiety, panic, addictions, guilt, and various other emotional and psychological maladies.

I firmly believe that emotional wholeness lies in the working out of the image of God within us. Paul writes that God has called us to be "predestined to become conformed to the image of His Son" (Rom. 8:29). But most Christians have difficulty figuring out how becoming Christlike relates to facing everyday emotional struggles.

Most of us assume that psychological symptoms, such as depression, panic, guilt, or addictions, have little or nothing to do with spirituality. We try to identify a problem as emotional *or* spiritual. If it is decided that one is struggling with an emotional problem, the Christian psychologist is called in; if it is a spiritual problem, we order a prescription of prayer, Bible study, and spiritual disciplines.

We need to reconsider this either/or approach, however. Because of the Fall, *all* of these problems are related to the underdeveloped image of God within the soul. The likeness of God in Joan, Stephen, Ted, and Sara was lacking in vital areas within them, and as a result, they experienced pain and functioned at a level far below their best.

God has passed on to us four aspects of His personality that greatly influence our psychological functioning: (1) bonding, (2) having boundaries, (3) resolving problems of good and bad, and

(4) establishing authority over one's life as an adult. If our development enables us to achieve these tasks, we are on our way toward wholeness.

The Four Tasks

Before we proceed further, let's clarify each developmental task.

Bonding

Bonding is the ability of a person to establish an emotional attachment to another person. The most important aspect of the spiritual life, it is the basis for repairing the isolation and separation that the Fall created in our souls. Paul describes its preeminence in this commandment: "But above all these things put on love, which is the bond of perfection" (Col. 3:14). He adds that we are to be "rooted and grounded in love" (Eph. 3:17). First John 4:16 tells us that "God is love," and we see that throughout eternity He has been in an unbroken bond within the Trinity.

Without a solid grounding in bonded relationship, the human soul is destined for psychological and emotional symptoms as well as failures in work functioning. The soul cannot prosper without emotional connectedness to others. It does not matter what other attributes one possesses or what other accomplishments one may achieve. We can see this in Joan's case. She had everything that one could wish for, yet she was suicidally depressed. Things happened in her development that prevented her from being able to attach to others in an emotional way; she was headed for a lifetime of depression unless her isolation could be ended. Perhaps you identify with the blackness Joan felt or the meaninglessness she experienced in her Christian life. Or maybe you are overwhelmed by anxieties and fears of people and the world, or you are addicted to substances. However your symptoms manifest themselves, *emotional isolation* may be at the root of the struggle, and we will examine the ways it can be resolved.

It should be evident that we need this attachment to others, for we know that nothing grows anywhere in God's universe apart from a source of strength and nutrition. When the Bible uses metaphors for growth, it frequently depicts plants so that we can visualize the process. To grow, plants must be connected to something outside themselves. Jesus talks of us as being branches connected to Him as the vine, and unless we stay connected to Him, we will fail to grow (John 15:4). He then points out the significance of being in relationship with one another: "This is My commandment, that you love one another as I have loved you" (v. 12).

A lack of emotional "abiding" and connectedness led Joan into a detached depression that took away the very life within. The good news is that she learned how to resolve her isolation and came out of her depression. Later we will look at how an unbonded person can come out of emotional unconnectedness, but the important thing to remember now is that *God has a solution.*

Having Boundaries

Having boundaries means realizing one's own person apart from others and knowing one's limits. This sense of separateness forms the basis of personal identity and rests upon our choices. It is the function of the likeness of God that says what one is and what one is not, what one will choose and what one will not choose, what one will endure and what one will not, what one feels and does not feel, what one likes and does not like. Boundaries, in short, *define* us. In the same way that a physical boundary defines where a property line ends and begins, a psychological and spiritual boundary defines who we are and who we are not.

We can see the problems Stephen had because he lacked boundaries. He could not choose what he wanted to do apart from what others wanted him to do. He wasn't able to say no. He could not be responsible for his life and service because he was overly responsible for others. His life and ministry were chaotic, and he felt resentment, panic at times, and depression. Because of the encumbrances on his will, he was out of control.

The Bible often portrays God exercising His will and asking man to do the same. Joshua stated it this way: "Choose for yourselves this day whom you will serve. . . . But as for me and my house, we will serve the LORD" (Josh. 24:15). He was defining himself by his choices for the good. While Joshua was choosing "for," we are also called to choose "against." In Matthew 18:15–18 Jesus tells us to put a limit or a boundary on the evil of others when they sin against us. We are to confront evil in love.

Many people struggle with their ability to discover, set, and keep personal boundaries. They suffer from lack of purpose, powerlessness, panic, identity loss, eating disorders, depression, irresponsibility, and a whole host of other problems, all of which lead to a lack of real intimacy with others. Probably the most destructive aspect is suffering abuse or being controlled by other people. They allow themselves to be repeatedly injured or controlled by others. This type of control is evident in Stephen's life or in brutal stories of spouse abuse or other sorts of inabilities of people to put a limit on the evils inflicted upon them.

If you identify with these symptoms, you may have a problem establishing and keeping boundaries. It is in your nature as a creature in the image of God to have boundaries, and He has specific ways that those can be repaired. We will look at how they are destroyed and how they are rebuilt. Rest assured that if God's ways are initiated, He can restore your damaged boundaries and your will.

Resolving Good and Bad

This problem plagues everyone born after Adam and Eve: handling the coexistence of good and bad. We were created to be perfect people and live with other perfect people in a perfect world. Genesis 1:13 sums it up: "Then God saw everything that He had made, and indeed it was very good."

God even went further to protect this state of "all good" by warning Adam and Eve that they were not to experience the knowledge of good and evil. But they did not heed His warning, and as a result, they found themselves in a world that, for the first time, had both good and bad together. Man was still created in the image of God; the beauty and the craftsmanship of the Creator were still present in both man and the creation. However, the created goodness was marred by the entrance of evil.

Everywhere we can see that we, others, and the world are both good and bad. Our loves, talents, and abilities have sometimes unimaginable potential only to be thwarted by our character deficits. Our spouses, friends, and work companions have many strengths that we are attracted to and want to share in, but they disappoint us with their sometimes glaring failures of our expectations and wishes. Our world is in some ways as beautiful as the day God created it, but at the same time it is full of decay and death. What are we to do about these contradictions?

Our natural tendency is to resolve the problem by keeping the good and the bad separated. But this split is not based on reality and cannot stand the test of time and real life.

This approach brings about an intolerance of badness, weakness, and failure. We end up having an unstable relationship with ourselves, others, and the world. We may think we are all bad when we fail, or we may think we are all good when we do well. Ted tried to build an image and a life that were "all good," and when the badness came, he felt immediately and hopelessly "all bad."

In addition, we may blame or punish others for not being all good, or we may deny their actual badness. We may require perfection and devalue any church, group, job, or aspect of society that fails our expectations and subsequently withdraw from it, or we may idealize situations in a way that blinds us to their bad points. In short, if we do not have the ability to tolerate and deal with the simultaneous existence of good and bad, we cannot successfully live in this world, for it and we are both good and bad.

God understands the tension we feel and wants to help us resolve it. Consider Jesus' words in John 16:33: "In the world you will have tribulation, but be of good cheer, I have overcome the world." He promises that this will not be an "all good world," but He also promises that within it we may experience abundant life. He says that we are not perfect, for "if we say we have no sin, we deceive ourselves, and the truth is not in us" (1 John 1:8), yet He offers us peace in that condition. God has provided us the means to resolve the conflict between good and bad through a combination of grace, truth, forgiveness, and time.

If perfectionism, impractical idealism, the inability to tolerate badness, weakness, or negative feelings in yourself or others is part of your struggle, to some degree you are a victim of this splitting of good and bad. Depression, self-image problems, guilt, anxiety, eating and substance problems, narcissism, midlife crises, and a whole host of other maladies can keep you from experiencing God's joy. We will explore ways to help you deal with the issues of good and bad.

Establishing Authority As an Adult

The last developmental task we will examine is that of becoming an authority or, in other words, an adult. Certainly, the first three tasks we've discussed pertain to growing up into adulthood—the process of bonding, the birth of the will that leads to one's sense of boundaries and limits, and the realization of goodness and badness that allows one to cope with a fallen world. However, it is possible to be a bonded, willing, good and bad person who is still in a one-up, one-down relationship with other adults and is functioning as a child in an adult's world. Therefore, I define this last task as the process of establishing equality with other adults, of becoming a peer to other adults.

We all start out as very little people in a big person's world. We aren't very authoritative as children because we have several problems. We have limited rights to exercise decisions, we have limited resources to act upon decisions, we are intellectually immature, we are emotionally dependent, and we simply have not had enough experience to play the real game of life. That's not a very strong start!

However, God has designed a path that leads us to an "age of accountability" when we are turned loose upon the adult world. Physical, intellectual, and emotional maturity and experience combine to play a part in the process. Paul puts it this way: "When I was a child, I spoke as a child, I understood as a child, I thought as a child; but when I became a man, I put away childish things" (1 Cor. 13:11). The writer of Hebrews shows us that this step to maturity comes from practice: "But solid food is for the mature, who because of practice have their senses trained to discern good and evil" (Heb. 5:14 NASB). Growing up to adulthood is a process that takes practice!

When one becomes an adult, one must take authority over one's life. If an individual is able to do this, adulthood goes rather smoothly. The person is responsible for making decisions, having opinions, establishing values not subject to approval or disapproval from parents or parental figures, and incurring legal consequences for actions. One does not need "permission" to think, feel, or act in any way from some fantasized superior person; one is accountable and responsible only for the consequences of one's thoughts, feelings, and actions. When someone takes this sort of equal stance toward other adults, he or she has become a peer and has come "out from underneath" human authority and is ready to be accountable to the authority of God.

Jesus said, "Do not be called 'Rabbi'; for One is your Teacher, the Christ, and you are all brethren. Do not call anyone on earth your father; for One is your Father, He who is in heaven. And do not be called teachers; for One is your Teacher, the Christ" (Matt. 23:8-10).

He called for adults to assume a position of equality. We are to treat other adults as siblings under the common parentage of God. Then, and only then, can we have a proper relationship to human authority.

Don't get me wrong; I am all for human authority, for it is God-ordained and supported: "Let every soul be subject to the governing authorities. For there is no authority except from God, and the authorities that exist are appointed by God" (Rom. 13:1). However, if one does not experience obedience to authority figures as a choice to submit to a God-ordained role instead of complying to a person out of guilt and lack of freedom, one will always resent and/or reject authority. One who cannot make obedience come from freedom has missed the essence of adulthood and will suffer guilt, fear, depression, performance anxiety, passive-dominant cycles, problems with anger, sexual problems relating to performance and approval, and/or other problems. Sara is a good example. She did not have the internal "permission" from herself, as the manager of her life, to do and think as *she* saw fit; she invariably needed approval and permission from some parent figure in her life. She was burdened by enormous and unending anxiety until she was able to come out from under the pharisaical domination of others.

Jesus declared that there was no greater man born of woman than John the Baptist (Luke 7:28). Certainly that comment had to do with the nature of John's mission, but John's distinctive qualities also made him a special man. The most apparent one was his ability to stand up to the authority figures of his community and give his opinion of them: "Brood of vipers! Who warned you to flee from the wrath to come? Therefore bear fruits worthy of repentance" (Matt. 3:7–8). Can you imagine the strength of independent thinking that his confrontation required? And yet he was able to submit to the authority of God: "I indeed baptize you with water unto repentance, but He who is coming after me is mightier than I, whose sandals I am not worthy to carry" (v. 11). He had the freedom of thought necessary to stand up against authority figures when he knew they were wrong. Daniel and Martin Luther were two others who did not bow to the authority of man; having authority over their own lives, they were free to bow to the authority of God and obey Him as bond servants.

In the same way that God takes authority over His life, He calls us to bear that likeness. We are to be the "boss" of our minds and submit to Him and to roles of authority over us without conflict. This task of development takes a lot of work, especially if one has struggled with either a lack of authority or a critical, controlling authority in the growing-up years. But the good news is that Jesus died to free us from the authority of the law, the devil, and the world, and if you follow His ways, you can be freed from one-upsmanship to join the ranks of adulthood. You can become one of the "big people" and embrace the freedoms and responsibilities that go with a hard-earned adulthood.

Those are the four tasks we will examine throughout this book. If you, or someone you know, suffers from significant emotional struggles, take heart. God has provided a way that will have you on the path toward wholeness. If you will do what He says, He can truly lead you to a better place, and you can exhibit His likeness.

One more word about the four areas. They present a reasonably comprehensive view of the human personality; therefore, because the Fall affected all of who we are, *all of us will have deficits in all of the areas.* Do not be discouraged if you can see aspects of yourself in each area. That is a given. However, one or two may be particularly troublesome to you. Accept the fact that you, like everyone else, were drastically affected by the Fall and at the same time are created in the image of God. Transforming the effects of the Fall and growing into His image comprise our task. Remember "that He who has begun a good work in you will complete it until the day of Jesus Christ" (Phil. 1:6).

CHAPTER TWO

Grace, Truth, and Time

Once upon a time in a faraway galaxy, a commission was established to come up with a god. The inhabitants were getting a bit bored with technology and science, and the fact that they had very little to do on Sunday made them a bit disgruntled, so they figured that the best solution was to get religion. They held some meetings and tried desperately to invent a god, to little avail. After all, what good was a god they could invent? They were intelligent enough to realize that the idol worshiper who invented the god was really in control anyway. They figured they had to find a god instead.

After much ado, they decided to send someone to earth to learn of the God of those primitive earthlings they had read about in their history books. So they sent their newly appointed bishop, Beezy, on a mission to find the God of earth and bring Him back to their galaxy.

Beezy took his task seriously. He visited many churches and religious institutions. After a while (he wasn't sure how long because of the time change), he returned with his report.

His friends were both excited and perplexed about his findings. Beezy brought back two gods. He said he went to some churches that had a very nice god, or goddess, he wasn't sure which because the name was Grace. She talked about love mostly, saying that it didn't matter much what had gone on during the week, for all was OK. Her main concern was that everybody get along well and be friends. She didn't much mind that her subjects were doing all sorts of questionable things during the week; they were forgiven. Beezy didn't quite understand what forgiveness was actually, for there really didn't seem to be any rules to be broken, but they were forgiven nevertheless, and all were very happy people.

Beezy was especially interested in what the followers of Grace did. They fed poor people, took in orphans, visited jails, stayed up all night with alcoholics, and did a lot of helpful things. However, he was a bit perplexed as to why so many of the followers of Grace seemed so lost. They just didn't seem to know where they were going most of the time. And when they got there, it seemed to have some destructive ending that Grace would forgive them for all over again, and they would repeat the cycle.

The second group of people followed another god. As far as Beezy could tell, this one was definitely a man, whose name was Truth. It seemed that as nice as Grace was, Truth was equally mean. He kept telling the people all sorts of things about themselves that made them feel very bad, and Truth's followers told people out of line with them to "get right with Truth." It wasn't that Beezy didn't like Truth; in fact, he found him helpful. Truth's people campaigned against his enemies: lying, cheating, murder, adultery, abortion, drunkenness, and so on. Wherever the disciples went, they were like a big religious street sweeper, sweeping away the enemies of Truth. However, Beezy noticed that the sweeper also swept away the people who were doing untrue things. The sweepers themselves had none of the smiling faces that the followers of Grace had; they mostly grimaced and yelled.

It is easy to see, then, why the space beings decided to continue to play golf on Sunday. Their only solution was some suggestion by a little kid spaceling that Grace and Truth should climb into one of those mixers his mommy made cookies with and be mixed together. Then they could come out as a cross between Judge Wapner and Mr. Rogers.

Grace and Truth Divided

God's grace and truth have many implications for the human struggle. What exactly are these two qualities? Why are they important?

Grace involves what is called unmerited favor, or unconditional acceptance. It has to do with love. Now, this is no small issue, for when we speak of the healing of the human condition, love is the foundation upon which all healing of the human spirit rests. Love is also the foundation of the nature of God.

Whenever we talk about the healing of the human personality, we must look at the basis for the personality as being primarily one of love. What this means is that love is the foundation upon which our personhood is to be built, for it is the foundation of who God is.

We will talk more later about the bonding process, but for now it is important to see that throughout the four tasks mentioned earlier, grace is a key ingredient to healing. In terms of the application of grace in the healing process, we will define it as unbroken, uninterrupted, unearned, and accepting *relationship*. It is love expressing itself to us, not as an idea, but as a real relationship of favor.

Mankind started out in an unbroken relationship with God in the Garden, and several things were passed on. Man was loved, provided for, given truth, sustenance, freedom, and direction. He was secure and had no shame, anxiety, or self-doubt. He could be who he truly was. Perhaps you have experienced this sort of grace with someone; it is the calming feeling of being able to be exactly who you really are

So, then, grace has to do with the relational aspect of God's character and manifests itself in His unconditional connection to us. This characteristic was evident in the nature of the first church that Beezy visited. It was a church of compassion and relationship. The people did all sorts of loving things for one another and gave of themselves freely. They tried to connect with people in pain and help them out of the pain. Everyone had a wonderful experience of togetherness.

There was only one problem with that church; very little truth was spoken, and the "loved" ones continued to fall into bad situations that required more and more grace. It's not that the goddess of Grace minded giving more, for we know that the God of grace is infinite, as Paul tells us: "Where sin abounded, grace abounded much more" (Rom. 5:20). There is no limit to the nature or the amount of God's grace to us when we sin. The relationship is secure.

However, Grace's followers in the story needed some direction. They needed to know some things to keep from repeatedly falling into the same old patterns. They needed some structure to their lives to keep them out of trouble. They needed limits.

This is where Truth enters the scene. The second god that Beezy found was very good at setting limits on bad things and bad behavior. He gave his people a lot of direction and structure and limits about what they could do or not do. They had what the followers of Grace did not have: they clearly knew the difference between what was right and wrong or, more accurately, what was good and not good. Truth gave them clear boundaries as to where they should play and where they should not. This quality was attractive to Beezy, for the things that Truth tried to stand against were very hurtful things indeed: lying, cheating, murder, adultery, drunkenness, and so on. Beezy did not have to stick around earth very long to see the devastation in people's lives that those things caused. He thought it was a good idea that Truth stood against them.

This is the second aspect of the image of God and the second ingredient necessary to the healing of the personality: truth. Just as grace is the *relational* aspect of God's character, truth is the *structure* of His character. It is the order of everything that is of Him, thus the order of everything that is good. It is His blueprint for the way that everything is to be built, and He is the master craftsman. His truth leads us to what is accurate. In the same way that our DNA contains the form that our physical life is to take, His truth contains the form that our soul is to take.

This all sounds wonderful, but as Beezy observed, Truth was mean. He didn't seem to care about the people violating his standards; he seemed to care only about wiping out the bad. He had none of the compassion that Grace offered. He had none of the relational aspects of God; he lacked forgiveness, favor, mercy, compassion, and all of the other attributes that seem to be derivatives of grace. Love didn't seem to matter very much to him. Therefore, just as Grace left Beezy wanting structure, Truth left Beezy wanting love.

All of us to some degree have experienced those two gods—the loving one who allows anything to go on and the tough one who lets nothing slide. Further, we have experienced those aspects of ourselves at various times; we may be on "strict diets" of life, coming down hard on our imperfections and the imperfections of others, only to be followed by a day or a month or a season of irresponsible behavior and a lack of limits on our bad sides, whether in thought or deed. There seem to be two of us, as there seem to be two gods if one listens to different "half churches" and their message of only one aspect of God's character.

Why is this? Most of us realize that these "two gods" are only aspects of God's nature that different churches emphasize, but we fail to realize that these gods are really symbols of the entire problem of the human condition and the Fall: *grace and truth are divided*.

When man was in the Garden, grace and truth were united, for he was connected to the One who is both. When man fell, he experienced separation from God and a lost relationship for the first time. He was without grace, and he felt ashamed: "And Adam and his wife hid themselves from the presence of the LORD God among the trees of the garden. Then the LORD God called to Adam and said to him, 'Where are you?' So he said, 'I heard Your voice in the garden, and I was afraid because I was naked; and I hid myself'" (Gen. 3:8–10). Without God's grace, shame and guilt had entered into the world. Man was no longer safe.

After man lost relationship with God, he was cut off from a connection to grace and truth. However, God did not let him stay there long. He decided to give man some direction, so He gave him truth in the form of the law. The law was a blueprint or a structure for man to live by. It gave him some limits within which he could function as best he could. There was only one problem: it was truth without grace, and it led to a performance orientation. Man soon found out an important reality: *truth without grace is judgment, and it sends someone to hell, both literally and experientially*.

Paul writes in Romans about the nature of truth without grace, the law, and the things that it does to us: "Now we know that whatever the law says, it says to those who are under the law, that every mouth may be stopped, and all the world may become guilty before God. Therefore by the deeds of the law no flesh will be justified in His sight, for by the law is the knowledge of sin" (3:19–20); and "For when we were in the flesh, the sinful passions which were aroused by the law were at work in our members to bear fruit to death. But now we have been delivered from the law, having died to what we were held by" (7:5–6). And Paul observes, "You have become estranged from Christ, you who attempt to be justified by law; you have fallen from grace" (Gal. 5:4).

Various scriptural references indicate that truth without grace condemns us, brings anger, arouses sinful desires, brings forth death, binds us, fails us, puts us under a curse, severs us from Christ, is perfectionistic in its judgment, and is useless. No wonder Beezy didn't like Truth! It is the nature of the law to interact with our sin nature to bring about all sorts of failure and destruction of the personality. Getting truth before grace, or truth before relationship, brings forth guilt, anxiety, anger, and a host of other painful emotions.

Susan was the daughter of missionary parents. She showed up at the hospital with her father, who forced her to come. She was twenty-two, using hard drugs and sleeping around. She showed no interest in God and would not talk to her parents. In addition, she was struggling in college. Mostly, she felt depressed. But I didn't discover all of that information during her first visit.

I asked what the problem was, and her father answered, "Well, it's pretty obvious. She's not living like she should."

"What does that mean?" I asked, as if I didn't have at least some suspicion.

"She ought to be reading her Bible, going to church, and loving God. It's no wonder that she's so depressed. She's not living right. She's not doing what a girl should do to please the Lord. All she wants to do is hang around those reprobate friends of hers."

"What would happen if she began to do all of the things you think she should?" I asked.

"She would be happy like her mother and me, and the Lord would bless her," he said.

I could see that I was not going to get very far with him, a feeling I'm sure that she'd had many times. I thanked him and asked if I could talk with Susan alone. When he was out of the room, she was still hesitant to talk, naturally thinking that I would side with him. When she refused to answer any of my questions with more than a yes or no, I began to feel her discouragement, and I told her so. "Susan, I think if I had to live with that, I'd take drugs too. Does his attitude have anything to do with your discouragement?" She nodded.

"You are an adult, and this is an adults' hospital," I said. "I don't see that you are a danger to yourself or anyone else, so you are free to go. But before you leave, let me tell you what I think is going on. I don't know all of the story, but I can tell that you're very depressed, and I *don't* think it is because you aren't doing the things your father thinks you should do. I think there are some other reasons that he doesn't understand. If you would like to stay, I think we can help you feel better. If you do stay, though, it will have to be your doing, and not his. If he is upset about something, he can get some help on his own."

She didn't respond, and I left her to think it over. After a while, she decided to check in, and what I had suspected was true. Susan had had many years of truth without grace and, as a result, was experiencing the same things that the Bible says that the law produces: bad feelings and failure. Everywhere she turned, she ran into some "should" and very little acceptance. The law of sin and death had taken its toll on her, and it was a slow process for her to become free. As I saw her struggle, I could not help remembering what the Bible describes about truth without grace. I only wished her father could have seen that; I don't think that Beezy would have liked living with him, either.

On the other hand, as we have seen in Beezy's world, relationship without truth led to less than successful living as well. When he went into Grace's church, he saw a lot of loving people who were without direction and limits. In actuality, Grace should not have been her name; in the same way that truth without grace should be named Judgment, grace without truth should be named License, and the Scriptures discuss her, also:

> For you, brethren, have been called to liberty; only do not use liberty as an opportunity for the flesh (Gal. 5:13).

> What then? Shall we sin because we are not under law but under grace? Certainly not! Do you not know that to whom you present yourselves slaves to obey, you are that one's slaves whom you obey, whether of sin leading to death, or of obedience leading to righteousness? (Rom. 6:15–16).

> He who disdains instruction despises his own soul, but he who heeds rebuke gets understanding (Prov. 15:32).

In the same way that Susan's home had been one of truth without grace that led to negative consequences, a home of grace without truth can also have devastating results. Sam was twenty-eight when he came to the hospital, but he looked eighteen. His features may have shown his age, but something in his dress and demeanor was immature. He was admitted for a physiological drug reaction that was accidental; he simply wasn't aware of how much cocaine he was using. His history revealed that although he had an IQ of genius level, he had flunked out of four colleges. He had never been able to hold a job because he was irresponsible and lacked discipline.

In his relational life, there were equal difficulties. He would almost totally lose himself in any relationship and abandon other areas of his life. Eventually, he would emotionally smother the girl and chase her off. At that particular time, his second wife had just left him.

He said that his father had died when Sam was four and that his mother had never remarried. She wasn't able to resolve her grief, and she had been depressed and withdrawn for many years. In an attempt to have some relationship in her life, however, she tried to be as nice to the kids as possible. Sam never had many responsibilities or chores and always had plenty of money. His mother bailed him out of jail and other situations "because he was such a loving boy."

It didn't take long to see Sam's patterns emerge within the hospital unit. He forever slept late and missed activities, didn't follow through on assignments, and was generally unkempt. The lack of limits in his life, the lack of truth and discipline, had led to a shapelessness of his whole existence. It took a lot of limits to help Sam gain some direction. His problem had been one of love without limits or, in Beezy's language, grace without truth.

It's pretty clear that the Bible doesn't commend either of Beezy's gods apart from the other. The suggestion from the little kid spaceling was a good one; he wanted to get Grace and Truth together and come up with a mixture: a nice guy who knew what was right and wrong. Fortunately, he wasn't the first to think of that: "And the Word became flesh and dwelt among us, and we beheld His glory, the glory as of the only begotten from the Father, full of grace and truth. . . . And of His fullness we have all received, and grace for grace. For the law was given through Moses, but grace and truth came through Jesus Christ" (John 1:14, 16–17).

In this statement we can see both the failure of man and his redemption, which is really a blueprint for healing. The failure was through the law; the redemption is through Jesus, because it is only through Him that we can realize the two ingredients together: grace and truth. It is in the essence of who our Savior is that we can come back into the same relationship that Adam had: an unbroken connection (grace) to the One who is reality (truth).

We have seen what happens when grace and truth are divided and how destructive that division is. Let's now look at what happens when they get together.

Relationship Promoted

The main effect of the Fall was separation from God and others and an introduction of isolation into the world. When grace comes onto the scene, it invites us out of that isolation, but when it is combined with truth, it invites the *true self* into relationship for the first time. It is one thing to have safety and relationship offered to us; it is quite another thing to be truly known and accepted in that relationship. When grace is offered alone, there is no intimacy, although there is safety from condemnation. When the one offering grace also offers truth and we respond with the true self, there is the possibility for real intimacy in a real world.

A wonderful example is Jesus' interaction with the woman caught in adultery. The scribes and the Pharisees brought the woman to Him and said, "Moses, in the law, commanded us that such should be stoned. But what do You say?" He responded, "He who is without sin among you, let him throw a stone at her first." At that, the men retreated, leaving Jesus alone with the woman. Jesus said to her, "Woman, where are those accusers of yours? Has no one condemned you?" And she said, "No one, Lord." Jesus replied, "Neither do I condemn you; go and sin no more" (John 8:3–11).

In that one encounter, Jesus showed what it means to realize grace and truth with Him. Because of grace, He offered her forgiveness and acceptance as she was. He said, in effect, that she did not have to die for her sin. She did not have to be separated from Him. He also indicated that the power of grace could end separation from others, for he showed that the Pharisees, like her, were sinners. He invited them to commune with her as members of the fallen human race, an invitation they declined.

Jesus accepted the woman with a full realization of who she was. He knew that she was an adulteress, a person of sinful desires and actions, and He accepted both her and the truth about her. Then He stated the truth that would form her future and mold her personality: "Sin no more." Grace and truth together bring the real self, the true person, into relationship, which is the only way that healing takes place.

Jesus said it in another way in John 4:23-24: "But the hour is coming, and now is, when the true worshipers will worship the Father in spirit and truth; for the Father is seeking such to worship Him. God is Spirit, and those who worship Him must worship in spirit and truth." We must worship God *in relationship and in honesty*, or we do not worship Him at all. The sad thing is that most of us come to Christ because we are sinners and then spend the next forty years trying to prove that we are not! It's no wonder that little growth occurs; the true self is still hiding.

The Fall took who we really were and who we really were created to be and separated that person from God and others. That real person today longs for relationship and healing, but is unable to come into either one unless grace and truth are experienced together. If relationship is real and honest, and God's truth is present and responded to, there is limitless healing. *Grace and truth together bring the real self, the true person, into relationship; therefore, the real needs can be met by God and His people. This is the essence of the incarnational gospel.*

When the real self comes into relationship with God and others, an incredible dynamic is set into motion: "Holding fast to the Head, from whom all the body, nourished and knit together by joints and ligaments, grows with the increase that is from God" (Col. 2:19). When there is a real abiding (a concept we will discuss later) with God, ourselves, and others, there is real relationship in spirit and in truth.

A coming together of grace and truth is our only hope, and it is a hope that does not disappoint. Jake, a friend of mine who had been in the church for years but had remained enslaved to alcohol, put it this way: "When I was in church or with my Christian friends, they would just tell me that drinking was wrong and that I should repent. They did not know how many times I had tried that and how many times I had tried to be a good Christian. When I got into AA [Alcoholics Anonymous], I found that I could be honest with my failure, but most importantly, I could be honest with my helplessness. When I found out that God and others could accept me in my helplessness *and* my drinking, I began to have hope. I could come forth with who I really was and find help.

"When I was in the church, as much as they preached grace, I never really found acceptance for my real state. They always expected me to somehow change. In my AA group, they told me that, by myself, I could not change! They told me that all I could do was confess who I truly was, an alcoholic, and that God could change me along with their daily support. Finally, I could be honest, and I could have friends. That was totally different, and it changed my life."

Jake found that when real relationship with God and others occurred with who he truthfully was, healing was possible. It is sad that his church did not provide an atmosphere of grace and truth earlier. He would have probably salvaged a few very difficult years.

We've examined four developmental tasks that need to be achieved in order for us to grow. A serious problem occurs when the real needs of the real self to mature in those areas cannot be met because the real self is hiding and is not connected to God and others. When this happens and the false self is in relationship, the four tasks cannot be developed. The false self, "conformed to this world" (Rom. 12:2), lives up to the expectations of and is molded by the world, a system where grace and truth are not integrated.

Paul speaks of the false self:

> But you have not so learned Christ, if indeed you have heard Him and have been taught by Him, as the truth is in Jesus: that you put off, concerning your former conduct, the old man which grows corrupt according to the deceitful lusts, and be renewed in the spirit of your mind, and that you put on the new man which was created according to God in true righteousness and holiness. Therefore, putting away lying, "Let each one of you speak truth with his neighbor," for we are members of one another (Eph. 4:20–25).

And again: "Do not lie to one another, since you have put off the old man with his deeds, and have put on the new man who is renewed in knowledge according to the image of Him who created him" (Col. 3:9, 10). There are numerous other ways that the false, deceitful self is referred to in the Scriptures, but the main theme is that as long as the false self is the one relating to God, others, and ourself, then we are not in relationship and truth, and that as a result, grace and truth cannot heal us.

The false self tries to "heal" us by its own methods. It tries to solve the problems of the real self by one of Satan's solutions of the lust of the flesh, the lust of the eyes, or the boastful pride of life. The false self always finds false solutions.

In terms of bonding, if one is not being honest in relationship about needing others, the real self is not receiving grace. The false self is in relationship with one's friends. As a result, the real, needy person stays unbonded.

One pastor said, "Before I came into the hospital, I was fifty-three years old and never needed anyone. I didn't think that I was supposed to need anyone. I thought that was the way it was. I never knew that my depression was because I didn't have any emotional bonds with others. I had plenty of friends and a church of one thousand people. It wasn't until I felt my need for others that I began to realize what a hole I was in. It's sad when you think that I could go fifty-three years without a significant friend. I had best friends, but no significant friends, because I could not allow them to make a difference in my guts."

Through an expression of the real self he began to find grace for his isolation. This was a coming together of grace and truth; he discovered he truly was a person with needs for bonding.

In terms of boundaries, if someone is not being honest about the true self's need to have limits and choices, the person cannot exert himself or herself in real relationship and develop appropriately. Jane was thirty-two when she realized that she had a God-given need for a will to be exerted in real relationship. She told me, "When the group didn't hate me for saying no to them over and over, I began to discover that I could have relationship with people and still have choices. It was a beginning that allowed me to get the strength to say no to my husband's abuse, and then I found that I really was a person after all."

Because Jane's will had always been outside the sphere of her relationships, her real self remained hidden. When there were grace and acceptance of the true self, her basic need to develop a will was met, and she got well.

Grace and truth are also essential in resolving good and bad. In her early fifties Joan developed headaches with no physical cause. When we began to look at her life, it was apparent that she was very angry, but she boxed in her anger because she had been taught to be "nice." She had grown up in a very strict Christian home where the expression of negative feelings wasn't allowed. Only good, positive, loving feelings were acceptable.

"It was hard for me to accept that I had angry feelings, because I knew that some of them were revengeful and bad," Joan said. It helped her to see that God and others had grace for that true part of her, and she began to realize that she was composed of good feelings as well as negative ones. When she learned to express those and receive grace for her angry, but real, self, her headaches disappeared. In addition, she gradually perceived herself and others as good *and* bad, and the pressure to be "all good" decreased.

As authoritative adulthood develops, grace and truth need to be realized. When one begins to have real adult thoughts and opinions, these need to be expressed to authority figures and accepted by them. Authority problems often develop when one fails to accept the authority that the real self is developing as it is growing up. Instead, one systematically denies authority over one's life.

Joe was in the hospital for depression. When we began to talk about why he was so passive and could not take charge of his family, it was clear that his father was still running his life. Though he had the years and a law degree to mask it, Joe was not an adult. He was still under his father's rule. In a joint session with his father, for the first time in forty-two years Joe disagreed with him openly and without guilt. He gradually realized that he could disagree with other authority figures as well. He understood that his pastor, though stern and authoritarian, could be wrong and Joe could actually know more about certain things. This process was greatly enhanced because the other adults had grace and acceptance for Joe's real authority over his life. They did not look down at him; they considered him an equal. His real authority muscle had received grace, and for the first time he could accept the authority of God.

In addition, grace and truth together are a healing combination because they deal with the main barrier to all growth: guilt. Basically, we have emotional difficulties because we have been injured (sin done to us) or we have rebelled (sin done by us) or some combination of the two. As a result of this lack of love and a lack of obedience, we are hidden in a world of guilt. We saw earlier that Adam and Eve had to hide themselves because of the guilt and shame of their sin, and also of what they had become (less than perfect). If we have to hide, we cannot get help for our needs and brokenness. When grace comes along and says that we are not condemned for who we truly are, guilt can be resolved, and healing can progress. Guilt causes us to hide, and hiding causes us to remain without grace and truth; it is a vicious cycle.

Oftentimes the church does not properly promote healing. Jake found an end to his hiding only after he found another "church," AA. When he did not have to be ashamed of his deficiencies and was forgiven for his sins, grace and truth had an impact on his life. It is interesting to compare a legalistic church with a good AA group. In the church, it is culturally unacceptable to have problems; that is called being sinful. In the AA group, it is culturally unacceptable to be perfect; that is called denial. In one setting people look better but get worse, and in the other, they look worse but get better. Beezy would have no problem figuring out which was the more biblical of the two. Certainly, there are good churches and poor AA groups. I am all for the church being the healing arm of the body. But it is true that for some problems, because of a lack of grace and truth in some churches, Christians have had to go elsewhere to find that combination and get healed. Nevertheless, God is honored. Grace and truth do away with guilt, and when that happens, real relationship that accepts the true self is possible, and the true self can develop along the lines God ordained.

In regard, then, to Beezy's dilemma, it is obvious why the spacelings decided to keep playing golf on Sunday. On the one hand was acceptance without direction, and that was not good; on the other hand was direction without relationship, and that stung! Only in a combination of Beezy's two gods, Grace and Truth, is the real Jesus present. And only when the real Jesus is present can we grow into the likeness of our Creator. Then the real self can develop in the four essential areas that we have been talking about: bonding, having boundaries, resolving good and bad, and accepting authority. We really can be healed if we have one more ingredient.

Time

Jesus told this parable:

A certain man had a fig tree planted in his vineyard, and he came seeking fruit on it and found none. Then he said to the keeper of his vineyard, "Look, for three years I have come seeking fruit on this fig tree and find none. Cut it down; why does it use up the ground?" But he answered and said to him, "Sir, let it alone this year also, until I dig around it and fertilize it. And if it bears fruit, well. But if not, after that you can cut it down" (Luke 13:6–9).

Jesus' picture of growth in this story illustrates that there are ingredients to producing fruit. We have already talked about two of them, grace and truth. Now let's look at a third one that is often neglected: time.

In the parable, the owner of the tree was looking for fruit, but it had none. He was disappointed and even angry. "Cut it down!" was his response, which is similar to ours when we examine our lackings and our fruitlessness in light of the truth. We look at the tree (ourselves), and we expect fruit (the ability to love and to work). When we see our failings, or bad fruit as expressed in certain symptoms, such as depression or overwhelming fears, we respond with the answer that truth without grace always gives. We say things like, "I should be able to do that" or "I shouldn't get so angry" or "I should be able to get close to people" or "I should be able to accomplish more" or "I should be like so-and-so." The angry assessment of the self is a sort of "cut down" in the form of guilt and an angry attack. At that point, we operate against ourselves. We want growth, like the tree owner, but we judge quickly without figuring out the problem. Susan's father in an earlier example did the same thing to her, with disastrous results.

Or if we operate in the realm of grace without truth, we say that it does not matter that a fruitless aspect of ourselves is taking up space in our lives (the vineyard). Either we allow it to go on as it is, continually rotting our lives and robbing us of much delicious fruit that God has for us, or we deny it and that aspect of functioning altogether with even more damaging results. Sam ignored the chaos in his life caused by a lack of truth. The fruitlessness was allowed to continue.

To some degree, we all do both: we yell "Cut it down!" and we ignore it. But one thing is certain. Neither approach produces growth.

In the story, grace and truth are symbolized by "digging around it" and "fertilizing it." We must dig out the weeds of falsehood and sin that keep the soil of our souls in disarray. This is an arduous process of confession and realization of the truth inside our souls, our soil, and an addition of the truth of God's ways. And some nutrients, fertilizer, are required to enrich the soil. Grace and truth give us the ingredients to be structured properly and provide the fuel that we do not have. (We will examine those in detail later.) But the Bible continually tells us that wherever grace and truth are together to produce fruit, there needs to be a third key element, that of time.

The vineyard keeper, who certainly symbolizes the Author and Perfecter of our faith, realized that time was necessary for the ingredients to have their effect upon the tree and cause growth. When the elements of grace, truth, and time are present and responsibly responded to by a person, healing and fruitbearing will take place.

The requirement of time is not just an act of grace on God's part; it is a necessity, born out of God's infinite love. Let's look at the reason time is so essential.

"OK, Out of the Pool!"

In the Garden of Eden, the first couple existed in the eternal, with God, and there were two significant trees: the tree of life, and the tree of the knowledge of good and evil. There was no such thing as fallen time, as we experience it, for God is eternal, and human beings lived with Him in eternity. There was also no such thing as evil, or at least a knowledge of it by man and the creation. Things were all good. (John tells us that eternal life is in the Son because He brings us back into relationship with God. When we are in relationship with God, we are in the eternal).

When man ate of the tree of the knowledge of good and evil, something terrible happened. For the first time, things were no longer "all good." Man "knew" both good and evil. The Hebrew word used there for *know* is the same word used when the Scripture says that Abraham knew Sara in the sexual sense. It means a total experience of knowing. That experience of knowing evil, or pain, is what God tried to protect man from. He knew that it would hurt.

Nevertheless, man was deceived by Satan. Satan held out the apple of omniscience and wisdom (Gen. 3:6), but instead, man received the knowledge of evil, the experience of pain.

Imagine for a moment the situation. God had created a perfect place with perfect creatures to live in eternity. And suddenly, evil was within reach of eternity! So what did God do?

He said,

> "Behold, the man has become like one of Us, to know good and
> evil. And now, lest he put out his hand and take also of the tree of

life, and eat, and live forever"—therefore the LORD God sent him out of the garden of Eden to till the ground from which he was taken. So He drove out the man; and He placed cherubim at the east of the garden of Eden, and a flaming sword which turned every way, to guard the way to the tree of life (Gen. 3:22–24).

God moved immediately to protect eternity, the tree of life, from anything evil. Thus in one move, He protected man from being in an eternal state of knowing evil, experiencing pain forever. He sent man into a new place called redemptive time, away from eternity, and that is where we live now. Again, in the wisdom of God, fallen time is the place where, for a period, evil was sent. There God could fix the problem; He could undo the effects of the Fall! He could redeem His creation and bring man back into eternity after he was again holy and blameless and would therefore offer no threat to himself or eternity. What an awesome plan! He even gave a clue as to how He would do this in the first prophecy of Christ, which is recorded in Genesis 3:15: Christ would protect woman's seed—us—from Satan's seed—evil. No wonder the writer of Hebrews calls it "so great a salvation" (2:3).

Philosophers and scientists have for centuries debated the nature of time, but for our purposes, let's define redemptive time as *an incubator that exists for the purpose of redemption.* Paul says it this way: "But all things that are exposed are made manifest by the light, for whatever makes manifest is light. Therefore He says, 'Awake, you who sleep, arise from the dead, and Christ will give you light.' See then that you walk circumspectly, not as fools, but as wise, redeeming the time, because the days are evil" (Eph. 5:13–16).

Think of it another way. God has a sick creation, and He needs to operate on it. He places us in the operating room of redemptive time and into that room, or that incubator, He pumps in the ingredients of grace and truth. In the context of that surgery, He transforms the evil. He will bring the transformed patient, His body, back into the rest of His world, eternity, in a holy state. We don't know how long that surgery will last; we ony know that we are to be active participants in the process.

You may be a bit taken aback by the idea that we are to participate in our own surgery. But that is an important difference between God's surgery of grace and truth and the way that we perform surgery. In our surgery, we go under general anesthesia to lose consciousness. In God's surgery, we are to gain consciousness. In the Garden of Eden, innocence was the commandment, and ignorance was bliss. We were commanded not to be conscious of good and evil. In the place where we live now, redemptive time, we are *commanded to gain consciousness, not lose it.* As Paul says, we are to expose the evil to the light, to bring it to consciousness through confession, for time is the only place where we can have redemption. Therefore, in time, innocence, or unconsciousness is what we are commanded against. That is probably why the next verse in Ephesians 5 deals with getting drunk, a loss of consciousness as is sleeping, mentioned in verse 14. In Eden, ignorance is bliss and consciousness is evil; in time, ignorance is evil, and consciousness leads to joy. Time, because it is a place of evil, works directly opposite from Eden and eternity.

We cannot ever go back to innocence, this side of eternity. We are to pursue consciousness of good and evil through a confessional process of grace and truth in time. The biblical record shows that the trip away from innocence is headed toward a destination, a city "whose builder and maker is God" (Heb. 11:10), and it can be progressively realized only through faith.

Time is an essential ingredient to growth that God has ordained so that His ways of redemption and growth can take place. Yet it will not last forever. Scripture tells us that time will end, and that God's delay will not last forever. He will at some point put an end to this redemptive phase called time and usher in the return of eternity. In the meantime, however, He has ordained it for the purpose of redemption and growth. Let's look at some more examples from the Bible.

Psalm 1 speaks of the ingredient of time as necessary for growth: "He shall be like a tree planted by the rivers of water, that bring forth its fruit in its season, whose leaf also shall not wither; and whatever he does shall prosper." In this psalm we learn of the biblical idea of seasons. It gives us a clue that there are different periods in our growth for different purposes, just as spring, summer, fall, and winter are necessary for plants to grow.

Some seasons are for planting, some for nourishing, some for harvesting, and some for death of some aspect of our way of being. Some Christians and teachers want every day to be harvesttime, without the other seasons required for growth. Oftentimes, therapists are asked, "Why does it take so long?" The real answer to that question has to do with the nature of time being God's way of bringing about the wholeness lost in Eden. It takes time to work the soil with His ingredients of grace and truth and to allow them to have their effect. These teachers sound like the owner in the parable who did not have the wisdom of the vineyard keeper. They yell, "Cut it down!" and put people under some undue yoke of slavery that is not from God.

The wise ruler Solomon understood that there is a season for everything:

> A time to be born,
> And a time to die; . . .
> A time to break down,
> And a time to build up;
> A time to weep,
> And a time to laugh; . . .
> A time to love,
> And a time to hate;
> A time of war,
> And a time of peace. . . .

I have seen the God-given task with which the sons of men are to be occupied. He has made everything beautiful in its time. Also He has put eternity in their hearts, except that no one can find out the work that God does from beginning to end (Eccles. 3:1-11).

We see here the necessity of time as well as the backdrop of eternity.

It follows, then, that there are different seasons for different processes of growing up, and that this takes time. Paul writes, "And I, brethren, could not speak to you as to spiritual people but as to carnal, as to babes in Christ. I fed you with milk and not with solid food; for until now you were not able to receive it, and even now you are still not able; for you are still carnal" (1 Cor. 3:1-3). There are different stages of growth for the Christian, and those stages require various methods until the necessary maturity has taken place to prepare one for the next stage. An infant cannot digest solid food until his stomach is mature enough to handle the next level of food. Unlike Paul, we do not often realize that people are *unable* to do or to understand what is being asked of them. It takes time for the spirit and soul to metabolize and utilize resources. Trying to rush it would be like adding the frame of a house to the foundation before the concrete had hardened. (The concrete would not be solid enough to handle the next step.) Similarly, an apple tree cannot yield fruit when its young limbs are too flimsy to bear the weight of ripe apples. (The limbs would break and be incapable of feeding, carrying, and sustaining apples.)

For some inexplicable reason we expect basically unloved and un-bonded people to be able to stand up against the attacks of the world, and under such a demand, they break. After they break, we often tell them it all happened because they didn't have enough faith or weren't walking with God. Such discouraging comments fail to take into account the developmental process to maturity.

God understands that process; He invented it; He uses time. But man prefers to leave time out of the equation.

Jesus said, "My time has not yet come, but your time is always ready" (John 7:6). He said the same sort of thing to Peter: "And He began to teach them that the Son of Man must suffer many things, and be rejected by the elders and chief priests and scribes, and be killed, and after three days rise again. He spoke this word openly. Then Peter took Him aside and began to rebuke Him. But when He had turned around and looked at His disciples, He rebuked Peter, saying, 'Get behind Me, Satan! For you are not mindful of the things of God, but the things of men'" (Mark 8:31-33).

Jesus knew that He had to go through a process that was to take some time and suffering: "Though He was a Son, yet He learned obedience by the things which He suffered. And having been per-fected, He became the author of eternal salvation to all who obey Him" (Heb. 5:8-9). Our model for growth is the Savior.

Think of what the devil did in the temptation (Luke 4). He offered Jesus instant relief from His hunger, but Jesus said no. He offered Jesus instant glory, but He refused. The devil offered Him instant safety, but Jesus rebuked him. Jesus knew that to gain those things, He had to go through a process that was God's way. And He learned obedience through the suffering.

We have always been susceptible to the shortcut. But the shortcut usually guarantees failure, and that is Satan's goal. Satan tempts with quick riches and schemes to make money, and God compares that to faithfulness that takes time: "A faithful man will abound with bless-ings, but he who hastens to be rich will not go unpunished" (Prov. 28:20). Satan tempts with instant intimacy through sexual passion, but God's way is faithfully building a loving relationship, which takes time. Diet fads tempt with quick weight loss, but quick diets inevitably fail, for people do not learn the discipline needed to maintain the weight loss. Drugs and alcohol offer immediate relief from suffering, but do not build character that can endure.

In the parable of the soils, Jesus warns against fast growth: "Some fell on stony places, where they did not have much earth; and *they immediately sprang up because they had no depth of earth.* But when the sun was up they were scorched, and because they had no root they withered away" (Matt. 13:5–6, emphasis added). Quick growth invariably has no firm root, and it will always be superficial and short-lived. As Jesus indicates, deep growth is always slower. Developmental psychologists always worry about children who begin to show drastic non-age-appropriate behaviors, for it usually means that those children are growing up too quickly because their environment lacks resources. God's way always takes time.

I am reminded of this truth frequently when people are referred to me for help with some deeply rooted problem. After doing an evaluation, I may tell them that I think they can get over it, but a certain amount of time will be required. The "quick-fix" type will say, "Oh, that's way too long. I can't wait that long. Can you refer me to a short-term therapist?" I usually try to explain why that won't work, and after they refuse my explanation, I refer them to someone who works that way. Then, in about a year or two, they will call me again and say something to this effect: "I went to counseling for a little while, and I seemed to get better. But the problem has come back again, and I need more help."

Unfortunately, those people think that in some way they have failed, that they should be better by that point. In reality, they opted for a guaranteed failure, growth without time, and that is what went wrong. I am not decrying short-term help, for it can be useful in sorting out issues that need work. That is very helpful. But by trying to take the short route, they end up taking longer than if they had taken the long route. Whenever people want something *now*, they will pay later.

In spiritual growth as new experience and information (grace and truth) are taken in, a transformation occurs over time. Something new emerges, most often without the individual knowing how it happened.

Stan came into therapy because of uncontrollable outbursts of rage. He had tried for years to get the anger under control. He repented often, prayed even more, studied biblical passages on anger, all the while focusing on the symptom, or the lack of fruit. Only after he changed his focus to the ingredients that led to the fruit did things begin to happen.

He opened up to grace in the form of a group. He found that the members were happy to accept him in his poverty of spirit; they had all struggled with similar things. Their acceptance slowly enabled him to face the truth about himself. He had some very lonely places inside that felt bad and unloved. He believed that he had no choices, and he was almost overcome by powerlessness.

As he experienced love from others, he felt strong enough to exercise choices in his life, and he was not so powerless. As his sense of mastery improved, he became less threatened by others and more relaxed. One day he said to the group, "My wife came at me today with all of these things to do, and something strange happened. I lovingly laughed at how big the list was. I didn't get mad at all. I don't know how that happened, but it did."

Stan experienced growth because of grace and truth working over time. He had the same sort of pleasant surprise that a farmer has on a spring day when he sees the first blossom. It just seems to appear. That is how fruit grows. It is something that is produced over time from ingredients, and how it happens is out of our control.

When Stan said he did not know how it happened, I was reminded of Jesus' words: "The kingdom of God is as if a man should scatter seed on the ground, and should sleep by night and rise by day, and the seed should sprout and grow, *he himself does not know how*. For the earth yields crops by itself: first the blade, then the head, after that the full grain in the head. But when the grain ripens, immediately he puts in the sickle, because the harvest has come" (Mark 4:26–29, emphasis added).

This passage reveals an important truth about the growth process. It cannot be willed or controlled. It can only be cultivated or enhanced by adding the ingredients, grace-truth-time, to the soil, and then God produces the growth as we sleep. Any system of growth that says we can "will" fruit is not biblical. If we are depressed, for example, it does no good to try to be "undepressed" or to somehow change ourselves. It does do good, however, to cultivate the soil of the soul with the ingredients of grace, truth, and time, and then we will gradually be transformed to greater stages of "undepression," or joy.

Sally entered therapy because of what she described as an inner emptiness. This sort of depression comes from a deep inner isolation. She had tried for years to focus on getting rid of the symptom, the depression. She memorized verses, served others, tried to change her state in some way. Yet the internal pain remained.

As she learned to allow other people, Christ's body, to be connected to her from a deep place inside, she opened up more and more, and the emptiness was filled with a sense of belonging and being loved. She was cultivating the soil, her soul, over time with a combination of grace and truth. Time had its effect in a healing way for the first time. Without grace and truth, time was doing her no good. This would be the first three years in the parable above. After she began cultivating her soul with the grace of others and God, along with the truth about her true self, time became a healing thing and was working for her. This change in focus, from the symptom of depression to the responsible cultivation of her soul by adding the ingredients, was what Jesus described in the parable and made the difference in her condition. She continued her therapy and her groups, her reading of Scripture and other materials about growth, and her faith walk with God. A good vineyard keeper diligently cultivates the soil with good ingredients and watches for the fruit to appear. Proverbs 4:23 instructs us: "Keep your heart with all diligence, for out of it spring the issues of life." As Sally became a cultivator of her soul, watching over her heart diligently by adding grace and truth, life began to flow.

Good Time and Bad Time

We have seen that time is an ingredient for growth. We can pass through time and get better (good time), or we can pass through time and not get better (bad time). Let's explore further its nature.

When we truly live in time, which is where we are now, we are present with our experience. We are present in the "here and now." We are aware of our experience. If we are not aware of our experience or are not experiencing some aspect of ourselves, that part is removed from time and is not affected by it. Change takes place only in time, and if we have removed some aspect of ourselves from it, grace and truth cannot transform that aspect. In the example of Sally, the bonding part of herself was outside her experience (or outside time) and was unchanged. When she experienced her need for others and their connection to her, time brought about transformation; growth commenced within her. We "gain time" by being connected to it, by participating in it. Then time is working for us and not against us.

A parable illustrates the difference between time working for us and time working against us. Before a man went on a trip, he gathered his servants and distributed his goods among them. To one, he gave five talents; to another, two talents; and to another, one talent. When the master returned, he discovered that the first servant had used the money and made five more talents; the second had gained two more; but the third had buried his money and had only the one talent to hand over.

The master rewarded the first two according to their profitable endeavors. But to the third he said,

> You wicked and lazy servant, you knew that I reap where I have not sown, and gather where I have not scattered seed. So you ought to have deposited my money with the bankers, and at my coming I would have received back my own with interest. So take the talent from him, and give it to him who has ten talents. For to everyone who has, more will be given, and he will have abundance; but from him who does not have, even what he has will be taken away. And cast the unprofitable servant into the outer darkness. There will be weeping and gnashing of teeth (Matt. 25:26–30).

The two successful servants who experienced growth brought their talents into experience; they brought them into time; they used them. The third servant took his away from experience, away from the realm of use where time could affect it. He buried it in the ground. Therefore, time was not affecting the talent, and time was not making it grow. Basically, that is what happens to our souls. When we take different aspects of our person out of time, that is, out of experience, they remain exactly as they were when they were buried.

Katherine was thirty-one when she was hospitalized for panic disorder. She experienced overwhelming panic at various times for seemingly no reason, and it interrupted her normal functioning. She was not usually a fearful person, having obtained a law degree and acclaim and prestige as a young attorney.

As she began to open up, she experienced feelings that were alien to her. She began to feel like she was twelve years old. She described wanting to go out and play games and be spontaneous and childlike. She also had some strong "anti-authority" feelings and had the urge to mock the authority figures in the hospital. In addition, she had the impulse to flirt with different men.

She began to understand that when she was twelve and her mother had left the family because of a divorce, she had instantly grown up and become a little adult. She turned into an overachiever and took care of the rest of the family as a mother would have done. She was never the teenager that she needed to be. Her teenage aspects went into hiding and were never expressed. They had not grown up or developed with the rest of her. That was why she wasn't able to relate to men as a sexual person. She had many good working relationships, but the sexual and flirtatious dynamic never had really entered into any relationships, for that is a developmental task of adolescence.

As she allowed herself to experience the split-off twelve-year-old and accepted that as a valid part of who God had made her, it began to grow up with the rest of her. After she got out of the hospital, she was under much less stress. Her sense of overresponsibility for the world was gone, and she began dating and having fun. Also, she was less subject to control from authority figures and had more options open up to her. God became less demanding to her, and she saw Him as Someone she could love. *When the twelve-year-old became available to time and experience, time and the experience of grace and truth transformed her.* Time began to be on her side once again. She was not hidden away from time, or experience.

In Katherine's case, some aspect of the personality was taken out of time because of trauma. This is nearly always the way it happens if our understanding of trauma includes a lack of resources in the environment. For Katherine, the trauma of losing her mother at a very important developmental time meant that she had no one to work out her adolescent struggles with. Therefore, she took the adolescent part of herself out of time and became an adult at age twelve. Obviously, an adult who has never completed the adolescent stage is subject to all sorts of lackings, particularly in relation to authority issues and sexuality. The same sex parent is integral to the development of an adolescent, and she did not have one. Therefore, she had to wait, outside time.

This is true to varying degrees for all of us. We need specific parental ingredients to negotiate our developmental tasks, and when these are not present or when we sustain injury, we take that uncompleted aspect of our personality out of time. Katherine's real self was stuck at twelve, and her false self was playacting at adulthood. When her true self came into grace-giving relationships, she began to integrate as a person, and she could be a "true adult." She was no longer faking it.

People often tell of their decisions to leave time. Tom said, "I remember when my big brothers and the other kids would make fun of me because I couldn't do the things they could do. I was not as strong, and I was very afraid. They would call me names and the hurt was so unbearable that I remember saying to myself, 'I will never try to have friends. It hurts.' I must have been about eight or nine at the time, and from that point on I became a loner."

By the time Tom became an adult, the loneliness was overwhelming, and he had missed out on some important developmental tasks. His work was suffering, and his marriage was shallow. It was hard work for him to regain the trust and vulnerability that he took out of experience at age eight, but he did it, and life began to change for him. His God-given personality developed, and trust caught up with the rest of his talents.

Others cannot specifically remember making a decision, but they were pushed outside time and into a place where they could not be present and experience the years with the true self. One woman, who had not been able to become an individual apart from her family, had difficulty standing separate from everyone else as well. Whenever someone had an expectation of her, she felt as if she had to fulfill it. Because she had skipped the stage in which the "choice muscle" develops in relation to one's family, she had hidden that function of her personality. That talent had not developed in a way that could exercise the choices needed with others. She was stagnated at an earlier level of development and could not get on with life until she learned to say no to her parents. After she brought that aspect of herself into being, she began to handle all of her relationships more maturely.

Another woman was very detached and angry as an adolescent because of an abusive father. He was so terrible to the family of ten children that she hardly left her room. But in late adolescence, before that passage was over, she became a Christian and thought she had to be nice. The angry adolescent went underground.

Years later, in therapy, that part of her surfaced. She described "time warp" as she experienced the world of the sixties in the early eighties. She had to meet me for the first time, even though I had known her for a few years. The adolescent did not know me at all, and we had to be introduced. She discovered all sorts of wonderful things about herself that the adolescent contained. She had more ability to play, to be creative, and to separate from her controlling mother. This helped her in her sales career.

This stagnation often characterizes people who abuse substances, such as drugs and alcohol. Their emotional development likely stopped at the age that they began to escape life through substance abuse. One cannot grow when one no longer participates in life and experience.

The Bible contrasts good time and bad time. When Paul says, "See then that you walk circumspectly, not as fools but as wise, redeeming the time, because the days are evil" (Eph. 5:15–16), it behooves us to see time as a precious commodity to use to develop into maturity. Paul calls us out of the darkness and unconsciousness and into the light of experience with Jesus and His body (Eph. 5:13–14). Then time can be good time; it can transform us and develop us as His children need to be developed. If we hide ourselves, time is bad time, for it is not being redemptive.

Another point about time is particularly hope giving. Because the aspect of ourselves that goes outside time in our childhood gets stored in its chronological state, it is still that same age when it returns. God will use our current relationships to provide the nurturance we didn't receive as children or the mentoring we missed as school-age kids or the companionship we needed as teenagers. It is literally never too late enough to open it to those who love us and care about our development. God has promised that He will develop us, and He does that primarily by providing what we never had. One of my favorite passages is Psalm 68:5–6:

> A father of the fatherless, a defender of widows,
> Is God in His holy habitation.
> God sets the solitary in families;

He brings out those who are bound into prosperity.
But the rebellious dwell in a dry land.

God can and does redeem the time for us. He can provide the experiences that we need to develop different aspects of ourselves through His body.

In reality, then, there is nothing sacred about "the first time around." Because of the nature of time being experience, we can affect any "past" aspect of ourselves in the present. We can reach the hurting, lonely child within in the present, even though that child supposedly lived in the past. "Pastness" is a foreign concept to God; He sees everything at once. That is why Paul can write in the past tense in Romans 8:29–30 that we have been glorified. Even though we have not experienced it "yet," in God's view, it just is. Everything is present to Him. He lives outside this reality we call time.

The lonely child, the hurting child, the untrained child, or whoever else we "were" is still alive; he or she is eternal and lives within us. This is relatively simple to see when we look at our reactions to different situations. We can see how we respond to some people or situations like a rejected or hurt child. Often that child is never reached by God's grace and truth because he or she is outside time. He or she is not brought into experience and is not allowed to grow up. People will tell the person to "stop acting like a child," but will never give what is needed to the "child" parts of the person.

When God says that He can redeem the time, He can actually make the past different. If someone missed out on essential developmental aspects, just because that stage is past chronologically doesn't mean that it cannot be grown up and transformed. We can all work through the trust issues of infancy, the boundary-setting issues of toddlerhood, the forgiveness issues of young childhood, the role issues of later childhood, and the separation issues of adolescence in our present adulthood, as we will see in the rest of this book. Those aspects of the likeness of God, our personalities, are still there in their pristine form if they have been separated from time. Through bringing them to the light of experience in grace-giving relationships with our true selves, they can be matured and redeemed in God's masterful process.

It never ceases to amaze me when a certain scenario happens to people who are desperately hurting because of a lack of good relationships in the past or injuries sustained in the past. It goes like this: they finally get some good help and some love and understanding from others for what they have sustained at the hands of irresponsible parents. Then, Christians who have never worked through their own issues will quote some verses totally out of context and tell them that they should get on with their lives. "Paul said to forget what lies behind and to press on," they will say. Or "If you are in Christ, you are a new creation; the old things passed away; behold, new things have come. Forget about your past; move on to maturity."

Certainly, we are to forget old ways of trying to be religious or relating to God; we are operating within a new system. However, we cannot forget the lack of development as persons that may have come from the past, for it has not "passed way." Our immaturity (or lack of learning important developmental tasks) has not magically disappeared; we carry it around daily. A dangerous heresy comes from the injunction to forget the past, and that is this: *it rules out the possibility for forgiveness.* Forgiveness always has to do with something that has already happened; therefore, it always deals with the past. All redemption deals with things that have already happened, and persons who advocate denying the past rule out redemption of what has happened. God is shut out of His creation. He isn't allowed to fix anything that has already happened.

Grace, Truth, and Time Together

By now, the significance of the ingredients of grace, truth, and time and the importance of their being experienced together should be apparent.

We have seen what happens when there is grace without truth, truth without grace, and time without either. When they all come together, we can for the first time have the true self loved and accepted and, through practice and experience, have the likeness of God grown within us.

Grace, truth, and time, working correctly, can bring forth the endurance that James talks about: "Consider it all joy, my brethren, when you encounter various trials, knowing that the testing of your faith produces endurance. And let endurance have its perfect result, that you may be perfect and complete, lacking in nothing" (James 1:2-4 NASB). In the way that we talked about good time versus bad time, there is good endurance versus bad endurance. The difference is whether our time spent suffering is the true self growing versus the false self enduring its pain. If we are on God's surgery table in grace-giving relationships with the real self, that time spent suffering will produce completeness; developmental issues will be resolved.

When the Lord interacted with Peter in the present, He predicted Peter's failure in the future but also saw his maturity in the more distant future: "Simon, Simon! Indeed, Satan has asked for you, that he may sift you as wheat. But I have prayed for you, that your faith should not fail; and when you have returned to Me, strengthen your brethren." And Peter said to Him, "Lord, I am ready to go with You, both to prison and to death." And He replied, "I tell you, Peter, the rooster shall not crow this day before you will deny three times that you know Me" (Luke 22:31-34). Jesus, who exists outside time, could see the present state of Peter, how he would fail in the future, and how he would overcome to the point of being able to help others after his failure. And in all of it, He totally accepted Peter. The Lord accepts us fully, knowing that we will need time and experience to work out our imperfections. The failures do not surprise Him, and if they surprise us, it is only because we have too high an opinion of ourselves. We have a standing in grace that gives us freedom to achieve truth over time.

The truth that we need to achieve is the truth of the developmental needs of the real self, the one made in the likeness of God. It takes the grace of relationship, the real needs of the person as related to the truth of how God created us, and the time to accomplish that process. Now, let's see how the combination of grace, truth, and time can bring about the likeness of God in our souls and cure the spiritual and emotional problems of depression, panic, addictions, and the like.

CHAPTER THREE

How to Become Bonded

"You don't understand. I have lots of friends," Robbie replied when I asked him about his emotional attachments. "I work with a lot of people, and I do a lot of things in my church. I have a lot of people in my life."

"OK," I said, "which ones could we call and ask how you have been feeling in the last, say, few weeks? Could they give me an accurate description of the amount of depression you have had?"

"What do you mean?" he asked.

"Well, when I think of close attachments, I think of the people who really know us and know when we are hurting and know how to respond to our needs," I replied.

"Are you nuts?" he asked. "No one wants to know about this! They would get tired of it. I can't tell them about this sort of thing. They would think something is wrong with me."

"There is," I said. "You're so depressed you can't function, and yet not one other human being knows how you are really feeling. How do you expect to get better in a vacuum?"

"I don't understand what you're talking about," he said with a puzzled look on his face.

And that was the problem. Robbie didn't have the vaguest idea what I was talking about, and yet it was the most basic idea in life: bonding. What is it?

The Biblical Basis for Bonding

When God created the universe, He did it His way. Before we can comprehend anything about growth, we need to understand that His way is, quite simply, *relationship*. Every living thing exists in relationship.

The Bible tells us quite plainly that God's essence is love. From that identity God does everything that He does. Love is essential to being a person and to being a Christian: "Beloved, let us love one another, for love is of God; and everyone who loves is born of God and knows God" (1 John 4:7). Paul says the same thing in Ephesians 3: "That you, being *rooted and grounded in love,* may be able to comprehend with all the saints what is the width and length and depth and height—to know the love of Christ which passes knowledge" (vv. 17–19). And he adds, "Beyond all these things put on love, which is the *perfect bond of unity*" (Col. 3:14 NASB, emphasis added). These ideas of identity, foundational grounding, and unity give us a good starting place to begin talking about the developmental task of bonding.

God's relational nature is basically one of attachment, or bonding. He does not exist alone; He exists in a Trinity. The Bible depicts the nature of this relationship beginning in Genesis when God says, "Let Us make man in Our image, according to Our likeness" (1:26). This idea is also in John 17:24, where Jesus declares, "You loved Me before the foundation of the world." Before anything that we know as the creation, God was in relationship within the Trinity, a bonded, attached relationship of love that gave a foundation of unity to existence.

Unity, or fundamental connectedness, is evident throughout the Scriptures. Jesus said,

> I in them, and You in Me; that they may be made perfect in one, and that the world may know that You have sent Me, and have loved them as You have loved Me (John 17:23).
>
> Abide in Me, and I in you. As the branch cannot bear fruit of itself, unless it abides in the vine, neither can you, unless you abide in Me. I am the vine, you are the branches. He who abides in Me, and I in him, bears much fruit, for without Me you can do nothing (John 15:4–5).

Jesus often discussed the connectedness of relationship. This fundamental truth of existence applies to the likeness of God. Even His truth comes under the domain of love, for when asked about the greatest commandment, Jesus put it this way: "'You shall love the

LORD your God with all your heart, with all your soul, and with all your mind.' This is the first and great commandment. And the second is like it: 'You shall love your neighbor as yourself.' On these two commandments hang all the Law and the Prophets" (Matt. 22:37–40).

When we understand that the basis of existence lies in relationship, it makes sense that love is the highest ethic. The rest of the law was a structure or a blueprint for love; it was the way that love was to be lived out. Paul stated that if he did not have love, he was nothing (1 Cor. 13:2).

We can see, then, that relationship, or bonding, is at the foundation of God's nature. Since we are created in His likeness, it is also our most fundamental need. Without attachment to God and others, we cannot be truly human or truly in the likeness of God. Relationship is the most spiritual activity we can engage in. Jesus told Martha that it was the only thing necessary and the only thing lasting (Luke 10:42).

Jesus often used metaphors of plants when talking about growth of the kingdom within. A plant grows in relationship. It must be connected to the soil and to the sunlight, or it will starve.

If we, for example, cap off its roots and prevent it from getting the grounding it needs to be stable, it cannot support its structure to feed its different limbs, etc. Nor can it get the food it needs from the minerals that are outside itself. If sunlight is blocked from it, it cannot thrive. If water is blocked from reaching its leaves and roots, it will wither. A plant cannot survive impediments to its connectedness with the rest of creation.

When Paul says that we are to be rooted and grounded in love, he means that we are to literally draw from the love of God and others. That love will fuel us to greater transformation and fruit bearing. We cannot grow in a state of emotional and spiritual isolation; we cannot supply all of our own needs. Attempting to do so violates the basic nature of the universe as God has made it, and as a result, sometimes we develop serious problems.

Out of the Garden and Into the Garage

We know what will happen to a plant when it is taken out of the garden, where it is in relationship, and put into the garage, or separated from what it needs. A similar thing happened to man in the Garden of Eden.

When we looked at the story of the Garden earlier, we saw that human beings were created in relationship with God and one another. God gave a basic value to human relationship when He said, "It is not good that man should be alone" (Gen. 2:18). Man needed and had unbroken relationship with God, others, and himself. He was fully himself and not in conflict, or "divided against himself." From these relationships came knowledge, or truth, and morality. All of man's needs were perfectly met. He existed in perfect connection.

When man fell, however, he was alienated for the first time. He lost his unbroken relationship with God, others, and himself. He experienced the pain of isolation. From that point on, alienation has been our primary problem. That fact is reflected in the way redemption is spoken of in the Bible; it is called reconciliation: "For it pleased the Father that in Him all the fullness should dwell, and by Him to reconcile all things to Himself, by Him, whether things on earth or things in heaven, having made peace through the blood of His cross. And you, who once were alienated and enemies in your mind by wicked works, yet now He has reconciled in the body of His flesh through death" (Col. 1:19–22).

The basic message of the gospel is restoration of relationship, which is primarily what bonding is all about. It is about restoring connection and unity with God, others, and ourselves.

In our fallen state, however, we are not born into emotional and spiritual connection. It has to be gained. It is an arduous developmental process, but without achieving connection, we are doomed to alienation and isolation. In that state, we do not grow; we deteriorate. And there is a reason for it.

A plant cut off from anything other than itself begins to wither, decay, and eventually die. In the field of physics the law of entropy states that any closed system left to itself will become increasingly disordered over time. In other words, any energy system, without energy and direction from the outside, will become more and more chaotic over time. In the psychological and spiritual sphere, the law shows itself dramatically. Anyone's internal world that is left to itself begins to wither and become more and more chaotic.

Susan came into therapy for depression and what she described as "terror." In her late twenties, she stated that she had been depressed "for as long as I can remember." Like Joan, she saw it as a blackness. The depression had gone on for years with little change, but after she graduated from college, it got worse, and she had deteriorated over the last few years. Recently, she had experienced such confusion and chaos inside that she would sometimes tremble and at other times have trouble thinking accurately. Occasionally, she would hear voices inside her head that would confuse her even more.

As she talked about her life, she revealed that she had never had a real emotional bond to anyone. She was beset by fears of people and situations that would require her to be close to others. Basically, she was in a position of having to wonder about herself and the world all by herself, and the confusion over the years had grown to be too much. She developed a host of phobias that plagued her much of the time. She wondered if she was really saved and if God hated her; many other things about her faith did not make sense to her. People would explain them to her, and she could grasp them for a while, but eventually the confusion would return.

Susan tried to connect with others, but it was difficult. Like all disconnected people, she had what are called paranoid fears, and she felt that others hated her or would hurt her. Gradually, however, she began to feel a sense of connection with a few safe people, and her world made more sense. She could feel a sense of belonging where before there had been only isolation. Her paranoia decreased over time, and eventually, she had some close friendships. She described the change primarily in two ways. First, she said that the depression had lifted. She still would occasionally get depressed, but it was not the blackness that had overwhelmed her before. Second, she said that her thoughts were not so disorganized. In short, the law of entropy had been reversed. Because she had gotten connected with others and had ceased to be a closed system, she was moving in a different direction, one of higher order instead of higher disorder. And her emotional bonding was creating the movement.

A Developmental Perspective

When we are born into the world as infants, we are in an emotionally isolated state. This is evident on the face and in the screams of an uncomforted infant. If you want a good picture of what hell, total isolation, is like, look into the face of an infant who is experiencing separation and unbondedness from his mother. The infant is in so much distress because of his internal isolation; he literally has no love inside.

When his mother or caregiver picks him up and nurtures him, a transformation takes place. He is able to receive comfort from the outside, and he goes through a transformational experience as he connects with the mother emotionally. Over a period of time, these countless transformations are gradually internalized through the process of memory traces, and the child literally internalizes the mother's care. He begins to feel comforted by the memory of mother that is stored in the emotional brain, and an internal self-soothing system builds up over time. The spiritual and emotional bond created between the mother and the child brings the child out of the isolation he was born into.

This emotional bond with the mother begins all sorts of physiological, psychological, and neurological processes within the child. He begins to develop physically and emotionally as he is nurtured. God has ordained the mothering process to call the infant to life. The connection of their spirits woos the child into the land of humanness, and the child develops a sense of belonging to the human race through his first relationship. He learns that there are safety and hope of being relieved from distress. As this bond matures, the child's normal developmental processes continue to mature, and he becomes more and more relational. He is being rooted and grounded in love.

Although mothers throughout the ages have known and experienced the importance of this bond, scientists began to study it only in this century. A famous body of scientific literature compiled findings about the significance of emotional bonding. They discovered that institutionalized infants were taken care of physically, that is, they were fed and bathed and so on, but only some were held and nurtured, or bonded with. The ones that did not have emotional bonds because of the shortage of caregivers showed drastically increased instances of physical illnesses and even death. In addition, their psychological development was retarded, or it ceased.

Recently, more and more research has been done on the effect of the bonding process throughout life, and the same findings have emerged. Emotional isolation has been shown to affect the entire range of physical illness and recovery: mortality rates, prolonged chronic illnesses such as cardiac problems and cancer, pregnancy complications and healthy infants, recovery rates from heart attack and stroke, for example. One study showed that one group of post-heart attack patients recovered more rapidly than another group because of one factor—they had a pet! It seems like a trite thing, but it illustrates the most important principle of the emotional, physical, and spiritual life. *When we are in a bonded position, a loving position, we are growing, and life is growing within us.* When we are isolated, death is growing within us. Recent evidence in the field of cardiology indicates that the nature of our emotional ties drastically affects the chemical processes that cause heart disease. Doctors are now including, as part of the treatment for heart patients, training in becoming more loving and trusting. It is becoming a medical as well as a psychological fact that the amount of love and connection with others is at the basis of health, both psychologically and physically.

The book of Proverbs frequently mentions the status of the heart that affects the rest of life: "Keep your heart with all diligence, for out of it spring the issues of life" (4:23); "A sound heart is life to the body" (14:30); "A merry heart makes a cheerful countenance, but by sorrow of the heart the spirit is broken" (15:13); "All the days of the afflicted are evil, but he who is of a merry heart has a continual feast" (15:15); "A merry heart does good, like medicine, but a broken spirit dries the bones" (17:22). Emotional and psychological well-being is related to the status of the heart, and that has to do with the depth of bonds with others and God. The Bible said it long ago, and science is proving it today.

In terms, then, of the developmental process, if we come into the world learning to attach to others and trust them, we develop emotionally, physically, and psychologically. We proceed along prescribed plans outlined by our Creator. If, however, we lose attachment with others, our development will be impaired, and we will become symptomatic in some way.

For example, an infant who has a good bonding experience in the first year of life learns some independence in the second year. In this stage of independence, however, the bonding process is still just as important, for the child needs the emotional security provided by the bonds to have the courage to try the newfound independence. If this goes along properly, the child can learn within emotional attachments the ways of dealing with good and bad and with failure. If this is successful, the attachments to parents allow him to identify with his father for sex-role typing and to respond lovingly to his mother.

The security of those bonds propels him out onto the playground to establish bonds of friendship that help him to develop mastery and competency as a member of the group. After he feels good about being one of the gang, he can develop further emotional ties with peers in adolescence and try out a deeper romantic bonding as dating becomes a reality. He will need his emotional attachments with friends to feel secure enough to separate from home and go to college to prepare for a career. There he will develop friendships that help him enter the world of adulthood where he will form the emotional attachments that are to support him for the rest of life.

In this very predictable scenario, development proceeds along normal lines *if and only if* the ability to form emotional attachments is present, for that ability underlies all of the other tasks. This is why the developmental task of bonding is the first and most important in growing into the likeness of God. It leads us to love, knowledge, and morality. By developing attachment to others, we can develop our talents and use them in the real world instead of fantasy, and we can learn values that have love as the basis from being in relationship with peers.

Lest we get too far ahead, let's return to the infant who is learning about relationship from the attachment with mother, or caregiver. There are some vital things to learn at this stage. As the child stores up memories of being comforted by mother, a relationship of memory is being stored inside. Literally, in a deeply spiritual sense, the child takes mother in and has her on the inside in memory. This leads to a greater and greater sense of security as this attachment is repetitively internalized. The child gets a storehouse of loving memories upon which to draw in the absence of mother. The "self-soothing" system is being formed through the growing internal relationship. In her absence he can literally have a relationship with the one who loves him. The memory traces must be built up in the bond through thousands of moments of connections. (This is why the idea of quality time instead of quantity time is a myth for very young children.)

As the relationship gets stronger, the child develops what is known as emotional object constancy. That is, he can experience himself as loved constantly, even in the absence of the loved one, and he can experience a loving self in relation to an absent loved one. If you have had warm feelings as you think of a loved one, you know the riches of this treasured ability. Perhaps during a time of fear or pain, you thought of the ones who love you and are pulling for you, and you gained a sense of courage and hope. Then you know the importance of emotional object constancy, which is crucial to life. It allows a two-year-old to play in the yard by himself without panic and the corporate executive to go to work without needing his wife by his side throughout the day. Both have a sense that their emotional ties are secure, and they are not isolated, even if they are alone.

In the spiritual sense, Jesus was praying for this when He prayed for the Father to be in us and for His love to abide in us. God is consistent in the way that He does things. We develop spiritual constant connection in the same way He gives it to us at the new birth, and we nurture it to fullness of love over time. The biblical writers often tell us to "remember when" God did something or fulfilled a promise; they call on our memory of spiritual experiences to give us the courage to go further with Him. Spurgeon wrote of the experience of the walk with God as allowing us to do more and more for Him. We build a sense of spiritual object constancy with God over the years as we have logged memories of trusting Him and having relationship with Him.

If you can identify with thinking of your deep bonds and thus gaining relief from internal distress, you are extremely fortunate. You have at least a degree of bonding and connection constancy. This degree, whatever it is, can be built upon. If you allow yourself to enter into deeper and deeper relationships, your emotional and spiritual development will get better and better. If, however, that is difficult or limited, there may be a degree to which your ability to bond has been injured or underdeveloped.

Terry gives us an example. He required therapy because of increasing tension and anxiety. At twenty-seven, he was enormously successful. As he became more and more successful, however, his tension increased. He related it to the stress of work.

As we began to examine his life, however, we found little real emotional attachment. He was married to a wonderful woman, but he was unable to emotionally feel much with her. He had married her for her "beauty, personality, innocence, and brains," he said. We discovered that his work was not creating the tension; it was protecting him from it. It allowed him to run from the panic that was underneath. (It would be interesting to know how many fortunes have been made by people running from pain.) But the older he got, the idealism protecting him was wearing off as he achieved his goals at a relatively young age.

We explored the depths of his isolation, which seemed almost bottomless. At a very deep level in his soul, he was an isolated child. We could see his absence of object constancy because he could not stand for his wife to be out of his sight. He went through prolonged depressions when he was separated from her or someone significant. He described the inability to remember what she looked like when he was in his isolated state, and he would need pictures of her to remember that he was loved.

One day, in a crying terror, he said, "I need my mother inside me. She's supposed to live on the inside where she can't get away!" He had never read a book on object constancy, but he knew it from his soul. As he allowed himself to attach in a dependent way to a few trustworthy people, he learned that attachment with loving others could comfort him. He also learned that, over time, he could have a loved self with him wherever he was.

Through the achievement of bonding, his relationships with his wife and three kids changed drastically. He showed empathy for his wife and her emotional needs because he had experienced his own. Before, the boys were easy to relate to, for they could do nonrelational things together like play football. His daughter liked those things, too, but she wanted more tender interaction with him and he was unable to provide that until he knew what bonding was about. With his sons, he was able to get them to express their feelings more openly, and their behavior problems improved.

Spiritually, he learned a vital lesson. When he was in the beginning of his pain, he would be angry and say, "It doesn't do any good to pray or read my Bible. It is not relieving my tension one bit." Later, as he experienced God loving him through His body, he said, "I didn't know how God works. He had to take me through experiences of emotional connection with others to get me out of pain. But I still wish He had done it an easier way."

I am always amazed when some spiritual leaders make this process difficult for the people under their domain. It is a common occurrence for a Christian counselor to see a very hurt, isolated person and for that person to realize for the first time the emotional need for others. The person then opens up to being available to other people in the body of Christ, thus getting into the process that fulfills "the law of Christ" (Gal. 6:2), the process of creating an abiding love within the body that Jesus commanded. Then, the "spiritual leader" will say that such "relational" teaching from the counselor is "humanistic and man-centered," and that the person should "depend on the Lord."

I have seen the disastrous results of people being in bondage to such commandments of their leaders. It is incredible to me that when the Bible teaches, *above everything else*, we need love and attachment, these leaders will declare that the emphasis on relationship is wrong! I would love to hear them say such things to the incarnate Christ when He taught that the entire law could be summed up in the law of loving God and loving others as oneself. He spoke to this problem when He said that some teachers and leaders "bind heavy burdens . . . and lay them on men's shoulders; but they themselves will not move them with one of their fingers" (Matt. 23:4). They won't "allow" people to seek help from those that understand their pain, yet they do nothing to alleviate that pain.

In this passage we see the dynamic of teachers against love. They give a burden of isolation to someone with realistic, God-created needs for connection with others, but they will not enter into the pain with that person. There is no relational aspect to their way of seeing sanctification; they want sanctification without relationship, without bonding. But sanctification rests upon the working out of our relationships with God, others, and ourselves. If there is a break in any of those three connections, we are in trouble. It is always an aspect of the "leaven of the Pharisees" to get us out of relationship with God, others, and ourselves, a process that we will deal with later. At this point, however, it is crucial to see that the teaching against relationship is not from God. "We know that we have passed from death to life, because we love the brethren. He who does not love his brother abides in death" (1 John 3:14). The teaching that we can have love for God without having love for others is a heresy against the Incarnation: "For he who does not love his brother whom he has seen, how can he love God whom he has not seen?" (1 John 4:20).

Generally, these teachers are task-oriented people who are much more concerned with the "rightness" of their theology and rules than with people's hurts. Jesus had this in mind when He said, "But if you had known what this means, 'I desire compassion and not sacrifice,' you would not have condemned the guiltless" (Matt. 12:7). Throughout Christendom, innocent, hurting people who need love and compassion are being commanded away from relationship and into sacrificial striving in order to gain wholeness. There is nothing further away from the heart of God than a theology without love and compassion at its base.

When we see the need for people to have emotional bonds in their lives, we can understand why so many people struggle so desperately and why any isolated view of spiritual maturity is not biblical. Someone like Terry can struggle for a long time against problems such as tension and anxiety and never resolve them until his heart gets rooted and grounded in love.

The quote that Jesus mentions above about compassion comes from Hosea 6:6. The Hebrew word there is *hesed*, which means a belonging love, or a faithful loyal love that has an emphasis on the "belonging together of those involved in the love relationship" (RYRIE STUDY BIBLE note). This is the basis for the ideas of abiding that we see in the New Testament, and it is the basis for emotional and psychological health. It is essential in our understanding of the Christian life.

That is why it is so important to distinguish between emotional isolation and physical isolation. Many people who have a lot of relationships are emotionally isolated. They may have many friends and be involved with a lot of people, but they are still emotionally isolated. *The key to attachment is vulnerability and experiencing one's needs for another.* In that sort of vulnerability, an emotional need for another, bonding is created. After twenty years of marriage, a partner may just walk out on the marriage and not feel anything because there was never really a deep need for the spouse; leaving has little effect emotionally. The Bible talks of a morality based on love, not on principles or rules. If we feel a connection with others and God, we feel the loss of relationship and need satisfaction when we wander away. We also experience the damage that we do to the one we love because of the bond. This is morality based on love and empathy, rather than rules, and it is the strongest morality in the universe. Paul says that the "love of Christ compels us" (2 Cor. 5:14). This is why Jesus said that the whole law and the prophets depended on the law of love.

A good mother does not think that she "ought" to hold her child; she wants to because she feels his discomfort. She loves out of attachment. A good friend does not visit a sick friend because she "should," but because she sympathizes with the friend's infirmity. It is based on compassion, and only compassion drives us to real sacrificial love. When we are giving out of any other reason, it is usually to satisfy a guilty conscience. According to the Gospels, Jesus was continually "moved out of compassion." The Hebrew word translated there conveys a deep attachment and empathy. It does not say that He gave because He should or thought it was the right thing to do. He did not give to get points with His conscience; He gave out of a deep empathy for others, and that comes only from attachment.

I often ask a group, "If I handed you a baseball bat and gave you total permission to bash my face in, would you do it?" Typically, they say no. Then I ask, "Why not?" There will be two answers. The first is something like this: "Because it's wrong to hit someone. It's not the right thing to do." The second sounds this way: "Because it would hurt you, and I don't want to hurt you." Then I ask, "Which one would you trust the bat to more easily?" The answer is obvious. The one that does not want to hurt me is much less likely to hit me because of the ability to empathize with the damage that would be caused.

On the other hand, we often do what we know is wrong, so the first reason is dangerous. Rules never keep us in line; love does a better job of keeping us moral. We think of the damage to the one we love instead of keeping some code. The Bible's answer to morality is always love. When we sin on that basis, it produces "godly sorrow," which is based on hurting our love object and losing relationship instead of being based on guilt or the "sorrow of the world" (2 Cor. 7:10).

Attachment also gives us a basis for the ability to handle stress. I will never forget one week when I witnessed an amazing comparison. I saw two men who were multimillionaires. Both were fifty years old. Both had many, many friends. Both were accomplished and respected in their fields. Both were popular in their communities and in their churches. Then in the same week, both went bankrupt. Both had their wives leave them; both lost three kids in the marital split-up. But there were major differences between the two.

The first one became suicidal and was in a depressive stupor. He locked himself in his house for a month and would not return phone calls to his friends. Finally, he couldn't handle the depression any more and began withdrawing from reality. His father had to take him in and care for his basic needs. It took about a year for him to return to work.

The second man called a meeting of a few close friends and told them that he was really going to need their support. He said that he wanted each of them to promise to have lunch with him on a different day so that he could stay connected and supported through the trouble and try to make a comeback. He called a counselor to help with his depression and grief over the marriage and his kids. In one year, he had restored his fortune and was on the way to rebuilding his life.

The difference was not just the way they handled the crisis. It was in the nature of their attachments. The first man had never let himself need anyone, and he had no deep attachments, even to his three children. When he lost everything, he had no deep love in his life and no way to survive. He had no model for deeply abiding bonds with others. He was alone when catastrophe hit, and because of his lack of bonding, he did not know how to ask for help.

The second man was a recovered alcoholic who had been involved in a support group for years. He had learned about the nature of deep attachments with others; he knew they would sustain him along with his relationship with God. His soul was full apart from his riches and his accomplishments, for he had the love of others within. As a result, he could reach out to them and draw on their strength in his time of need. His bonds of love with others and God, as well as himself, brought him through. He vividly illustrated Jesus' word picture:

> Whoever comes to Me, and hears My sayings and does them, I will show you whom he is like: He is like a man building a house, who dug deep and laid the foundation on the rock. And when the flood arose, the stream beat vehemently against that house, and could not shake it, for it was founded on the rock. But he who heard and did nothing is like a man who built a house on the earth without a foundation, against which the stream beat vehemently; and immediately it fell. And the ruin of that house was great (Luke 6:47–49).

In terms of overall development, when we have a lot of abiding love, we internalize that abiding. This emotional object constancy gives us several abilities. Bonding gets us out of the pain of isolation and enables us to handle stress, as we have seen through research and example, and it gives us the basis for empathy, which plays a major role in morality and relationship. Bonding is also the basis for accomplishment. As we shall see later, bonded people are able to tolerate, and even use constructively, time alone. Being alone does not mean that they are isolated because they have the love inside for whomever they are attached to. They can accomplish things because they don't fear loneliness and work. Bonding puts work into the proper perspective of accomplishing things for the family of humanity instead of running from pain or selfish pride of grandiose accomplishment.

I remember one man in the real estate business who complained of his profession not having any meaning, for it was "just one of making money." His sense of accomplishment was totally task-oriented. Just because he wasn't "in the ministry," he couldn't experience meaning in what he was doing. His words made an impression on me because he was an emotionally detached person. Later, another man, a very relational, loving one, said this: "I love my work in real estate. It is an opportunity to exercise my talents and create good communities for families to raise their kids in. I love the feeling of building developments that will provide jobs, offices, and safety for others." It was a startling contrast. The one who was attached to others felt loving in his work; the detached one did not. Paul affirms that, rooted and grounded in love, we can accomplish everything. But if we don't have love, "it profits . . . nothing" (1 Cor. 13:3).

Attachment gives meaning to accomplishment. It also fuels the rest of development, as we will see in later chapters. When we cannot at the same time be dependent and independent, we are in trouble. When we work on developing our ability to work through badness, without attachment, we have nothing to transform our shame and guilt. When we begin to exercise authority over our lives, we need mutual relationships in the body as brothers and sisters give us an accountable community within which we can grow and exercise our talents. Many people in the adolescent phase of development drop out of life because they cannot attach to a peer group and develop the relationships that move them into adulthood.

Isolation creates an inability to attach, and there are tragic results, for the basic nature of God's likeness is not functioning. What does that look like in real life?

Symptoms of Inability
to Become Bonded

A person who is isolated internally is unable to make emotional attachments or cannot feel the ones he or she has. Thus, an internal need is unmet. In the beginning, the individual protests this isolation through anger or sadness. A good example is a lonely child or an abandoned lover. That pain, or protest, is a good thing, for it signals that there is a need. If we did not have hunger, we would all starve to death. Our hunger is what tells us that we need some food. That is seen in Jesus' statement "blessed are those who hunger and thirst for righteousness, for they shall be filled" (Matt. 5:6). It is our hunger that leads us to get what we need. Proverbs 16:26 says the same thing, "The laborer's appetite works for him; his hunger drives him on" (NIV).

However, if the isolation continues too long without relief, the next stage is depression and despair. The hope of having the need met begins to wither. Someone who feels isolated looks hopeless and longs for something that seemingly will not come. In reality, this is still a good stage, for the person is at least in touch with what is wanted; he or she just doesn't think that it will materialize. They are in the stage that the Bible refers to when it says, "Hope deferred makes the heart sick" (Prov. 13:12). They are experiencing a sick heart because of their unanswered need for relationship, but they still experience the need. They are still attached to the needy part of their makeup.

If depression and despair go on long enough, without anyone intervening to relieve the situation, a third stage—detachment—sets in. There is detachment both from the internal need for others and from the outside world. They are then out of touch with themselves at a very rudimentary level. At times they no longer even feel alive. This does not mean that they are necessarily in pain, but they are not experiencing being alive and all of what that means.

One woman put it this way, "If I can't feel my pain, then I just start to feel dead inside. That is why I have to cut myself, in order to know that I can still feel something." Her action may sound extreme because of its self-destructive nature. But in reality it is a move toward staying alive. She wanted to know that she was at least physically alive, for emotionally she felt dead. She had gone into a detached state. (Incidentally, this woman had been taught by her spiritual leaders that her emotional needs were not important and that she just needed to be more disciplined.)

It may be easier to visualize the detachment of the successful businessman who focuses all of his unfelt isolation into driving achieve-

SYMPTOMS OF INABILITY TO BECOME BONDED

Addictions
Depression
Emptiness
Excessive caretaking
Fear of being treated like an object
Fears of closeness with others
Feelings of badness and guilt
Feelings of unreality
Idealism
Lack of joy
Loss of meaning
Negative bonds
Outbursts of anger
Panic
Shallow relationships
Thought problems (confusion, distorted
*   thinking, irrational fears)*

ment. This is a more acceptable way in our society to be detached. One can even get awards and large salaries for it, but his spouse and children can tell a different story. Let's look at some specific symptoms of a lack of attachment.

Depression

The depression of an emotionally isolated person can be enormous. The example of Joan, at the beginning of the book, shows how painful it can become. Some describe it as a "blackness" surrounding them or a "feeling of being really low." This is the withering of the plant. It consists of repressed feelings of sadness and anger, the two ingredients of the God-given protest against lack of love. That people have the capacity for depression really says something hopeful: it says that relationship matters to them and they are longing for it.

This depression can manifest itself in a quieter way than a deep blackness. It gets masked as a dull ache or a grayness to life. The range of emotional functioning is lost, and the entire world begins to look gray. A lot of people prefer gloomy weather because it matches the way they feel inside. Oftentimes, a sunny day can make them more depressed, for it seems so far removed from their reality.

They experience a loss of interest in doing things, and being with people doesn't really interest them because it doesn't get to the root of the need. Therefore, they usually withdraw from social activities and relationships, which only furthers the isolation and creates a cycle.

Loss of Meaning

Another frequent symptom of isolation is the feeling of meaninglessness. Emotionally isolated people often confuse this meaninglessness with not having purpose, and they pursue some activity or ministry. But they only get further from a solution, for they do not lack purpose. They lack meaning, for the meaning of life is love. In a real sense, life means love, and people in a disconnected state lose a sense of this meaning. One single, detached man said, "I work hard to make a lot of money and be successful, but it doesn't mean much. I don't have anyone to share it with. It's kind of empty, actually."

Many times meaninglessness overcomes people after they have experienced a loss and that relationship has not been replaced. In the depression of the loss, they have not just been in grief, but have gone into isolation. As a result, what they are doing does not give them meaning, for they cannot feel any attachment to others. Meaninglessness is a terrible symptom of isolation and can drive individuals to suicidal feelings because they envision a life without meaning and hope. They do not realize that isolation is at the root.

Feelings of Badness and Guilt

To understand this symptom, we have to recognize a basic fact of the emotional world: a lonely self is a bad self. Isolated people aren't bad; they just think they are bad. A lonely self seems to be an unloved self, and that translates to a "bad self." We have seen that in the Garden Adam and Eve were ashamed when they lost relationship. Isolation equals guilt and feelings of badness, and that is a state we are all born into.

Whenever we do not feel loved, we feel badness. It translates in the emotional brain something like this: *I feel alone, I am unloved. If I am unloved, it must be because I am unlovable. I am bad, or someone would love me.*

Young children who feel "good," which means basically full, dry, and comforted, have the beginnings of worth. When they feel "bad," or distressed, they internalize that into a description of the self. We all retain some aspects of that very early, bodily way of thinking with the emotional brain. It is a basic physiological and psychological fact that when we feel crummy, as we do when we are alone, we feel that we are bad.

Many people perceive that feeling as guilt and try all sorts of methods to get out of the guilt. They confess and confess and confess and try to realize their righteousness, but cannot seem to feel forgiven. The root of this guilt is not sin or some sort of badness; it is isolation.

Addictions

Addictions plague our society. Usually they are to a specific substance, such as alcohol, cocaine, or even food. But there are also addictions to sex, gambling, work, destructive relationships, religiosity, achievement, and materialism. By definition, an addiction is something that someone needs to survive, but it never satisfies because it does not deal with the real problem. For example, there is no such thing as a real need for alcohol or street drugs or millions of dollars. We can live very well without those things.

However, there is such a thing as a real need for relationship, and we cannot live very well without it. We have seen what happens in its absence. In addictions, as in other symptoms, a real need is getting a false solution based on the lusts of deceit, as Ephesians 4 tells us:

> [They are] alienated from the life of God, because of the ignorance that is in them, because of the blindness of their heart; who, being past feeling, have given themselves over to lewdness. . . . the truth is in Jesus: that you put off, concerning your former conduct, the old man which grows corrupt according to the deceitful lusts, and be renewed in the spirit of your mind, and that you put on the new man which was created according to God, in true righteousness and holiness (vv. 18–24).

The important thing about curing addictions is returning to sensitivity and humility, for example, AA's steps of admitting powerlessness and the need for God and others, softening the heart toward those one has injured, and realizing deceitful desires. The desires of addictions are not real desires. They are substitutes for some other need of the real self that is like God. An essential step in the healing of addictions is finding out the real need of the true self that is being negated because of a deceitful desire. In this section, we are focusing on the need for attachment.

What happens is that emotionally isolated people can't get relationship, so they go for something else. Satan convinces them that they really want the food or the sex or whatever, and they order their whole lives around it. But they truly need for their emptiness to be filled up with loving feelings and connections with others. Don't get me wrong; I am not saying that as soon as people realize this, they can stop the addiction. Anyone who works with addicts knows better than that. I am saying, however, that addicts must discover their real need and have it fulfilled to get free from the addiction, and more often than not, the need is for emotional connection with others and God.

When the inner hunger for relationship is filled with love, the driving force for many addictions goes away. Not all addictions, as we shall see, come from isolation, but many do. If someone cannot have a bond with another person, he or she will bond with a prostitute's body, a bottle, an ideal image of success, or some other pseudo-connection, all the while going hungry inside. One woman, who had struggled with an addiction to food, said, "I remember the first time that I chose to call someone instead of eat. I could feel the pull toward the refrigerator, and I interpreted that as a pull toward love. So I called someone in the group. After going over to her house and feeling some real interaction, some warmth, I wasn't hungry anymore. Since that time, I've learned to do that more and more, and I'm finding out it's not really food that I want at those times. It's love."

Thought Problems

Earlier we discussed the law of entropy, which states that any system left to itself becomes more and more disordered over time. This is what happens in emotional isolation. The rage and depression of isolation interfere with the person's thinking processes. The circuits get overloaded, if you will, and the thought processes become distorted, especially in some sorts of paranoid thinking. The inner isolation becomes so great that one feels attacked by the pain, and it is projected outward so that others can't be trusted. Therefore, they are avoided, and more isolation results. That is why paranoid states don't get better on their own and why someone can't be given an assignment to change his or her thinking. That is an isolated assignment, and isolation is the problem!

Often in Christian circles when people have confused ideas about God, they are expected to just memorize verses in order to see Him clearly. That definitely helps, but it must be in the context of love so that they can realize the truth incarnationally. That way, the real problem of isolation is being addressed, and the force behind the thinking problem is diminished. If people are isolated, they will come up with all sorts of delusions and obsessions to explain their pain. They have to make sense of it some way, so they imagine that the world must really be the way that they feel inside. When their internal world begins to change, the way they think about the outside world begins to change, also.

When we hurt inside, we always have some interference with our thinking. David described it this way:

> Thus my heart was grieved,
> And I was vexed in my mind,
> I was so foolish and ignorant;
> I was like a beast before You (Ps. 73:21–22).

The hurt always causes strong emotions of rage and sadness, which interfere with our thinking. There is no greater hurt than isolation; therefore, it follows that isolation causes many thought problems. One must work with the real problem, the isolation, to get sounder thinking.

Emptiness

Probably one of the most painful things a human being can feel is emptiness. Over and over the Bible talks of being filled, which is the opposite of being empty. Paul writes, "[And I pray] that you, being rooted and grounded in love, may be able to comprehend with all the saints what is the width and length and depth and height—to know the love of Christ which passes knowledge; that you may be filled with all the fullness of God" (Eph. 3:17-19). We come into the world empty, and love fills us up.

Some people, disconnected from God and others, feel very empty. They have no experience of bonding inside that fills up the vacuum. Although some people believe that someone else is going to "fill them up," this is impossible. What does "fill them up" is their experience of the bond to others. People who feel empty cannot sense their own feelings of need and love for the other. When we begin to experience our own feelings of connection, then we are "filled." Someone can love me perfectly, and unless I experience my need and reception of the love, which is really a response to that love, I will still feel empty. Many people who are greatly loved will continue to feel empty until they experience their need of and response to others and the love inside begins to grow. That is why cardiologists are teaching people to trust, for the trusting heart is a heart full of feelings of connections with others.

Paul received comfort from his relationships within the body of Christ:

> Great is my boldness of speech toward you, great is my boasting on your behalf. I am filled with comfort. I am exceedingly joyful in all our tribulation. For indeed, when we came to Macedonia, our bodies had no rest, but we were troubled on every side. Outside were conflicts, inside were fears. Nevertheless God, who comforts the downcast, comforted us by the coming of Titus, and not only by his coming, but also by the consolation with which he was com-

forted in you, when he told us of your earnest desire, your mourning, your zeal for me, so that I rejoiced even more (2 Cor. 7:4-7).

Paul gives us an example of the incarnational way that God loves us and works for us. Paul had a need, and God comforted the depressed apostle by sending him Titus.

Compare God's way to the command of many to hurting people that they do not need others; they should just pray and study Scripture! That is cutting off the hand of God who wants to comfort the empty by sending His body to minister! That is what James said when he wrote, "If a brother or sister is naked and destitute of daily food, and one of you says to them, 'Depart in peace, be warmed and filled,' but you do not give them the things which are needed for the body, what does it profit?" (James 12:15-16). Many times someone needs the presence of another, as Paul did, and that is the way God wants to love that individual.

But there is another side, and that is the response of the hurting people. All sorts of people can love them, but they should respond and humble themselves to feel the need for others. When they do this, they begin to be filled with the bond that develops. That is how emptiness is cured. When the need is evacuated, when one denies the need and the filling, then emptiness is the result. When one owns the need and responds to others' love, then the bond inside fills the emptiness. Emotional object constancy develops.

Lack of Joy

From what we've learned so far, it's apparent that a lack of attachment results in a lack of lightheartedness and joy and instead produces a feeling of gloom. Joy comes through connection and relationship with God and others, as well as being connected with oneself, one's feelings of needs and love. John affirms, "That you also may have fellowship with us; and truly our fellowship is with the Father and with His Son Jesus Christ. And these things we write to you that "our joy may be full" (1 John 1:3-4).

Fears of Closeness with Others

It is a natural thing to fear what we do not know. The same is true for attachment. If people are isolated and have always been that way, they fear intimacy. Many fears are associated with this, but the bottom line is that isolated people tend to avoid closeness with others.

Feelings of Unreality

Sometimes we can get so detached that we literally feel disconnected from the world around us. We can see and hear others and our environment, but we cannot feel them. Therefore, they seem unreal.

Because God has created a relational world, we can only know our true selves in relationship. Our true self is a relational self. If we are out of relationship at a deep level, then we can't experience what is true, and this gives a feeling of things being false, or unreal. It is very common, yet if not understood, very scary. It is a frightening thing to live in an unreal existence.

Fear of Being Treated Like an Object

When people have not been loved, they have not experienced empathy and a respect for their needs and personhood. They have been depersonalized and often treated like "things." As a result, they avoid relationship, for they do not want that process repeated. For bonding to occur, we need to respect each other's vulnerability.

Panic

Many panic attacks have isolation at the root. The human soul must be connected to others and be filled with love. If this does not happen, the emptiness is so great that some people can literally fall into it. Some describe it as a "black hole." They feel the panic of utter isolation, the most terrifying experience known to man.

Negative Bonds

For many people, isolation comes from having negative bonds, bonds that do not feed their real needs. But because they consider a bad bond better than no bond, they will stay in hurtful relationships and patterns. Behind almost every bad connection is a fear of isolation. The problem is that bad connections are not real connections, and they lead to isolation as well. As someone once said, "If I am going to be alone, I prefer to be by myself." The person with bad connections says in effect, "If I am going to be alone, I prefer to be with someone."

Shallow Relationships

Many people described as being shallow deny their deeper feelings and thoughts. But often such people are so isolated that they are unable to connect on an emotional level, and as a result, there is no deeper bonding. When we are with someone like this, we often feel like we haven't really been with anyone—"the lights were on but nobody was home." There is not much ability to connect at deep levels. This can be very frustrating in a marriage.

Outbursts of Anger

Angry outbursts and problems with anger are often related to isolation. The most clear example of how this works is with an infant who is left alone and expresses pure, unadulterated rage. As we get older, we tend to hide the rage of isolation, and it comes out in other ways such as cynicism or bodily illness. But the rage, or natural protest against isolation, is there nevertheless.

Excessive Caretaking

Some people feel very isolated inside, and the only way that they can feel close to others is to give to them. This tendency is sometimes not apparent because we don't think of "givers" as being in need. However, underneath many givers' masks are desperate needs for relationship. By always giving and never receiving, they are denying part of who they truly are.

Idealism

Some people enter into a fantasy for the ideal. We will talk more about this in the section on resolving good and bad, but often a deep sense of isolation causes excessive idealism and romanticism. One can have a safe relationship with an ideal fantasy, but it never fulfills; only the real can do that.

The ideal self avoids attachment. Being narcissistic is one way of avoiding trusting others, for the person believes all that is good is inside himself. Everything outside the self is inferior. It is a way of distancing and staying invulnerable.

Other Problems

This is in no way a comprehensive list of the symptoms of isolation; isolation masks itself in many ways. If you are struggling with anything, perhaps emotional isolation is at the root.

Barriers to Becoming Bonded

As we can see from the Bible, Barbra Streisand was right when she sang, "People, people who need people, are the luckiest people in the world." The Bible asserts that only from a humble place of need can we receive and be filled. Truly, needing others is the highest stance for mankind, for it is the humble place where God and others can meet us.

But if it is the cure for so many awful maladies, why don't we just attach to others and be filled? Oh, if it were that easy! Because of the Fall, a whole host of problems render us unable to attach to others and leave us isolated. Let's look at some of those now.

Injury

We come into the world as very vulnerable people. We are totally dependent as little children, and everything that we receive depends on our innate ability to trust and how trustworthy the world around us proves to be. Even from the outset, it is a relationship. We cannot come into the world full of love, we must have that given to us. As John tells us, "We love Him because He first loved us" (1 John 4:19). Anything that we have inside is given to us from the outside, and we receive it. That is the way grace works. It is that way with love, it is that way with salvation, and it is that way with abilities. We must be given talents in order to develop them. "And what do you have that you did not receive? Now if you did indeed receive it, why do you boast as if you had not received it?" (1 Cor. 4:7).

So, by the design of God, no one enters life as a god. We are humbled, needy people. We need others. If we are fortunate to be given to and we humbly receive what we are given, we become grateful givers of what we receive. This is the path of maturity. But if we are not given to, we get injured. This can happen through hurt to our developing "trust muscle."

If a child trusts and is hurt, abandoned, beaten, abused, neglected, criticized, hated, or resented for existing, the very ability to trust is injured. Attachment is based on vulnerability and need. It is easy to see, then, why a child is in trouble if that ability to be vulnerable and experience need is damaged. It is the key to life. In developmental terms, it has been called basic trust.

If we find the world a trustworthy place, we learn that being vulnerable is wonderful, for it gets us lots of good things, like love. When this happens, we just get more and more. Loving people tend to find love.

On the other hand, if we find the world to be untrustworthy, we develop pretty accurate beliefs about our survival depending on our ability not to be vulnerable. We get into the "I don't need anybody" stance, which is a smart and natural thing to do in a nontrustworthy environment. In fact, it is unavoidable, for God wired us with a memory so that we could learn what satisfies us and remember it in order to get it again. Hope comes from remembering that good things have come our way in the past; therefore, they are likely to come again.

That function of memory works the same way when things are bad, and we expect more of the same. We develop a map of the world, and we order our journey around it. This is not something we really sit down and think about; it is much more automatic than that. The problem is that our map is constructed in one sort of setting, a hurtful one, and when we are older and out of that setting, we still have the same map, which is a barrier to relationship.

These convictions are barriers that keep us in isolation. They are outdated maps of the territory around us. They once were accurate, but that is no longer the case. However, we haven't had enough experience to change them in our hearts, so we still operate by them. They govern our deepest behavior patterns.

Often God will introduce us to communities and relationships that can heal our isolation, but our internal barriers built up from another time keep us from bonding to others in the present. There, in the new land that Jesus has transferred us to, we must prayerfully examine our barriers to relationship and ask God to help us see the world His way.

Remember though, lest this sound too easy, it is imperative to have good relationships available to us to begin to face barriers and give them up. It would be silly for the puppy to open up to abusers. But if God has given us opportunity for good relationships, then we must acknowledge our distortions of the truth and bring our real self into attachment with others. In addition, these are distortions that I would call convictions, not beliefs. Oftentimes people are told to change their thinking when that is impossible. Thinking is a more

mature process than trusting. It develops later in life. The real problems lie in our convictions, for these are held in the heart.

Some people expect others to somehow change their minds about
others and themselves. This is very shallow. Our minds are only a
part of who we are. Proverbs tells us that it is deeper than that; it is in
the heart. "For as he thinks in his heart, so is he" (23:7). We form
our view of relationships long before we have the capacity to reason
with our minds. They are carved into our hearts. There can be no real
change outside relationship and trust, for that is where the heart enters in. I'm sure you've heard someone say, "I know that in my head,
but I don't know it in my heart." For the heart to know something, it
must return to the vulnerable place where it was when the rules were
written on it; then it can learn new rules. And that, my friends, is no
easy process.

But God promises to do it if we can be vulnerable again. James
puts it like this: "Lament and mourn and weep: let your laughter be
turned to mourning and your joy to gloom. Humble yourselves in the
sight of the Lord, and He will lift you up" (4:9-10). We must humble
ourselves before His hand and allow Him to rework our distortions
with His Spirit and His body. Listen to the way that David prays for
himself:

> Search me, O God, and know my heart;
> Try me and know my anxious thoughts;
> And see if there be any hurtful way in me,
> And lead me in the everlasting way (Ps. 139:23-24 NASB).

What are some common "hurtful ways" that we see things?

Distortions in Our View of Others

"No one is trustworthy." If we have trusted our real self to others
in the past and they have failed that trust, we develop this sort of
conviction. We do not open our vulnerable heart to anyone, for we
think others will misuse us.

"People will always leave me." If we are isolated because of abandonment that we have suffered, we will fear that others will emotionally abandon us, also. That is our map for relationship: it always ends
as soon as we trust. That is a heartfelt conviction, because that is what
the heart experienced.

"People are mean and critical." If our picture of others shows that they were abusive and criticized our real self, the needy one, we are not likely to be vulnerable to that sort of abuse again.

"People will disapprove of certain parts of me." Some feel they have things inside that others will disapprove of. As a result, the real self cannot bond with another, for it fears judgment. It must stay in hiding. Others believe that other parts of themselves are not desirable enough to bond with. They may be angry parts or sad parts; these are different for different people. These people feel that no one could ever accept them.

"People will control me." Many isolated people have been impinged upon and controlled in relationship; therefore, they learn that being isolated is the only way they can really have freedom. They can't believe they can have freedom within relationship, for they have never experienced it. Their choices, which we will talk about in the next main section, have never been honored within their bonds, so they gave up bonding in order to have freedom.

"People are faking their care." Sometimes individuals grow up in a home of "duty bound" parents who feel obligated to "love" their child, but in reality wish they didn't have to. It is not unusual for people to perceive that others are insincere about their love if they came from such a situation. Thus, they doubt everyone.

Distortions in Our View of Ourselves

"I am bad." We talked earlier about how a lonely self feels like a bad self and how many guilt feelings really have their roots in isolation. If the isolated person is alone, he feels bad; and if he feels that he is bad, he stays away from others on a deep level. It is a vicious cycle.

"I am fundamentally unlovable." This is similar to badness, but it is more directly involved in relationship. The person is aware of the need for love but at the same time feels unworthy of it. The truth is, the person is unloved, and that truth gets distorted into lovability.

"Something about me makes people move away." Many times people will have a conviction that something "in" them is faulty, and that it "causes" others to move away from them. This may go deep into their history, when maybe as an unwanted baby, their mere existence "drove" the overwhelmed mother away. Who knows what it was. But there was something about the environment's response that got internalized as a conviction about the self.

"My sins are worse than other people's sins." Some people finally open up to a group only after finding out that they were not the only ones in the world who felt "that way." They find out that their conviction—such as "No one is as irresponsible or as immoral or as big a drinker as I am"—about themselves was not true. This distortion keeps people isolated.

"I don't deserve love." We often feel that we get what we deserve. It is the basic "law of sin and death" in operation. We are on a works salvation, and we think that if love does not present itself to us, we must not have earned it. The truth is, we can't deserve love. It is just something that someone decides to feel toward us. We can deserve approval, but not love.

"My love is too great and will overwhelm anyone." When people are convinced that their needs will ruin a relationship, they often stay in isolation instead of letting those needs be made available to other people. In fact, people want to see needs so they can get a chance to love in return.

"My need for others isn't valid." Many believe that their need for connection is not something that someone should feel. They think that it is not biblical or strong or whatever, and that it really is not a valid thing to feel. *I should be able to make it on my own,* they think.

"My feelings would overwhelm anyone." This conviction is common among people whose isolation comes from a denial of feelings by people in their past. They think that if they show emotion, it will cause a problem in the connection. They fear their anger or sadness, for example.

Distortions in Our View of God

"He really doesn't love me." Rarely do isolated people feel that God loves them. Since one of the ways that God loves us is through His body, those who are cut off from that body certainly can't feel His love in that way. Also, they usually have few experiences of connection to draw on.

"God doesn't care about the way I feel. He just wants me to be good." Often others have so neglected the inner life of the person that he or she assumes that others are not concerned about it. The individual perceives that others are more interested in performance.

"He just wants 'good Christians.'" Sometimes isolated people try to make sense out of the fact that others seem to be close to God.

Usually they are convinced that other people are somehow better, and that is how God sees them as well. They feel doomed to a life of being left out.

"He gets angry with me." Many people have been driven into emotional isolation by angry attacks from others. They learned that the "other" is always angry or can at least be expected to become angry soon. This expectation of anger from the other, in this case God, keeps them from trusting Him.

"He doesn't hear me." God shows us His love by offering His presence, even when He does not intervene supernaturally. But people who feel isolated cannot sense His presence. They cannot see Him doing anything, and since they can't sense Him, either, they think He must not be listening.

"He doesn't answer prayer." This distortion is similar to the previous one. Since God knows that emotional isolation is at the root of the problem, He is probably answering by offering connection with others. Since this answer is not immediate, it seems that no answer is coming.

"He will control me and take away my freedom." People fear God's control as well as other people's control.

"He won't forgive me for . . ." Often isolated people conclude that God has deserted them and doomed them to hell. They may suppose that they have committed some unpardonable sin. This is really a way to get their theology to match their experience, for they seem to be in hell already. Since they are unconnected, they have not experienced a lot of grace, and forgiveness is something they always have trouble feeling. It is helpful to explain that there is no such thing as a sin that God will not forgive, except the rejection of Jesus, because He makes forgiveness possible. Even when they know this intellectually, they will need human connection to feel it emotionally.

Defenses Against Bonding

We have also built up defense mechanisms against relationship. In the beginning, it made sense to have them, for we may have been surrounded by hurtful relationships. It is a bit like putting on a heavy coat in winter for protection. It is a smart thing to do. But in the summer, taking it off makes sense. It is not needed anymore.

In a similar way, we wore psychological coats to protect us from the cold, and they were needed. But then God rescues us from the cold and transports us to a warm land with possibilities of warm relationships. If we are still wearing our coats, more problems are created than solved. David describes it this way: "A father of the fatherless, a defender of widows, is God in His holy habitation. God sets the solitary in families; He brings out those who are bound into prosperity; but the rebellious dwell in a dry land" (Ps. 68:5-6).

God promises to give us new relationships in His family, but we have to take off our coats to make use of the new. Different people have different types of "coats" to protect them against bonding, but these are some of the more common ones.

Denial

Denial of the need for others is the most basic type of defense against bonding. If individuals come from a situation, whether in childhood or later in life, where good, safe relationships were not available to them, they learn to deny that they even want connection. They slowly get rid of their awareness of the need. Notice that I said get rid of their *awareness* of the need instead of get rid of the need. As long as they are alive, the need is present. It is part of the image of God. But they can dull themselves to the experience of the need.

I'll never forget an attorney who was in the hospital for depression and angry outbursts. The second day he said, "What's all this stuff about needs? I don't need anyone." As the weeks went by, anytime a group would talk about isolation, he would demand a tranquilizer. It eventually became apparent to him that those discussions were difficult for him because they got him closer to experiencing his long-forgotten needs for others. As he gradually gave up his denial, he was able to connect with others, and he found that "macho needs love, too!"

Devaluation

Devaluing available love is a defense used by most people who struggle with emotional isolation. It works like this: love presents itself, and relationship is available. Then instead of responding, the people change it from something positive to something negative. They will say something like "You don't really care," or say something else to make the good into bad. This is a horrible defense because it makes relationship unavailable.

In the Gospels, the only unforgivable sin against God was blaspheming the Holy Spirit. The Holy Spirit, the Spirit of grace, was trying to reach into the world and draw people to Jesus by proving who He was. But instead of responding to the Spirit's grace, they turned the good into bad and stayed away from love. The sin was unforgivable because it kept them away from grace.

It isn't unforgivable to reject human love, but it has the same effects. The blasphemy, or rejection, of the human spirit would be to devalue love on the human level when it comes to us. It is to stay in isolation when love is at hand. It would be like starving to death, someone giving us a steak, and our saying, "It's probably poisoned." Because of the devaluation, we remain in a starving state, never able to get food, and in a state of isolation, because the risks of love are so great.

Projection

Sometimes, we project our needs onto others instead of owning them. This happens in caretaking when we vicariously have our needs met by seeing them in others instead of ourselves. For example, when the self-righteous person thanked God that he was not like the sinner, he did not realize his own need. This is not the biblical way, for Scripture says that we are to "comfort those who are in any trouble, with the comfort with which we ourselves are comforted by God" (2 Cor. 1:4).

Reaction Formation

This term means to do the opposite of what is true. In the sense of isolation, people may try to become overly independent. They may appear to be extremely strong and will often preach against dependency and neediness. They will construct an entire theology around the denial of needs for relationship, going in the opposite direction of what they unconsciously need. This reaction is rampant in Christian circles.

Mania

If persons stay busy enough, they can deny the need for others. They imagine that if they are able to do all of those things, they must not have any needs. Many workaholics tend to be somewhat manic.

The more grandiose they can be, the more they can deny their needs—until they crack.

Idealization

We talked about this as a symptom, for it is sometimes presented as a realized problem, especially in people who have trouble falling or staying in love. They search for the ideal self, or the ideal other, and thus the fantasy is supposed to make up for the state of being without. It is like a very lonely person getting lost in fantasy, except this person is really looking for the "ideal" other that will fulfill all needs.

Substitution

When people cannot get real relationship, they will find some substitute to take its place. We mentioned this in terms of addictions. For example, food or sex may be substituted for love. This is spoken of throughout Scripture in many ways, such as "deceitful desires," "lust," and "idols." First John tells us about "the lust of the flesh, the lust of the eyes, and the pride of life" (2:16). Telling someone to repent and stop a certain behavior is a good idea, but unless the person has the need met, the behavior will return (Luke 11:24–26). It is imperative to fill the soul with the love of God and others.

Withholding Love

A heart remains closed off from others when love is withheld. Whenever we conceal love and appreciation from someone, we further the closed system. When we openly express the care that we feel, we open our hearts to others, and there is connection.

Proverbs 27:5 affirms that "open rebuke is better than love carefully concealed." Only what is in the open, in the light, in time, as we said earlier, can grow and lead us to connection with others.

A Further Word About Injuries, Barriers, and Defenses

All these problems are direct results of the Fall, and everyone has them to differing degrees. The Bible speaks directly about them, and it is in the nature of redemption to address all three—injuries, barriers, and defenses. Early developmental injuries take time to heal and time to grow. We are talking here about the most vulnerable aspect of our hearts, and it takes time for that to be strengthened. Paul understood this when he said, "Now we exhort you, brethren, warn those who are unruly, comfort the fainthearted, uphold the weak, be patient with all" (1 Thess. 5:14).

Injury to the heart is like any other injury. First, it will be very painful and go into shock. Then, after time, if there is support, the heart will thaw out and the pain will return. Then as the pained heart comes back into relationship, it will be strengthened and grow, but that process is one of exercising a very sore limb or muscle. Therefore, we must be patient while we are rehabilitating.

Barriers in the form of our distortions are inherited from the system of relational values wherever we were raised. The family was set up by God to be a spiritual system and to impart spiritual laws to children. It was to be a place where God's ways of loving attachment, freedom of choice, forgiveness, and growing in skills and talents could be learned. There are commandments along these lines. However, we do not live in perfect families, and in many families, the rules are much different from God's.

I sometimes ask group members to write out the ten commandments of their families in terms of what was lived out emotionally. Jesus tells us that sometimes we live according to the traditions of our elders instead of the ways of God (Matt. 15:6–9).

Here is an example of someone's list:

1. Thou shalt not let anyone get emotionally close to you. Keep your distance.

2. Thou shalt not tell the truth about how you are feeling. If you are hurt, keep it a secret.

3. Thou shalt always lie if it will keep the peace.

4. Thou shalt try and look good on the outside. It is more important anyway.

5. Thou shalt achieve highly and bring honor to the family name instead of be close to loved ones from the real self.

6. Thou shalt never leave and cleave, for that would make the rest of the family very sad.

7. Thou shalt not talk about any family matter outside the home or any hurt that you sustain here. Breaking loyalty is an abomination.

8. Children are to interfere in the parents' conflicts. They are to take the focus off the struggles that the parents are having. This is a loving and acceptable sacrifice to the parents.

    9. Tender feelings are an abomination.
   10. Thou shalt be emotionally independent from birth.

This list is far from God's list. However, many people do not turn away from the tradition of their elders and operate according to God's rules. Even though they can be professing Christians, they can still live according to false religions, the original family religious system. They must renounce the theology of the dysfunctional family of origin and adopt the spiritual principles of God's family.

When this shift happens, then the dynamic that Jesus mentioned in Matthew opens one up to a family of connection:

> While He was still talking to the multitudes, behold, His mother and brothers stood outside, seeking to speak with Him. Then one said to Him, "Look, Your mother and Your brothers are standing outside, seeking to speak with You." But He answered and said to the one who told Him, "Who is My mother and who are My brothers?" And He stretched out His hand toward His disciples and said, "Here are My mother and My brothers! For whoever does the will of My Father in heaven is My brother and sister and mother" (Matt. 12:46–50).

Jesus continually taught that we have been transferred from one kingdom to another (Col. 1:13–14). A vital part of this transfer is to realize who our "family" is to be. In a real sense, God is saying that we need to get our "family" support from the ones who do His will. We have to renounce the rules of relationship that were learned in the first spiritual system, and learn God's ways of connection and abiding with the real self so that it can be nurtured into a fruit-bearing state.

When we start to make this shift, we may enter into conflict with many "friends," spiritual "leaders," and even our family of origin. The Bible speaks to that conflict in many places and asks us to make that shift. Jesus says the conflict may come about when we begin to value love if our "loved ones" do not hold to God's values: "Do not think that I came to bring peace to earth. I did not come to bring peace but a sword. For I have come to 'set a man against his father, a daughter against her mother, and a daughter-in-law against her mother-in-law'; and 'a man's enemies will be those of his own household.' He who loves father or mother more than Me is not worthy of

Me. And he who loves son or daughter more than Me is not worthy of Me" (Matt. 10:34–37).

He does not mean that we are to turn against friends or relatives who do not believe in God's ways of love. We are to "love [our] enemies . . . and pray for those who . . . persecute [us]" (Matt. 5:44). However, we *must* see those who do not believe in the importance of love as enemies of our souls, for they reject God's ways if they reject love. Then and only then can we get from the family of God what we need and then only from those within the family that do His will.

David lists attributes of certain people he will not tolerate and then says something very powerful:

> My eyes shall be upon the faithful of the land,
>   that they may dwell with me;
> He who walks in a blameless way is
>   the one who will minister to me (Ps. 101:6 NASB).

In the same way, we must seek out people who can lead us toward the likeness of God, not away from it: "Beware of false prophets, who come to you in sheep's clothing, but inwardly they are ravenous wolves. You will know them by their fruits. . . . every good tree bears good fruit, but a bad tree bears bad fruit" (Matt. 7:15–17).

We are to examine the fruit of our relationships and see if those people are leading us to a greater image-bearingness with regard to attachment. Paul says the same thing to the Corinthians: "O Corinthians! We have spoken openly to you, our heart is wide open. You are not restricted by us, but you are restricted by your own affections. Now in return for the same (I speak as to children), you also be open" (2 Cor. 6:11–12). Paul could see the problems of their affections, their "bad bonds." He exhorted them to connect, to "open wide" to the people who had loved them freely.

Saying no to bad relationships and yes to good is difficult if someone is tied to the bad. The psalmist states that when someone has been oppressed from youth, "furrows" are created in one's back. Every emotionally abused person knows what those feel like. But he says that God can deliver one from those cords, keeping one connected to relationships of ungodly isolation (Ps. 129:1–4). Then the individual can "open wide" his heart to those who walk in the ways of the Lord.

Skills Needed to
Become Bonded

Having good emotional connections is as natural as a plant taking in water. But we are not plants living in the Garden of Eden. Therefore, we require some serious gardening in order to bear fruit in this area of life. Let's look specifically at some skills that are helpful in creating bonding in one's life.

Realize the Need

Many people do not realize that their symptoms come from a lack of bonding and attachment. They have grown up in a situation where closeness was not a value, or their theology has not allowed it, or they have been injured to the point that it has been forgotten as important. In any case, the first skill needed is a realization of the essential nature of attachment. We have explored several reasons for its significance. But there is much more. I encourage you to examine the Bible to begin to see the value that God places on an abiding love from the heart. As Paul says, "And the eye cannot say to the hand, 'I have no need of you'; nor again the head to the feet, 'I have no need of you'. . . . And if one member suffers, all the members suffer with it." (1 Cor. 12:21, 26). We are a body, and we *cannot* be emotionally amputated from the blood flow and expect to thrive. This connection brings about a body that "being fitted together, grows into a holy temple in the Lord, in whom you also are being built together for a dwelling place of God in the Spirit" (Eph. 2:21–22).

Move Toward Others

It is wonderful when others move toward us and seek out our hearts, for that is what God did. Often, though, others cannot see what we need and how emotionally isolated we really are. Therefore, to the best of our ability, we have to actively reach out for help and support. Earlier, we saw how alien that idea was to Robbie. He could not imagine how someone would be interested in connecting with him at a deeper level.

Be Vulnerable

We can move toward others, get involved socially, and have relationships, but still be isolated. We must be vulnerable. We saw earlier how the realization and meeting of needs is the key to growth. This is real humility and vulnerability, and it is absolutely necessary for bonding to take place at a deep level.

This vulnerability may be too threatening on a social level. Maybe we have to start with a pastor, counselor, or support group that is a bit safer. But it is a skill that opens up the heart for love to take root. When we can admit that we need support and help, and disclose the hurt and isolation that we feel, a dynamic is set into motion that can literally transform our personalities and lives.

SKILLS NEEDED TO BECOME BONDED

Allow dependent feelings
Be empathetic
Be vulnerable
Become comfortable with anger
Change distortions to the truth
Move toward others
Pray and meditate
Realize the need
Recognize defenses
Rely on the Holy Spirit
Say yes to life
Take risks

Change Distortions to the Truth

We looked at some distortions that block us from relationship with others. They essentially cause us to repeat what happened to us in the past. That is why it is so important to challenge our distortions keeping us in bondage. To the extent that we continue to see the world with the rules that were learned in an unhealthy situation, our past will be our future.

For example, if someone does not challenge a belief that "all people will leave me," an abiding attachment will never be created, and the isolation from the past will be re-created. The Lord has promised to reveal truth to us, and if we ask Him to show us our particular distortions, He will.

The distortions were learned in the context of relationship, and that is where they are unlearned. We need new relationship to undo the learning of the past; there the real self can be connected in grace and truth and thereby be transformed.

Take Risks

To learn new relational skills and the way of attachment, we must take risks. Listen to Jesus' invitation: "Behold, I stand at the door and knock. If anyone hears My voice and opens the door, I will come in to him and dine with him, and he with Me" (Rev. 3:20). We have a responsibility to hear the voice and open the door. People and God will call to us, but if our distortions and our resistance to risk get in the way, we will keep the door closed so that attachment cannot happen. We must allow ourselves to risk valuing someone emotionally. For the isolated person, this is difficult, but essential.

Allow Dependent Feelings

Whenever we allow someone to matter to our isolated hearts, needy and dependent feelings that are uncomfortable will surface. These are the beginnings of a softening heart. Though uncomfortable, the feelings are a key to attachment. Many times we will feel the need to "keep a stiff upper lip," but allowing our tender sides to show to the ones we need will cement the attachment and allow it to grow.

Recognize Defenses

Each of us must recognize our particular defenses against attachment. As soon as we can spot the old familiar patterns, we can notice them in operation and take responsibility for them. We may say something like this: "Oh, there I go again, devaluing others trying to love me. I'll try to let them matter this time."

All growth involves some responsibility on our part. We must challenge our old ways of being and allow the Holy Spirit to empower us to resist our defenses.

Become Comfortable with Anger

Oftentimes people will avoid attachment because they fear their angry feelings toward the one who is needed and loved. As a result, the feelings lead them into isolation to protect the loved one. It is natural to feel angry toward people we need. The more we can feel comfortable with angry feelings toward "good" people, we can integrate those feelings into the relationship and not spoil it. We will cover more on this subject in the section on resolving good and bad, but it has implications for attachment, too. The angry self is an aspect of personhood that many people prefer to leave unbonded; they believe that it is an unlovable aspect of who they are.

Pray and Meditate

David in the psalms asked God to reveal who he was at a deep level. As he said in Psalm 51:6, "Behold, You desire truth in the inward parts, and in the hidden part You will make me to know wisdom." God will reveal the true state of being in our hearts if we allow Him to. Praying and sitting before God to have Him unravel our problems with bonding are important. He has assured us of His desire to do this.

Be Empathetic

Being able to empathize with others' needs tends to soften our own hearts. Many hardened people have melted into their own neediness by getting close to the hurts of others. I am not implying a give-to-get syndrome or one that says "get your mind off yourself." I am talking about identifying with other strugglers so that we can be aware of our hurts as well.

Rely on the Holy Spirit

The role of the Holy Spirit in the life of the believer is essential. He empowers us to change and to come out from the bondage of old ways of being. We must ask Him to free us from the hold that our defenses have on us to keep us in isolation, and ask Him to give us a place of freedom from which we can make attachments to others.

Every time we find ourselves at a crossroad of either responding defensively in an old pattern or risking the new, we must ask for help. When we reach our inability to attach, we can confess that inability and ask the Spirit to help us in our infirmities and give us courage to return to life. We cannot change on our own power. We must rely on Him to help create what was lost earlier in life.

Say Yes to Life

The task of bonding to others and God is one of saying yes to life. It is saying yes to God's invitation to attach to Him and others' invitations to have connection with them. People who struggle with isolation say no to relationship in numerous ways.

When we utilize our defenses, we are saying no. When we avoid intimacy, we are saying no. Connection requires us to say yes to love when it presents itself. This may involve accepting invitations to be with people instead of withdrawing from them. It may mean giving a different answer when asked, "How are you doing?" It may mean opening up and responding in empathy to others' vulnerability. Attachment always involves saying yes to relationship when it presents itself to us.

An Inventory of Progress
Toward Becoming Bonded

Before the days of computers, businessmen had to set aside a time to take an arduous count of what they really had in order to see three things: (1) What did we start with? (2) What do we have now? (3) What do we need to get for the future? Let's use these questions to take a personal inventory.

The Past

To discover what we started with, we must look at the nature of past bonding in our lives. This is not for the purpose of blaming; it is for the purpose of understanding.

Whatever is not understood tends to get repeated. Because of the tradition of the elders, we invalidate the truth of God. The sins of the fathers are carried on throughout generations if they are not confessed and repented of.

We need to discover our rules of attachment and where we learned them to change the generational pattern holding us back. It does not involve just family, but church or school or influential friends or whoever gave us a map for our bonding experiences. Doing this will help immensely in two ways.

First, we can understand the internalized voices of the past and reject them. Many problems of attachment have to do with projecting past figures in life onto present relationship. In marital counseling it is a sad thing to watch a person distort a spouse with a figure from the past, for it blocks present intimacy. Someone can describe a spouse as being uncaring or emotionally unavailable or critical or whatever, but a figure from the past is actually projected onto the present loved one.

Every counselor has heard the response in successful marital counseling: "I can see now that he (or she) is not as bad as I was seeing him (or her). My unresolved relationship with Father (or Mother or sibling or whomever) was getting in the way." When transferences from the past are learned about and the distortions corrected, intimacy can follow.

This understanding allows one to be more realistic about people in the present. It also permits one to choose new patterns of relating that have to do with God's way. One learns where "everyone will leave me" comes from and realizes that not everyone is like the one from the past.

Second, we can identify the people we must forgive. Thorough healing involves forgiving people from the past. Unforgiveness binds one to the person who inflicted the original injury. It is a handcuff that creates a negative tie to the original hurtful "other." It keeps one in that relationship for years, even if the abuser has died. Unforgiveness ties a cord to the one who injured the person, and forgiveness is the way out of that destructive relationship.

A lack of forgiveness also keeps one from opening up to new persons to love. We saw earlier how Paul asked the Corinthians to let go of the old bonds, or "affections," and to open up to the new. If there is unforgiveness from the past, it keeps one tied to the old and makes the new impossible. Forgiveness allows the part of the self that is "bondable" to be available to make new, good attachments that replace the old.

Here are some questions to use in taking an inventory of the past.

They allow you to remember what was good in order to re-create those things now and to recognize what was bad so those aspects can be avoided in the present and future.

1. *With whom did I have a good bonding relationship in the past? What ingredients of that relationship allowed me to make a connection?*

2. *Who hurt me in terms of my ability to bond and trust? How? What were their personality traits that were hurtful?*

3. *What convictions of the heart did I develop about myself and others from those attachments? What convictions did I develop about relationship in general?*

4. *Have I been able to forgive the persons who have been hurtful? What is blocking me from forgiveness (waiting for them to apologize or change, wanting revenge, enjoying punishment of them internally, never having admitted how mean they really were, feeling guilty over telling the truth about how bad they were)?*

5. *Have I been able to realize God's acceptance of the parts that they hurt in me and labeled "bad"? What is blocking that (distortions, lack of vulnerability, lack of sharing it with someone else to feel acceptance, etc.)?*

6. *What parts of my bonding self did I take outside time as a result of those bad bonds from the past? Why are they still hidden?*

The Present

Any good inventory values the present status as well. The past allows us to gain insight and forgiveness for ourselves and others, learn where our distortions come from to choose new ways and clear up projections, express hurt from others that has never been expressed in order to bring that hurt part back into time, and so on. But archaeology never built a new building, and that is the focus of sanctification, building something new.

If we are in the process of building something, we must take an inventory of our materials to see if we have what we need. We have identified the ingredients as grace, truth, and time. Here are some questions that may help.

1. *With whom do I have a good bonded relationship now? What elements help create that? How can I increase those elements (be more vulnerable, take more risks, show more need, etc.)?*

2. *With whom do I presently have a negative bond? Why am I remaining in that state and not changing the nature of the connection? What elements of the connection are hurting me and leaving me isolated?*

3. *How am I allowing the components of the present negative bond to reinforce my original distortions about myself and the rest of the world? How is that relationship reinforcing my defenses and injuries?*

4. *What distortions and barriers do I allow to dominate my current picture of relationship?*

5. *Am I showing my real self to someone who can give grace to me?*

6. *If I believe that time is an element of growth, how much time do I invest in creating these attachments each week? If very little, what can I do to change that?*

7. *Who is available that I am not connecting with?*

The Future

One thing is certain: if we do not make plans to change what has been, it will continue into the future, and that "bad" future will someday be more of a "bad" past. This is what we talked about earlier when we looked at "bad time." Time that is not being used is wasted, and we are not growing.

To create attachments in life, we have to do something different from what has been done. The bonding aspects of the self have to come out of hiding and get into relationship with others. This takes some real strategy and commitment to self and to God. It behooves us to plan for the future! The following questions may help in making the future different:

1. *As I look "out there," who is available, and how am I going to increase my relationships? What concrete steps am I going to take?*

2. *What structured situations can I take advantage of? What are some available support groups, prayer and sharing groups, or group therapies that I could pursue?*

3. *In what specific ways am I going to challenge my distortions and barriers?*

4. *What difficulties do I envision encountering as I challenge my isolation? How am I going to handle these when they arise, as they most assuredly will?*

5. *How can I allow God to be a part of ending my isolation?*

6. *Who will I share my plan with and get feedback from? Who can I ask to pray for me?*

7. *What negative attachments of truth without grace or grace without truth do I need to either change or avoid in order to grow?*

8. *How am I going to make the time that is absolutely necessary for bonding to increase with others?*

9. *What am I going to do when my defenses arise?*

Conclusion

Bonding with others and God, as well as the different aspects of ourselves, is essential. There is no such thing as spiritual growth without attachment. Without it, we have missed the foundational aspect of what it means to be human and what it means to be in the likeness of God.

We have seen some of the disastrous symptoms of a lack of bonding. If you feel those things, my prayer for you is that you can work with God to redeem the trusting, attaching, needy aspect of yourself and come into a deep, abiding relationship with Him and others.

But to do that, you must be willing to overcome your past, evaluate your present, and work on your future. This involves a diligent commitment to guarding the heart and includes the digging around and fertilizing of the tree that Jesus referred to. Because you must bring aspects of yourself back into time, you must deal with injuries, barriers, distortions, defenses, and lack of forgiveness. If you are willing to do that, you will establish a rooting and grounding in love, and love never fails.

Joan

This book began with Joan, who was isolated among an army of friends, and her only companion was the never-ending depression that led her to try to end her life. Let's get an update.

Joan's initial time in the hospital was tumultuous. She daily fought off attempts by the staff to get to know her. She remained isolated in her room, and even when she was out of it, she wouldn't talk about her plight. However, she apparently was warming up as she saw others feeling the same sort of pain that she had.

Slowly, she allowed some people to get close to her. At first, it was on the same surface level that she had built her life on—her wit, her charm, her attractive personality, her intelligence. Later, she opened up to a few trusted ones and told her story.

She had been raised in a strong Christian environment that taught her right from wrong and instilled a strong sense of values in her, which she had followed all her days. The one value that was absent, however, was attachment from a deep emotional level. Her mother was too passive and ineffectual for her to want to attach to, and her father was "interested only in righteousness." She grew up well on the outside, but on the inside she was empty.

At a young age she married a bright, promising seminary student and thought that he was all there was. He was everything she had ever hoped for. It turned out that he was a perfectionistic, hard driver. He had omitted the more relational aspects of life, also. After building a successful ministry with him, she found herself alone, unable to know that she needed him or anyone else. In fact, she had learned to omit that need, first at home, then later in marriage and with friends.

By opening up to her peers in the hospital and with the staff, she found that her more vulnerable parts were the ones most appreciated. She was bewildered when people would want to talk to her, even after she had been seen crying. She really believed that no one would accept that aspect of her. Other times when her needy self emerged, people found her extremely lovable.

She explored the barriers and distortions of her hyperindependence and slowly allowed others to matter to her. She even reached into the painful world of her fellow strugglers. This allowed her to see that even though she was becoming "needy," her strong parts did not disappear. She confronted other defenses that she had against vulnerability as well and invited some old friends to visit her. She was amazed when they did not reject her in her vulnerable state.

In addition, she explored the reasons for the lack of vulnerability in her marriage, and she and her husband worked hard to gain the intimacy they had never enjoyed because of their individual backgrounds and fears. Gradually, they established a connection.

Over time, her blackness lifted. She found some reason to live, for she could experience the thing that adds meaning and hope to life: relationship. She could finally feel the love of others and God, and although it began slowly and painfully, it multiplied over time.

She continued to work hard after her long hospital stay, and she made more connections with others. Since I was not her therapist, I did not see her after her stay at the hospital, but she would visit us from time to time. Years have passed since then, and she is still doing well.

Joan's battle was to regain her life. When she began to fight to regain the emotional connectedness that she had lost years before, grace, truth, and time were on her side. One day she will be able to face her Savior and be proud that she "fought the good fight," the one of love, and regained the lost likeness of God that the Fall and her background created. Until then, she and her family will enjoy being rooted and grounded in love as well as giving that love to others. She moved from the despair of isolation to the hope of connection.

CHAPTER FOUR

How to ── Create Boundaries

"**W**hy don't you just tell your mother that you don't want to come home for Thanksgiving? You're thirty years old. I think that's old enough to spend a holiday with your friends," I said.

"But that would make her very angry," she replied. "I could never do that. It's mean."

"How can you 'make' her angry? Why do you think you have that much power?" I asked.

"Well, if I didn't go home for the holidays, that would make her mad. That's how I have that much power."

"Then I guess you think you have the power to make her happy as well. Is that right?" I wondered aloud.

"Well, of course," Sandy responded. "If I do what she wants, I can make her happy."

"You're a very powerful lady," I said. "It must be frightening to have that much power. But if it's true that you are that powerful, why don't you have the power to make yourself feel good? This mixes me up."

"I don't know the answer to that. That's why I came to see you. So you could make me feel better."

"Oh, I see. You make your mother feel good, and that makes you feel bad. Then you come to see me, and I'll make you feel good. What am I supposed to do if that makes me feel bad?" I asked. "Maybe I could call your mother and she could make me feel better."

"You're crazy," she said. "How's she gonna make you feel better?"

"I don't know," I answered. "But as long as everyone is responsible for everyone else's feelings, I'm sure she would find a way."

If you felt a little mixed up by that conversation, imagine what it must feel like to be responsible for someone else's feelings or behaviors or attitudes but out of control of your own. Looking at Sandy's situation more closely, we see a basic problem: she did not know where her responsibility ended and someone else's began. She did not know her life apart from her mother's. That is the essence of boundaries: determining where you end and someone else begins.

The Biblical Basis for Having Boundaries

We have just seen how the most important thing is to be attached to others and to say yes to connection. But how does one establish an attachment and remain an individual? How does one determine what is actually oneself versus the other? How does one set a course within an attachment and know that it is personal choice? And on the negative side, what happens when one is connected to others and does not agree? Or wants to do something different from the individual connected to? Or does not want the negative aspects of the loved one to inflict pain anymore? Or wants some time and energies spent apart from the friend or spouse they feel close to? Sounds complicated, doesn't it? It is. Let's examine the second developmental aspect of the likeness of God: establishing boundaries and a sense of separateness.

The model for personality structure, God, reveals an incredible truth. He is a bonded person; the Father, the Son, and the Holy Spirit are always in a connection. They have an eternal "oneness." However, just as unity is the most basic quality that they possess, diversity is seen within that unity. They have separate personhoods; they are not fused so that they lose their individual identities. There are boundaries between them that make them distinct. They each have their own talents, responsibilities, wills, and personalities. They can be in different places at the same time and do different things without losing relationship.

In addition, God is separate from His creation. He knows what is Him and not Him. He is not a pantheistic God fused with creation. He is a separate person from us. He can have relationship with us, but He is not us, and we are not Him. There are boundaries between our identities, wills, and responsibilities. Real relationship is possible because His will is separate from us.

Likewise, on the human level, as we are created in His likeness, we are separate from one another. We have distinct personalities, wills, talents, and responsibilities. There is diversity in our unity of connection. Therefore, separateness is a significant aspect of human identity. We are to be connected to others without losing our own identity and individuality. We are to be like Him in this respect. We are to master the art of "being me without losing you."

But just as our sense of connection was marred in the Fall, so is our sense of separateness, boundaries, and responsibility. We are all confused as to where we end and someone else begins. We have difficulty having a will of our own without getting it entangled with someone else's. We often don't know who we really are as opposed to who someone else says we are. Sometimes we don't know what we think or feel unless the culture identifies it first. The boundaries between us and the world get blurred. These are all conflicts of separateness and boundaries, and this section will look at that problem from a biblical basis to rediscover our boundaries within relationship to the ones we love.

The Elements

Boundaries are a property line. They define who we are and who we are not; they have a positive and a negative function. They say positively, "I am this, and this, and this." And, they say negatively, "I am not this, nor this, nor this."

When one thinks of relationship, one thinks of love. When one thinks of boundaries, one thinks of limits. Boundaries give us a sense of limits as to what is part of us and what is not part of us, what we will allow and what we won't allow.

In the Bible God continually defines Himself to the world in both positive assertions and negative ones. In these examples, He defines Himself by saying who He is: "I am your shield" (Gen. 15:1); "I am a jealous God" (Exod. 20:5); "I am Almighty God" (Gen. 17:1); "I am the LORD" (Exod. 6:6); "I am gracious" (Exod. 22:27); "I am holy" (Lev. 11:44); "I am the First, I am also the Last" (Isa. 48:12); "I am your Savior" (Isa. 60:16); and "I am merciful" (Jer. 3:12).

In another way, He defines Himself by saying what He feels and thinks: "My heart makes a noise in me; I cannot hold my peace" (Jer. 4:19); "I am weary of relenting" (Jer. 15:6); "I knew that you were obstinate" (Isa. 48:4); "I love justice" (Isa. 61:8); "I was crushed by their adulterous heart" (Ezek. 6:9); and "I am glad" (John 11:15).

He defines Himself by saying what He will choose to do: "But I will establish My covenant with you" (Gen. 6:18); "I will make you a great nation; I will bless you" (Gen. 12:2); and "I will give you a new heart and put a new spirit within you" (Ezek. 36:26).

And there are numerous ways that His attributes, feelings, and thoughts are defined in the third person:

> The LORD executes righteousness,
> And justice for all who are oppressed.
> He made known His ways to Moses,
> His acts to the children of Israel.
> The LORD is merciful and gracious,
> Slow to anger, and abounding in mercy (Ps. 103:6–8).

His definition comes from what He is—His attributes, talents, feelings, thoughts, behaviors, and will. All of these things are who He is; they form His identity.

In the same way that the positive affirmations of who He is define Him, so do the negative affirmations. He defines what He is not by saying what He hates:

> These six things the LORD hates,
> Yes, seven are an abomination to Him:
> A proud look,
> A lying tongue,
> Hands that shed innocent blood,
> A heart that devises wicked plans,
> Feet that are swift in running to evil,
> A false witness who speaks lies,
> And one who sows discord among brethren (Prov. 6:16–19).

The biblical writers name things that the Lord loves and hates so that we can understand who He is. What He chooses and what He wills, what He wants and what He does not want, what He thinks about things and what He does—all of these things define the boundaries of who He is. In the same way, we define ourselves by the same functions.

Our Physical Presence

This aspect of identity comes from the physical self. Our body has physical boundaries, for instance. Our body's boundaries define our self, keep the good in, and keep the bad out. That is probably the best definition of the function of boundaries that I can think of. The skin is the clearest picture of a boundary that exists for a person. It defines where we begin and end. It has color and texture. It has shape.

It functions by keeping the good in. For example, it keeps blood and organs inside so that they can work for us. The skin also has the ability to open itself up to good things from the outside. By opening my mouth, I can let in a glass of milk that will nourish me, or I can open my eyes to see something beautiful that will add to my soul. I can choose to let my boundaries down. This is what we do when we say yes to love in the spiritual sense. We let our boundaries down.

At the same time, the bad is kept out. Our skin prevents poison elements from invading our bodies and contaminating us. It keeps germs on the outside so that we do not become infected. If I pour some infectious liquid on my arm, for example, and if I do not have a cut, my skin boundary protects me. If, however, I have a cut in my boundary, the bad gets inside and I become infected. My boundaries have been crossed by the bad stuff, and I am in trouble.

I can sneeze when air is bad, I can shut my eyes to something offensive, or I can cover my ears to evil sound. The physical boundary keeps the body safe, and in some ways, the soul as well.

I am responsible for taking care of my body. I must "guard it," as the Bible says about the heart. I best know what it requires to get needs met. For example, I feel my hunger, and I take responsibility for knowing that and for doing something about it. If I feel pain, I am responsible for telling someone about the pain who has knowledge to help it. That responsibility is mine even if I did not inflict the pain, for it is my pain, it is in my body. Since it is in my body, I must own it and be responsible for it. I am the steward over it.

Any other boundary works in the same way. If I own a farm or a piece of property, there are boundaries to my ownership. I am responsible for what is inside the line. Similarly, my responsibility ends where my boundaries end. If something is wrong with my neighbor's farm, I cannot be so presumptuous as to climb over his fence and begin to work without his permission. If I want to help, he can choose to allow me to cross his boundary line. But it is still his responsibility and choice.

With the physical boundary as well as other boundaries, whatever is mine is my responsibility and I must own it.

Our Attitudes

The second aspect of our personhood that lies within our boundaries is our attitudes. God defines His attitudes and beliefs throughout Scripture. For example, the Ten Commandments give a pretty good idea of where God stands on certain issues. His beliefs and attitudes really form the structure of His personality, as we mentioned when we talked about truth. God's boundaries are drawn intrinsically as part of who He is. They are firm, although flexible; they can bend with the needs of reality. One of my favorite examples of God's boundaries, although spoken to the ocean, occurs in Job 38:10–11: "When I fixed My limit for it, and I set bars and doors; When I said, 'This far you may come, but no farther, And here your proud waves must stop!'" One can hear and feel the solid nature of His boundaries, where He puts His foot down.

We are to own, or be responsible for, our attitudes because they exist inside our property lines. They are within our hearts. God repeatedly tells us to examine and take responsibility for the attitudes and beliefs governing our lives. They form the structure of our personality. In the beginning of life, they are "soaked up"; as we mature, we are to take more and more responsibility for making sure they are ours and not someone else's. We will take a closer look at that process, but for now it is important to see that our attitudes are our responsibility and not someone else's. They are part of who we are. In the book of Joshua we are told: "This Book of the Law shall not depart from your mouth, but you shall meditate in it day and night, that you may observe to do according to all that is written in it. For then you will make your way prosperous, and then you will have good success" (1:8). If our attitudes are God's, our way will be prosperous.

We will look at many of those attitudes as they apply to relationship and personality functioning, but suffice it to say that *every family or individual dynamic that produces symptoms in people is some violation of God's attitudes.* That is why we can trust them; they will get us out of pain. When we take responsibility for our attitudes, we can make sure what we have inside our property lines is what we want.

We saw how, in the area of attachment, some attitudes can be harmful. Joan had an attitude proclaiming, "All my weakness is bad," and it was causing her great depression. When she began to see that she could take responsibility for the attitude and work on it, that it was part of her, within her boundaries, she could get it in line with God's attitudes about relationship and need. As it was changed, she came out of her isolation.

In the case of Sandy at the beginning of this chapter, she was taking responsibility for the attitude of her mother, which said something like this: "Everyone must do exactly what I want. I should always get my way." When her mother's attitude made her mother angry, Sandy felt responsible for that anger. She grossly misunderstood the boundaries involved, however. Her mother's attitude, not Sandy's behavior, was making her angry. But her mother's attitude was outside Sandy's property line and therefore outside Sandy's control *and* responsibility. Sandy was in a bind; she was trying to control her mother's state of being, trying to "make" her happy.

Because she was taking responsibility for her mother's attitudes, Sandy was being irresponsible for her own. She had an attitude that was not of God, and it needed changing. It went something like this: "I am responsible for another person's pain that results from her self-centeredness. I should always give in to people's demands." She ignored her own unbiblical attitudes and beliefs, and she was not working on what she had the responsibility to change, namely, herself. That is why she felt so "overpowerful" and powerless at the same time. She had taken responsibility for something she could not control and deleted something she could control.

By becoming aware of what the Bible really says about attitudes and beliefs, we can align our internal structures of truth with reality. Those attitudes are within our own boundaries, they are part of us, and they dictate much of our identity.

Our Feelings

Another aspect within our boundaries is our feelings. In the same way that our physical feelings of pleasure or pain are on "our property," so are our emotional feelings. Thus, we are responsible for them.

Basically, feelings are signs of our state of being. As part of the likeness of God, they tell us how we are doing, what matters to us, what needs changing, what is going well, and what is going badly. To disown feelings, to not take responsibility for them, is one of the most destructive things we can do to ourselves and others. David knew how destructive closing one's heart could be. "They have closed their unfeeling heart; with their mouth they speak proudly" (Ps. 17:10 NASB). Solomon also was familiar with the ways of people who do not take responsibility for their feelings, those who do not "own" them. He says in Proverbs 14:13, "Even in laughter the heart may sorrow." And in Ecclesiastes 7:4, he shows the importance of owning feelings. He says that "the heart of the wise is in the house of mourning." He knew that people who did not deal with their feelings were not wise and that they could lose touch with themselves. He wrote, for example, of people who do not take responsibility for their anger and hatred and thus become dishonest flatterers:

> Fervent lips with a wicked heart
> Are like earthenware covered with silver dross.
> He who hates, disguises it with his lips,
> And lays up deceit within himself;
> When he speaks kindly, do not believe him,
> For there are seven abominations in his heart (Prov. 26:23–25).

David indicates in Psalm 51:6 that God desires truth in the innermost being. That is where our feelings lie, and we are commanded to be honest about them. We will look in depth at coping with feelings in another section, but it is important to realize that they are an essential aspect of boundaries. They are within our property lines, and we are responsible for them. If we think someone else is responsible for them, as did Sandy's mother, we are in big trouble, and we will cause big trouble for others.

In the Gospels, Jesus clarified the boundary issue and commanded people to take responsibility for their feelings. His story about the servants being hired at different hours and getting the same wage is a good example (Matt. 20:1–15). The ones who did not get what they wanted were angry with the landowner. But Jesus made the point that their anger came from envy, and they needed to deal with it.

On the other hand, feelings can let us know when something really has been done to us, and then we can move to remedy the problem. Our feelings tell us our state of being, and if we are out of touch with them, we do not often know that something is wrong. We need to know what they are in order to know what to do. They are our key to our heart, both good and bad. We need to see them as within our boundaries, or property line, and take responsibility for them, as God does.

Our feelings are one of the most important aspects to the "likeness" of God. They can move us to righteousness and compassion, as they did Jesus on many occasions. They provide the basis for empathy, which connects us to others as we discussed in the section on bonding. They give us joy, which has serious considerations for our state of physical, mental, and spiritual well-being. At the same time, they can alert us to something that needs changing. By owning our feelings, we will keep our property in order and be better neighbors to others.

Our Behaviors

Another aspect lying within our boundaries is our behavior. In the Law, and in the New Testament, the Bible continually talks of our taking responsibility for what we do. This is an important aspect of identity and boundaries, for if we disown our responsibility for our behavior, we are out of control.

People who are out of touch with this truth feel powerless because they have no faith in the law of cause and effect. They do not operate by the law of sowing and reaping, which governs the entire universe. Paul explains it: "Do not be deceived, God is not mocked; for whatever a man sows, that he will also reap. For he who sows to his flesh will of the flesh reap corruption, but he who sows to the Spirit will of the Spirit reap everlasting life" (Gal. 6:7–8). Irresponsible people hate this law and, as a result, suffer greatly, but responsible people thrive on it. It says that God has set up an ordered universe, and that if we behave in a certain way, certain things will happen. This law of natural consequences is the basis for our security, for it gives us control of ourselves. Let's briefly consider how it works.

God has set up a dependable system. Within it, for every action, there is an equal reaction. If I do something, something happens; if I do nothing, nothing happens. If I am hungry and want to eat, I can depend on the law of cause and effect. That is, I can do work, for which I will be paid. If I want to build a good relationship, I can give someone a smile or a hug. If I want to have a career, I can gain skills that will pay off for me later. God intended for us to have that feeling of power. We can cause things to happen with our behavior.

On the other hand, certain behaviors will cause bad things to happen to me. This is the law of natural consequences of behavior. If I do not steer my car, I will have a wreck. If I am lazy and do not study, I will flunk out of school. If I do not show up for work, I will not get paid and thus I will go without food and shelter. If I beat my loved ones, I will enjoy little intimacy. Therefore, to a large degree, my well-being depends on my behavior. If I learn the law of sowing and reaping, I can trust it to give me satisfaction as well as prevent pain.

People who are firm believers in this law feel in control of their lives, to the extent that human beings can feel in control. God wants it that way. If they have a need, they behave in a way that will meet their need: they pray, they go to work, they ask for help, they exercise, they make friends, they behave in ways that bear fruit in their lives, and they get somewhere. I saw an ad on television for a financial seminar in which someone said, "I realized that I did not have any money, and that if I kept doing what I was doing, I was guaranteed to continue having no money." That's a good summary of the law of cause and effect. Proverbs 9:12 says, "If you are wise, you are wise for yourself, and if you scoff, you will bear it alone." In other words, if we take responsibility, we reap. If we shrug it off, we will bear the consequences.

When people are denied ownership of their behavior and the consequences for it, they feel enormously powerless. A false dependency is created that leaves them with no sense of security in their ability to cause an effect. This is why Paul says in 2 Thessalonians 3:10, "If anyone will not work, neither shall he eat." He knows that there is dignity and joy in good behavior. "A desire accomplished is sweet to the soul" (Prov. 13:19).

People raised without the law of cause and effect are destined to be in a continual battle with reality and have a life of chaos. Owning our behavior is important to knowing our boundaries, as well as to knowing that others are responsible for their behavior as well. It clears up identity problems. We are always better off if we do not allow Adam and Eve's example of saying, "Someone else made me do it!" If we do that, we will create more and more "falls of Eden" in our own lives.

Our Thoughts

Our thoughts are an integral part of who we are. God has given all of us some capacity for thinking and has called us to love Him with all our minds. The greatest commandment is to "love the LORD your God with all your heart, with all your soul, with all your mind, and with all your strength" (Mark 12:30). Paul said that he was "bringing every thought into captivity to the obedience of Christ" (2 Cor. 10:5).

In part, to love God with our minds and thoughts is to grow in knowledge. To do this, we must take responsibility for our thinking and the development of our minds. Many people do not think very often about what they think about. They just let their thoughts live there, inside their head, without observing them or questioning them. In short, they do not own their thoughts. But by bringing our thoughts into captivity, we are taking responsibility for them and evaluating them, considering what they mean about the status of our minds and hearts. We are owning them.

Challenging our distortions in order to grow would be an example of owning our thoughts. If I think, for example, that you are going to do me harm, but I have never met you, I need to take responsibility for the way that my thinking affects my life. I need to work on the way that I distort reality and acknowledge that as my problem. Or if I find out that I do not have understanding in some area, I can admit that lacking and seek understanding in that field. This relates to the aspect of thinking that we call knowledge.

Sometimes, our passing thoughts indicate other things going on inside us, and it is helpful to own those thoughts and understand them. If we often think of dying or wish for death, that means something about what is happening inside. Or if we often think about how to get revenge, that points to a condition of the heart, which needs to be owned and worked with.

The thinking involved in expectations one has for others often affects interpersonal relationships. A classic example occurred when the boy Jesus remained behind in Jerusalem, but Mary and Joseph did not immediately discover His absence (Luke 2:42–49). When they found Him, Mary said, "Son, why have You done this to us?

Look, Your father and I have sought You anxiously." Jesus replied, "Why did you seek Me? Did you not know that I must be about My Father's business?" Mary made an incorrect assumption about His whereabouts. She should have checked on Him before leaving town. The account says that they supposed "Him to have been in the company." That was their expectation, but it wasn't reality. As a result, Mary was angry with Him and anxiously blamed Him for His behavior, but He knew who had assumed wrongly.

Many times we assume things or think things without checking them out, and then we blame others for the results. We must take responsibility for our faulty thinking and work to correct it. Paul declares, "For who among men knows the thoughts of a man except the spirit of the man, which is in him?" (1 Cor. 2:11 NASB). No one except God can read our thoughts; God has built that boundary into human existence.

When we take responsibility for someone else's thoughts, we invade their boundaries; we interfere with their property. Likewise, if we expect them to take responsibility for ours, there is an equal problem.

This dynamic of owning one's thoughts is important in establishing an identity, for what we think is an essential part of who we are as people. If someone such as Sandy does not own her thoughts about the nature of holidays, for example, and what she thinks about what her mother thinks, she is in bondage to her mother, and that is idolatry. If people cannot separate their thoughts and opinions from those of others, they have ceased to be persons in their own right and have denied something that God will one day hold them responsible for.

Our Abilities

Another aspect of identity involves talents and abilities. The Bible speaks of these in several ways, but it holds us responsible for using them and developing them. Many people have never taken inventory of the gifts God has given them. They accept others' definitions of themselves. Also, some people deny their gifts and live vicariously through the gifts of others.

Many frustrated people try to live their lives as someone else defined them. I remember one extremely gifted teenager who was artistically skilled. His parents, both physicians, decided very early in his life that he would continue the medical tradition. He tried to fight their labeling, to little avail, and could not perceive his talents apart from his parents' wishes for him. He tried to be a doctor, but his medical school education was fraught with difficulty because he didn't have that kind of talent. He finally finished school, but was in serious trouble in his residency because of his lack of functioning.

After his failure as a physician, he eventually became a separate enough person to figure out what he was gifted to do. He could own his true talents and forsake the feeling that he should have the talents his parents wanted him to have. He carved out a satisfying career in the creative arts. But he had to go through the arduous task of "finding himself" apart from the ones he loved.

God has not made all of us alike, and we are responsible for discovering that separateness and developing it. Peter understood this truth and wrote, "As each one has received a gift, minister it to one another, as good stewards of the manifold grace of God" (1 Pet. 4:10). Jesus stated it like this: "And to one he gave five talents, to another two, and to another one, to each according to his own ability" (Matt. 25:15).

A noteworthy principle appears in Paul's writings. He says that the foot is not to compare itself to the hand nor the ear to the eye (1 Cor. 12:15-16). That is, there is a grave danger in losing one's sense of separateness and identity; it offers opportunities for confusion, guilt, failure, and irresponsibility. He reiterates the point in Galatians: "But let each one examine his own work, and then he will have rejoicing in himself alone, and not in another" (6:4). If we are making the most of our God-given talents, we should have pride in assuming that responsibility, but we are not to gloat or feel guilty in relation to someone else. This is not false pride; it is an acknowledgment of reality.

Many people, afraid to own their abilities for one reason or another, have some disturbance in their identity. Realizing our talents and abilities and taking responsibility for them is crucial. We will one day be held accountable, and we want to hear, "Well done, good and faithful servant." If we never know what is within the boundaries of our own farm, then we will be unable to develop it. In the same way, we need to reject wishes that we be something we are not. Individuals cannot find happiness or satisfaction in not being the true self, the one

God created. The true self is lost when it so conforms to others that it loses its identity, which is the essence of fusion. Paul writes about this process:

> Do not be conformed to this world, but be transformed by the renewing of your mind, that you may prove what is that good and acceptable and perfect will of God. For I say, through the grace given to me, to everyone who is among you, not to think of himself more highly than he ought to think, but to think soberly, as God has dealt to each one a measure of faith. For as we have many members in one body, but all the members do not have the same function, so we, being many, are one body in Christ, and individually members of one another. Having then gifts differing according to the grace that is given to us, let us use them: if prophecy, let us prophesy in proportion to our faith; or ministry, let us use it in our ministering; he who teaches, in teaching; he who exhorts, in exhortation; he who gives, with liberality; he who leads, with diligence; he who shows mercy, with cheerfulness (Rom. 12:2-8).

We must not conform to someone else's wishes that are not the reality God has designed for us. We must own the true self and allow God's grace and instruction to develop it.

Our Wants

Our wants and desires are another aspect of what lies within our boundaries. Each person has different desires and wants, wishes and dreams, goals and plans, hungers and thirsts.

God speaks many, many times of our wants and desires, for they are a major part of what it means to be created in His likeness. He has given many of them to us; we have chosen some others. Both kinds can be good. But we have some wants and desires that are not so good. In either case, however, we must own them to straighten out what is good and bad as well as choose between the good and the best.

Whenever we do not own our wants and desires, we have cut ourselves off from who we are, limited our future satisfaction, our future service to God and others, our motivation, and our sanctification. Think of how frustrating it must be for the biggest giver in the universe to be unable to give to His children because they do not feel free to have wants!

The Scriptures frequently describe God as a "desire meeter":

You have given him his heart's desire,
And have not withheld the request of his lips.
For You meet him with the blessings of goodness;
You set a crown of pure gold upon his head.
He asked life from You, and You gave it to him (Ps. 21:2–4).

Delight yourself also in the LORD,
And He shall give you the desires of your heart.
Commit your way to the LORD,
Trust also in Him,
And He shall bring it to pass (Ps. 37:4–5).

He will fulfill the desire of those who fear Him (Ps. 145:19).

Only when we acknowledge our desires and wants can God work with us to meet them, delay them, encourage us to give them up, or whatever the helpful thing would be. But we have to own them before He can do something with them.

James names some consequences of not taking responsibility for our desires: "You lust and do not have; so you commit murder. And you are envious and cannot obtain; so you fight and quarrel. You do not have because you do not ask. You ask and do not receive, because you ask with wrong motives, so that you may spend it on your pleasures" (James 4:2–3 NASB). Mixed up in many lusts and quarrels are unmet desires, and according to James, there are two sorts of them: those that are not asked for, and those that are confused with wrong motives. An example of the first would be persons envying others' talents but not asking God to help them go to school to develop their own. In other words, they have not because they ask not. The second sort occurs when the motivation to go to school stems from a desire to get a degree to flaunt, not a desire to develop the true self. For example, most of us know a doctor who is fulfilled in practicing his profession and exercising real gifts. Most of us also know a doctor who acts like a "mini-God" and thinks that everyone should bow down to his position. One desire to go to school is good; the other is not. But either way, the desire must be owned and given to God to work with.

It is the same way with sports figures, housewives, ministers, machine workers, and everyone else. God is delighted to give us good things if they fit who we really are. Those kinds of desires accomplished can be sweet to the soul, and that sort of pride is good (Prov. 13:19; Gal. 6:4). On the other hand, He is not delighted to help someone inflate an ego.

God is a good parent who will grant your desires to further your development and His work. But it takes a real relationship between you and God to determine what is good desire and bad. Therefore, you need to own your desires and take them to Him. This relationship is pictured in Philippians 2:12–13: "Work out your own salvation with fear and trembling; for it is God who works in you both to will and to do for His good pleasure." God is at work in your desires, and you should bring them into relationship with Him as a part of yourself.

Also, you should own your desires in relationship with other people. You've likely had the frustrating experience of being with someone who would not tell you what he or she really wanted. You know that the wishes and desires are there somewhere, but it is difficult for the person to own them. If you ask about a place to eat or a movie to see, the response may be, "It doesn't matter. Whatever you want is OK." If you ask which piece of pie he would like when there are only two, he says, "You pick." It is usually easy to see his discontent when you pick the "wrong" restaurant, movie, or piece of pie, but he will not own it. It begins to make you uncomfortable. You fear he may resent you for always having your way. For any relationship to thrive, two separate people need to be working out particular likes and dislikes, giving and receiving them accordingly. That is the only way to build love and intimacy and gain knowledge of the real person you are in relationship with. If one person never "owns" his or her desires, then intimacy and knowledge of the other are limited. Those who do not define themselves remain "non persons."

Owning our desires gives us a stronger sense of where we stand on things. When we are with persons who are clear about what they want, we get a sense of being with solid entities. Their personhood has definition, and their personality has edges. These edges do not have to be rough and hurtful, but they need to be present nevertheless. If people are not definite about themselves, there is little feeling of having been with them at all.

If the colonists had not desired a better land, there would be no U.S.A. as we know it. If the pioneers had not desired westward expansion, there would be no western states. People throughout the ages have pursued their dreams and followed their desires, and that has led to a better life for all of us. Solomon puts it this way: "And follow the impulses of your heart and the desires of your eyes. Yet know that God will bring you to judgment for all these things" (Eccles. 11:9 NASB). There is a call for us to be aware of our desires and at the same time to include God in the working out of our plans and goals.

Our Choices

The next aspect of identity that we need to be aware of and own is our choices. Just because this aspect is so far down the list doesn't mean it is less important than the others, however. Nothing could be further from the truth. *Choices are not true choices unless we are aware of all the feelings, attitudes, behaviors, wants, thoughts, and abilities that go into them.* To own and make our choices, we must be aware of all the aspects of ourselves that go into any decision. In addition, we must be aware that we are making a choice about almost everything we do. There is no stronger element to forging an identity than owning and taking responsibility for choices. It is the cornerstone of freedom, love, and responsibility.

Let's take Sandy, for example. If she wanted to go with her friends for Thanksgiving but felt that her mother "made her" come home, she would not feel responsible for missing her trip. She would believe that her mother was responsible for her missing out. Sandy's mother did not have a gun to her head to make her come home. Sandy would be choosing to please her mother instead of herself, but if she did not realize it was her choice, she would resent her mother for the holiday. This loss of freedom, or more accurately, giving away freedom, is entirely Sandy's responsibility, and whatever feelings that her choice leaves her with are her responsibility, too.

Biblical writers are very clear about this dynamic. Listen to what Paul says about giving: "Let each one give as he purposes in his heart, not grudgingly or of necessity; for God loves a cheerful giver" (2 Cor. 9:7). Whenever we give anything—money, time, energy, talents, or possessions—we need to give only what we have purposed to give. That is the aspect of choosing we need to take responsibility for.

We need to realize that we gave it "on purpose." If we don't, we are giving out of a feeling of obligation or compulsion because we feel that we have no choice.

Few dynamics in life wreck people more than this one. It ranks second only to isolation. If we do not believe we own our choices, we feel out of control of our lives, and we resent the ones that we perceive as being in control of us. It is the opposite of freedom and the opposite of love.

Choices have two directions: yes and no. We can choose to do something, or we can choose not to do it. We can choose to give to someone, or we can choose not to give. In either case, we are responsible for the consequences. This is the essence of having a sense of limits and the cornerstone of love.

Many people give out of obligation and compulsion, which leads to resentment. They go to lunches that they can't say no to; they spend weekends they resent spending; they give others time and energy motivated out of guilt instead of love.

Such actions can bring about the martyr syndrome. Parents sacrifice time and money for their children and then act as if their lives are ruined: "Well, if it weren't for your schooling, we could have traveled more" and so on. Some people begin to feel guilty for their very existence, as if they somehow have the power to ruin others' lives by receiving a "gift." Jesus strongly words a commandment to make sure we do not blame or ask for repayment of a gift: "But when you do a charitable deed, do not let your left hand know what your right hand is doing" (Matt. 6:3). This admonition rules out the possibility of "giving" others time or energy and then griping later as if they "made" us do it.

I remember one woman whose mother would almost beg to babysit her children and then gripe about the inconvenience for weeks. She could not own the fact that she had chosen to take care of her four grandkids and her daughter did not "make" her do it.

Further, we negate that we have choices as to how we spend our time. We may complain about our level of enjoyment and boredom, but not accept responsibility for our reluctance to learn a new skill or hobby. We may gripe about the "crummy" pastor at the church, but not take responsibility for looking for a new church or writing the pastor a letter or getting on the board or making numerous other choices. There certainly are determinants in life, but we always have a choice as to how we will respond to them. Our choices have a lot to do with our direction in life, but if we do not own that fact, we do not know where we are going, and we resent where we end up as if it is someone else's fault.

In the story about the laborers hired at different hours, the angry one tried to negate the fact that he had made a choice to work for a certain amount. Jesus answers his complaint, "But he answered one of them and said, 'Friend, I am doing you no wrong. Did you not agree with me for a denarius?'" (Matt. 20:13). In other words, "Did you not make the choice to work for this wage? That choice is your responsibility. Own it." Complaining and griping without making an effort to do anything is the essence of negating choice, and it renders us powerless and resentful.

God wants us to own our choices and thus realize who we are. Joshua said it clearly,

> And if it seems evil to you to serve the LORD, choose for yourselves this day whom you will serve, whether the gods which your fathers served which were on the other side of the River, or the gods of the Amorites in whose land you dwell. But as for me and my house, we will serve the LORD" (Josh. 24:15).

He then goes on to describe what a significant choice that is and that there would be consequences either way.

It has been said that not to make a choice is to make a choice, and that is true. God has set up existence in such a way that we will be accountable for every choice we make, even when we do not think we are making one: "But I say to you that for every idle word men may speak, they will give account for it in the day of judgement" (Matt. 12:36). We may think that some action or word is unconnected to any substantial meaning about life, but Jesus says that everything has meaning; everything that we do or don't do is fruit. Therefore, we have a choice: "Either make the tree good and its fruit good, or else make the tree bad and its fruit bad; for a tree is known by its fruit" (v. 33). Our lives have fruit; we have no choice about that. But we have choices as to the nature of the fruit.

Our Limits

When we examine our boundaries, we discover our limits. The physical boundaries of a farm limit what it contains; there is a finite amount of property and possessions. In the emotional, psychological, and spiritual realms, we have limits, also. God has designed us in His likeness with one exception: He is infinite, and we are finite. This truth has some serious implications for our boundaries.

In terms of responsibility, we may be unclear about our boundaries if we are not certain of our limits. We all possess finite amounts of capability, time, money, energy, and so on. The amounts aren't static, however. We may get more or less as time goes on, but it is still true that at any given moment, we have somewhat fixed amounts. If we know our salary, for example, we need to know how much we can spend on different areas, including giving. If we know our energy level, we can figure how many projects we can take on and which ones we need to turn down. If we know how much energy we have available, we can take care not to exceed that amount.

Because many people do not own their limits, they get overextended in some area or another. It takes time to learn our limits in the various areas of life, but they can be learned if we are aware of our feelings, attitudes, and behaviors. If we feel overburdened, for example, we must realize where we have overextended our limits and say no. Sometimes, we don't know the limits of our love, and we love past where we should.

Others have too narrow limits. They "sow sparingly," as Paul writes (2 Cor. 9:6). They do not extend their boundaries far enough to contain the possibility of what they can give or possess. They too tightly restrict their feelings, attitudes, behaviors, thinking, and choices. They narrow their perception of what is acceptable to them. Paul talked about this in much of his teaching on legalism and the weak conscience that limited the type of food someone would eat. Many Christians do not take advantage of the room God has given them to experience all that is within them. They think, as I heard one man say of his legalistic background, that "any sensation stronger than an itch is sinful." They don't experience the limits of their feelings, both positive and negative, and thus narrow their experience of the likeness of God.

We can make an error in either direction—and we usually do. It takes a lot of grace, truth, and practice in time with others to discover limits and be responsible for them. This is the balanced life. We should not overextend or underextend ourselves. If we are going through a season of depression, for example, we must recognize that we have limited amounts to give and cut back accordingly. If we are "rich in love" for a season, we have a lot to give away. It takes responsible assessment before God to determine limitations.

We also must limit the effects of others on us. That is an important aspect of realizing our boundaries. If someone's behavior leaves trash on our property, we must limit the effects of that. We can draw the line on our property as to what we will allow and what we will not. Dr. James Dobson has called this a line of respect. It says basically, "I will not allow myself to be treated this way."

Our Negative Assertions

As we have seen, much of our identity comes from the positive assertions of who we are. From experience, we realize our feelings and our attitudes, and we own them. We make positive assertions about what is true about us. When I say, "I believe Jesus is Lord," I am asserting a positive truth about who I am. I am a person who believes in Jesus as Lord.

We have also seen how God asserts His identity positively. In the same way, He makes negative statements about who He is not. He says, for example, "God is not a man, that He should lie, nor a son of man, that He should repent" (Num. 23:19). Peter declares, "The Lord is not slack concerning His promise, as some count slackness, but is longsuffering toward us, not willing that any should perish but that all should come to repentance" (2 Pet. 3:9). We know who God is by who He says He is and by who He says He is not.

We describe our boundaries by negative assertions, also. When I say, "I hate injustice," I am saying what I am against, and that is an important identity statement. If I say, "I do not like science," I am making just as important an identity statement as when I say, "I love philosophy."

Many people are not in touch with their "not me" experiences. They take too many things into their boundaries. In an earlier example, the boy who was not medically talented did not assert strongly enough a negative statement of his identity. He needed to scream at the top of his lungs, "I hate medicine!" until someone finally heard him. The truth is, our negative assertions always come out in one form or another. His came out in poor performance in school and failure in residency.

A beautiful example of negative assertion is found in the story
Jesus told of two sons who worked for their father:

> But what do you think? A man had two sons, and he came to the
> first and said, "Son, go, work today in my vineyard." He answered
> and said, "I will not," but afterward he regretted it and went.
> Then he came to the second and said likewise. And he answered
> and said, "I go, sir," but he did not go. Which of the two did the
> will of his father? They said to Him, "The first." Jesus said to
> them, "Assuredly, I say to you that tax collectors and harlots enter
> the kingdom of God before you" (Matt. 21:28–31).

In effect, the second son did not know who he really was. He was
against his father, but he could not say, "I am not for you. I will not
go." Thus, he was out of touch with himself. The first, because he
could make a negative assertion, was in touch enough to later make a
positive one. This kind of person can say no and then the yes means
something. James puts it like this: "But let your 'Yes' be 'Yes,' and
your 'No,' 'No' " (James 5:12). We must be in touch with our "no"
and in control of it; otherwise, it will control us. The second son
could not own his "no," so it owned him. It always comes out in some
form or fashion. In his case it was in his procrastination.

Some negative assertions would be: "No, that talent is not me."
"No, I do not like it when you do that." "No, I will not work for that
amount." "No, I will not allow that sort of behavior." "No, I do not
like cocaine." "No, I do not want you to touch my body." "No, I do
not agree with your theology." "No, I do not like that movie (or restaurant or whatever)." By being in touch with our "not me" experiences, we further define ourselves to others and the world. If we
cannot say what is "not us," we have no hope of holiness, for we
cannot hate evil and be separate from it. People with weak boundaries
in this area cannot reject what is not them. It would be like skin that
would not reject foreign bodies; the blood would forever be infected.
If we cannot say what is "not us" in terms of all of the above
elements—body, feelings, attitudes, behaviors, thoughts, abilities,
choices, wants, and limits—we cannot keep the bad out of our souls.
We own things that don't belong within our boundaries. Some of
them are good things that just don't belong there; some are bad
things that don't belong anywhere. In either case, they are "not us."

For Sandy, a "not me" statement would be, "Mother, I love you, but I don't want to spend this Thanksgiving at home. I want to be with my friends." If her mother became angry, Sandy could assert, "I'm sorry you are angry with me, but that's something you'll have to deal with. You are going to have to figure out what else you plan to do for Thanksgiving besides visit with me. I will not be there."

This approach seems mean to some people, and too straightforward, but with many controlling people who won't take responsibility for their disappointments and do something about them, that sort of instruction is often required. In reality, that statement helps Sandy more than her mother. She can recognize who is responsible for what. A mother who is that controlling, to the point that she would blame her daughter for her disappointment, probably wouldn't hear it anyway. (We will look at this further in the crossed boundaries section.)

It is essential, however, to be able to assert negatively. Each of us must be able to say what is "not me" in order to have a "me." What we like has no meaning unless we know what we don't like. Our "yes" has no meaning if we never say "no." My chosen profession has no passion if "just any one would do." Our opinions and thoughts mean very little if we disagree with nothing. We are defined just as much by what we are not, and what we refuse, as by what we are. It is an important aspect of identity formation.

A Developmental Perspective

As we learned in the area of attachment, growth takes place in a process of development. This is true of boundaries as well. Let's see how that happens in God's plan.

Oneness

Attachment is the first and foremost stage to growth. We must be able to have relationship and join one another to be alive. This unity underlies the relational aspect of the image of God.

If we cannot have attachment, separateness has no meaning. It is a "no" without a "yes." We must be able to be "a part of" before we can be "apart." The attachment gives us the safety and the strength to be separate. That is why salvation, reconciliation, is the first step in beginning intimacy with God. First John notes the first developmental phase of faith: "I write to you, little children, because your sins are forgiven you for His name's sake" (2:12). Forgiveness brings us into bonding.

In a person's development, the first year is one of bonding; there is very little separateness. That foundation of being rooted and grounded in love will provide him safety and connectedness so that he can venture out in separateness. We can never require separateness from someone who has not first been bonded. Separateness without bonding either is impossible or must turn one into a nonhuman.

Jane came into therapy because of "panic attacks," as she put them. Her husband's increased drinking was causing several problems in the home. She tried to be loving and supportive, but that was doing no good. It only made matters worse.

She read some literature on learning to set limits on abusive behavior and how not to be codependent. She learned that she must set limits on his behavior and its effect on the home. She figured out that she had to say no in several ways to his behavior, and that she must separate from him when he was on a binge.

However, when she said no and put limits on his behavior, she experienced severe panic. She described it as "falling into a hole." She would shake and feel terrified, sensing that some awful loneliness was going to "swallow her up."

She gradually understood that she did not have very good bonding inside herself. She was isolated internally and did not have the ability to maintain her emotional connections with other people in their absence (what we referred to earlier as emotional object constancy). If she were not in the presence of the one she loved, she felt horribly alone, and that was why she was having panic attacks whenever she would separate from her husband or put a limit on him.

But by sticking to him, she was enabling his abusive behavior. Therefore, she was in a double bind familiar to many people in abusive situations. They literally can't live with him and can't live without him. They can't live with him because of the abuse, and they can't live without him because of the isolation. *There must be internal bonding before one can establish boundaries.* Without it, boundaries as they were meant to be cannot exist.

As Jane began to comprehend why she could not set and keep limits on her husband, she worked on her lack of attachment. She joined an AL-ANON group and established supportive relationships with others that would reinforce her setting limits on his drinking. She found that she could have a sense of separateness without isolation, and that just because she had limits did not mean that she had to go without love. Her support group loved her greatly, and they stood by her in her separateness.

As a result, her husband was not enabled any longer to be abusive. Before, because of her lack of attachment, he could pretty much do whatever he pleased, and she would go along. When she gained other support, she could stand up to his abuse, and he was forced to deal with himself. He had to realize that his behavior was causing him to be alone, and for the first time he had to take responsibility for it because there were consequences. Consequences change behavior, and she was not able to give him consequences before then. Gradually, he got sober, and they were able to work things out. But without the intervention of a group to provide her bonding needs, she would not have been able to establish separateness from his evil behavior. Bonding must always precede separateness.

Twoness

For the infant, after about a year of bonding and attachment, the process of separateness begins to kick in. The child displays new abilities called secondary processes because they develop secondarily to primary processes, such as feeling and loving. They involve things that promote separateness and identity and are based in mobility; development of language, thinking, and language-based thought; realization of consequences and the law of cause and effect; more ranges of behavior; realization of increasing physical and emotional separateness; and beginnings of the process of "willing." Since all these sound wonderful, it's strange that we call this time the terrible twos! (A friend of mine who has great kids calls this time of life the terrific twos, for she relishes her child's budding autonomy and separateness. It's a refreshing comment to hear.)

As these processes unfold, the entire world turns around for the child and the mother, for what was formerly a unit is about to become more of a relationship between two separate people. Think of the way in which God designed the process. There is an initial bonding period in which trust and relationship can be established, and from that trust can come the working out of a separateness that is not frightening because of the safety of the attachment. It is the basis for what He calls bond servanthood in the New Testament. Because of our love—our bond to God—He can give us the freedom of our separateness. The love constrains us.

In the same way, as love is established between infant and mother, the child slowly works out his sense of separateness from her. He begins to realize his boundaries, what is "me" and what is mother. As the infant gains the ability to move around more, he walks away from mother. He learns to have a life of his own, albeit a small one. He explores the world "apart" from the one he was "a part of." The budding faculties aid in this process, for as he gains mobility, he can venture out. For the first time mother does not cause all separateness. *His* wishes to move away and explore by himself cause it.

With his greater capacity for thought, he can better negotiate the world and even name things. This adds an increasing sense of order to the world, which begins to have some structure to it. He can realize what things are and how to use them in a goal-oriented way. He can talk about them, ask for them, demand them, scream when he does not get them, and so on. He learns how to think about and talk about a world apart from mother.

He learns separateness from mother in other ways. When he walks, he falls down as a result of his actions, not hers. His behavior and limitations have some effects on his life if he is allowed to be separate. When he falls down or finds joy in his discovery, he has his own feelings about that, and as mother shares those experiences with him, he learns to value and own them.

Similarly, through his discovery of his abilities, he gains competency and goal-directedness. Along with that, he learns that he has limitations and sometimes needs help. This aspect of boundaries is quite healthy: the child feels both the accomplishment and the consequences of his separateness and behavior. He needs to realize that there are limits to what will be allowed and there are consequences of his omnipotence. In this way, he learns to cooperate with the world.

He finds out that he can want some things and get them, either through his efforts or through someone's help, but he will not get everything he wants. Thus, internal boundaries on desires are being created.

He discerns that he is responsible for his choices. If he chooses to hit his sibling, for example, there are consequences. If he chooses to wander into the street at a little later age, there are consequences.

(Remember that this is a description of a process of gaining separateness, not a full description of child development. Therefore, I will not go into specific age levels and consequences for certain behaviors.) If he walks to the window, he experiences the good consequence of seeing a beautiful flower. This is a wonderful discovery of the law of cause and effect: "My choices to be mobile can bring me pleasure." At the same time, choices can bring pain: "When I choose to touch the heater, it hurts."

Through every action, feeling, and choice, he recognizes that he owns those things. He also learns that his thoughts and feelings are not always the same as mother's. He may think it is a great idea to stay in the sandbox for a longer time, but she does not agree. He learns that it is his wish and not hers. If he is allowed to have his thoughts and wishes without all of them being gratified, he learns a healthy ability to own what he thinks, feels, and chooses without being out of control. It is a delicate balance of being allowed to "be all of who he is" without being able to be "all that there is." This is the balance of having a self without continuing to be self-centered.

Failures in development of boundaries occur in both extremes. Occasionally people's boundaries are confused because they are not allowed to own their feelings, thoughts, and behaviors, so they never own who they are. They cannot know how to deal with those things later; they have no map for it. Other people, not limited enough in their feelings, thoughts, and behaviors, tend to think they are the only ones who matter. These two types in adulthood become the overresponsible and the underresponsible people. (Usually they find each other and get married!)

Three or More

From the second year of life onward, bonding and separateness must work hand in hand. As children reach age four or five, they increase the separateness to include more and more people in their world. They learn to relate to three people at a time instead of only two. They have playmates and kindergarten friends, as well as more and more experiences. Their world away from their primary attachments is growing, and they can stand to be away from them for more than twenty minutes. They can spend a half-day at kindergarten and enjoy it instead of being overwhelmed.

As abilities, thoughts, behaviors, and feelings increase in their development, separateness extends into the world of school. They have more and more responsibility as they own more things within their boundaries. Later, they move out of the house and go to college, and then move from the safety of college into the "real world." All along, there has been a process of learning to stay in relationship, but increase in the ability to be a separate person from the ones they are bonded to. This enables them to lead full, productive work lives and to be relational people. Love and work come together through the balancing of bonding and separateness.

People who are not allowed to own their thoughts, feelings, attitudes, behaviors, choices, and desires never develop a true biblical sense of responsibility. They have conflicts between bonding and separateness. They don't know how to have a relationship and at the same time be separate.

On the other hand, if they are not limited in the realization of those elements, the boundaries extend too far and encroach on other people's property, which was the case with Sandy and her mother. Sandy's time belongs to her, and her mother's time belongs to her mother. However, because of guilt and control, Sandy never learned to limit her mother. For years, she allowed her mother to think that her mother owned her (Sandy's) time as well. As a result, Sandy was not free to give time to her mother as she purposed in her heart; she was obligated and compelled to give to mother what mother owned anyway: Sandy's life. The wish to control someone else's life and not allow separateness is a serious relationship destroyer. It is the source for more parent-child struggles, friendship friction, marital break-ups, work conflicts, and struggles with God than any other dynamic.

Remember that in the Fall, our boundaries were destroyed. Since we no longer had grace, we could not tell the truth about who owned what. Adam said it was the woman's fault, not his. She "caused" him to do it. She said it was the serpent's fault, not hers, for he "made her do it." They could not admit that their desires, attitudes, and behaviors led to their choices. They could not take responsibility for themselves. It was their desire to have the fruit and to become Godlike. It was their attitude that they should have whatever they wanted and that God really did not know what was good for them. It was their choice to reach past their allotted boundaries. Therefore, God held them responsible for all of those things.

Since that time, we all tend to disown what is ours and try to own what belongs to others. Sandy's mother disowned several things. She disowned responsibility for existing in a world where children grow up and leave their parents, clinging to others in adulthood. She disowned that her wish to have Sandy there was disturbing her, not Sandy's behavior. There was nothing wrong with wanting to be with Sandy; that was a good desire. But when she negated that it was her responsibility to deal with, problems arose. Just as the two-year-old has to cope with his disappointment at not being able to stay up all night with mommy, Sandy's mother has to own the disappointment of not having Thanksgiving the way she wants it.

She also tried to own things that were not hers, such as Sandy's time and course of life. Parents, children, friends, and spouses have trouble working this out. There are two wills in any relationship, so allowances have to be made for that if love and responsibility are to be forthcoming. I saw a bumper sticker that read, "If you love something, set it free. If it really loves you, it will return. If it doesn't, HUNT IT DOWN AND KILL IT!" This is how we all feel in varying degrees. We may want the people we love to make their own choices, but many of those choices are going to limit us in some way. And when they do, we do not naturally want to deal with those limitations responsibly. We would rather place blame. For instance, if Sandy had chosen to continue with her plans to be with her friends, her mother would have to choose to deal with her own wishes being limited by Sandy's choices. She would have to grieve that wish and carve out some sort of satisfactory holiday apart from her daughter. Instead, she was probably going to blame Sandy and play the victim, crying out about how her daughter was ruining her holiday.

It is easy to say that we love others, but difficult to allow them the freedom inherent in love. When they do not want to do what we want them to, we "hunt them down and kill them" in various ways. It happens in the form of pouting, angry outbursts, guilt messages, and attempts to control. These are forms of "killing," for they kill freedom and will, and whenever that happens, they kill love. Love cannot exist where there is no freedom, and freedom cannot exist where there is no responsibility. We must take responsibility for what is ours, and that includes our disappointments of not getting everything we want from another person. The disappointment that comes from our loved one exercising freedom is our responsibility. That is the only way to keep love alive.

This is true even when others' freedom leads them to sin against us. The pain that we feel is not our fault, but it is our responsibility to deal with. Sandy wasn't sinning against her mother. Her mother was sinning against her, for she was coveting Sandy's life. But many times when others exercise their freedom in a way that they sin against us, we are responsible for dealing with the injury caused by that. If we don't, we can remain stuck in a blaming position, powerless against their sin. That is the essence of the victim mentality keeping many people stuck in their pain.

Jane's husband was sinning against her, drinking to an extent that it was affecting the family. The sin was his responsibility; there was no doubt about that. The pain that she was feeling was his fault. But it was her responsibility to deal with the pain he was causing her, and she did a wonderful job of that. In effect, she said, "I cannot control his behavior, but I can take responsibility for dealing with the way that it affects me and this family. I can own the hurt and the pain and use it to motivate me to change some things around here in the way I deal with him. In that way, I can limit the effects of his behavior on me."

Jane dealt with her hurt and anger and set some limits on him. When she found that she had some isolation as a result of that, she again took responsibility and worked on that problem. She was no longer under his power and control, and she could begin to be happy in her support groups apart from his sin. Because she had taken responsibility, *not fault*, for her pain, she found freedom. In her situation, it did work out that he changed. Some do not work out that favorably.

Many, however, do not take responsibility for their lives. (Again, I am not saying fault; I am saying responsibility. It is not my fault if I get hit by a truck, but it is my responsibility to learn to walk again. No one can do that for me, but others can help me. I must own the injured legs and exercise them.) They remain stuck because they want other people to change. They want others to make it better, and often those persons will not. As a result, they are in bondage to others. Freedom always comes from taking responsibility, and bondage comes from giving it away. Many spouses of alcoholics will not do what Jane did, but will continue to blame someone else for their misery. That is the essence of powerlessness.

I recall one woman whose husband left her abruptly with four small children. What he did to her was horrible, and she had every reason in the world to feel betrayed, angry, abandoned, depressed, and overwhelmed. As she expressed those feelings of "look what he's done to me," there was no movement for a long time. Those are natural feelings to have when one has been sinned against, but they should lead to a sense of ownership of the situation and a grief of letting go of the loss. That was not happening. She would hear nothing of a suggestion that she was going to have to do some things to get out of her situation. She would get angry with me for suggesting that she had the power to make some choices to help herself. Instead, all she wanted to own was the right to blame him for the situation. She continued to blame for quite a long time and then left therapy. I heard much later that she was still blaming—and still miserable.

She was in the same situation that others find themselves in, but with much different outcomes. They go through the appropriate blaming stage as well, for that is needed. It is part of the forgiveness process to call sin, sin, and it must take place. They must confess how they have been sinned against in order to forgive. They should never deny how someone has sinned against them, for then they cannot forgive and move on. However, after an appropriate period of blame, they take responsibility (not fault) for the mess that someone else's sin has left them in, and they deal with it. Their situation is part of their property; they must own it and deal with the feelings, attitudes, and behaviors necessary to get unstuck.

Bobbie's husband "left her for the secretary," and she was left alone without much child support or many marketable skills. He had virtually stolen everything through the divorce. In the entire situation she was truly victimized and mistreated. She went through all the proper attempts to reconcile and to work on the relationship, to no avail.

When it was clear that the marriage was over, she was devastated. Twenty-five years of marriage had ended overnight, and Bobbie was in distressing circumstances. She had not been to school in two decades and had done mostly volunteer work, with some other minimal employment. Her depression was serious, and her financial needs worse.

But after recognizing the reality of the sin against her, and all the while processing the feelings, she began to own her plight. Even though she had not caused it, she was responsible for dealing with it.

She got out of the blaming stage and got busy. She arranged to take some courses at night while working during the day. She networked with other single parents at her church to carry one another's load. She did some creative part-time work that did not take her away from her children.

After quite a while, she finished her classes and was able to get back on her feet financially. She had created a new body of relationships and had developed several supportive bonds with people. She attended workshops on recovering from divorce and working through painful emotions; she learned about the patterns that had led her to choose someone like her husband, and also the ways that she had slowly allowed him to isolate her emotionally and render her powerless.

Even though the divorce and abandonment were not her fault, she took responsibility for her situation. She owned what fell within her boundaries. She assumed responsibility for her feelings, attitudes, and behaviors and developed them. In addition, she pursued some desires and wants, and she made responsible choices that led to greater degrees of happiness for herself and her children. Where she found herself alone and isolated, she took responsibility for that and created support and regained her ability to trust people. Through it all, she found God to be faithful to His promises to sustain her.

Crossed Boundaries

What happens when we don't own the things that are ours? Let's examine some examples of crossed boundaries and the problems that come from not owning ourselves as separate people.

Body

The most basic boundary is the body. The Bible asserts that it is a vessel and that you are to possess your own vessel "in sanctification and honor" (1 Thess. 4:4). When you possess your body, you know that it belongs to you. You can feel it, you can own the pleasure that it brings you through your senses, and you are basically in touch with it. To be out of touch with one's body causes all sorts of problems spiritually, emotionally, and psychologically.

When people have had their bodily boundaries invaded by abuse or control, they may disown them in some way. They learn that their bodies, in a sense, do not belong to them; they belong to others. This is most often true with people who have been sexually abused or mistreated, even as adults.

To invade another person's body boundaries is the most basic act of abuse. To forcefully use someone's body is an awful thing indeed. It does away with the person's basic feeling of owning his or her own life, and everyone who has been violated has some sort of injury to personal boundaries.

The first effect of a crossover in these boundaries occurs when someone feels like a "thing" instead of a person. If our bodies are not respected by others, if they are "owned" by others, then we feel more like a thing than a person. This can happen in several ways. Sexual abuse is a horrible instance of boundary crossover. Our sexual functioning was meant to be freely given as a gift and a shared experience with a partner of our choice. It was not meant to be stolen against our will.

In physical abuse, the same kind of violation happens. One person crosses the boundary and touches another in a hurtful way. Abused persons may lose touch with their bodies and not be able to experience them in meaningful ways. They learn that others can do what they want with them.

Sometimes in marriage one spouse uses the other's body sexually with no concern for what feels good or bad to the other. This is an example of an invasion instead of respect.

In the single world some people take what is not theirs to have and use someone's body instead of respecting the individual's ownership of it. Many women feel that they lost their bodies in teen years and young adulthood, as they were used physically. They must work determinedly to regain them again and declare dominion and authority over what is theirs.

Parents may not allow their children to own their bodies. They have no adequate say in what they will wear or what they will eat. Certainly, there are limits to what is acceptable, as God puts in His law. But people are to have some choices about their bodies. Instead the parents may make the child's body an extension of their own narcissism and may not allow the child expression in regard to the body.

Many people are not allowed to experience themselves as sexual persons because of rigid teaching. They have so much guilt about their sexual feelings that they disown that part of the body. They were taught that those feelings should not be a part of them instead of being taught how to own them properly.

Some people learn that admitting pain is wrong. They lose touch with their ability to sense their bodies. Consequently, both pleasure and pain have little meaning for them.

These are all examples of how problems arise when people do not own their bodies. Sometimes they must work on reclaiming lost parts of the body in order to be fully functioning. For example, sexual counseling may be necessary before people can relearn how to feel pleasure; they have to reown what is rightly theirs.

Feelings

When we feel something, whether good or bad, that is our property. It falls within our boundaries. Our feelings are part of that property, and they are our responsibility; likewise others' feelings are their responsibility as well. If someone is feeling sad, that is his sadness. That doesn't mean he doesn't need someone else to be with him in his sadness and to empathize with him, for that is a certainty. It does mean he must own it. Sandy was confused about her boundaries because she felt that she was responsible for dealing with her mother's feelings. She thought that she had to change her mother's anger to happiness by changing her behavior, which basically puts her mother's anger in control of Sandy's life. That is a scary way to live. One day Sandy will give an account for her life. My guess is that Jesus will say something like this: "I want to know why you didn't take responsibility for your life." And she can only reply, "It would have made my mother angry."

If we conclude that we are responsible for other people's feelings, we cannot make decisions based on what is right to do; we make decisions based on how others feel about our choices. Jesus said, "Woe to you when all men speak well of you" (Luke 6:26). If we are always trying to keep everyone else happy, we cannot make the choices required to live correctly and freely.

When we feel responsible for the displeasure of others, we are controlled by their feelings, and not God. This is a basic boundary disturbance. If Jesus had tried to make everyone happy, we would all be lost. If self-centered people are angry with you, that is a good sign. It means that you are learning to say no to evil. If pharisaical Christians judge you, rejoice. It means that you are like your Savior. If your parents do not like the decisions that you feel God has led you to make, be thankful, "leap for joy! For indeed your reward is great in heaven, for in like manner their fathers did to the prophets" (Luke 6:23).

Whenever I speak to a Christian group, I can tell how I did by the reactions. If the people who are hurting feel understood *and* the noncompassionate critical types hate me, I know I have done my job. If the hurting people hate me, I have missed God's heart, and I must reevaluate. I have failed to be empathetic and give grace and truth. But whenever people hate us for being compassionate and offering forgiveness and truth, we know we are on the right track. God is against the proud types who have no compassion for hurting people.

Jesus said that families would often be divided when someone follows His ways (Luke 12:51–53). Following Him, in all of His ways, often leaves others with negative feelings. For example, He says to "leave and cleave," but how do some parents feel about a child separating and becoming an adult? If the child takes responsibility for the empty nest, he or she can't become an adult and follow God's leading.

God says to speak the truth, but how does an alcoholic feel when his spouse stops lying to the boss for him? If his spouse takes responsibility for those feelings, he can't obey God.

God says that if a man doesn't work, we are not to let him eat. How does an irresponsible twenty-five-year-old feel when his parents cut him off? If they feel responsible for the tough time he will have, God is not allowed to grow him up through consequences.

God says to give as we purpose in our heart instead of from compulsion. How does a controlling person feel when his spouse decides that next weekend is not one she is going to give to the family? Instead, she wants to go shopping with her pals. If she feels responsible for the spouse's abandonment rage, she will stay home out of compulsion and be guilty of the sin of resentment.

God describes a woman as someone who is diligent and prosperous outside the home and inside the home, and He says that she should be busy. How does a controlling husband feel when she gets a job that requires some time away from home? If she feels responsible for his immaturity, she can't develop as God has asked her to.

Most controlling people are stuck in the stage of development where they think that they can control others by getting angry or sad.

The problem is, with some boundaryless people, it works. Therefore, the person's immaturity is reinforced. We must all take responsibility for our disappointments, and then we clear up our boundaries. Assuming responsibility for others' feelings is a problem of crossed boundaries.

Perhaps you think that this approach is mean and insensitive. You may be saying, "That sounds so uncaring." Please hear something loud and clear. We are always to be sensitive to others' feelings about out choices. We must always empathize with them. But *we can never be responsible for how they feel*. That is wrong, and it is the most insensitive thing we can do. I am in no way saying to disregard others and do whatever you want. I am saying that when you make choices, some of those choices will take you away from loved ones and illustrate your separateness from them. If they are responsible, they will process the disappointment from that and own it. If they are not, they will blame you for their disappointment, and that is their responsibility to deal with.

It is a truth of life that none of us gets everything desired, and we must deal with that. When that is made untrue, we are in trouble. Jim came into therapy because he was unable to get things done at home. He said, "I am an irresponsible person, and my wife is displeased with me. I can't seem to follow through on anything."

When I asked what sorts of things he was talking about, he listed making more money, repairing the patio, working in the yard, remodeling the kitchen, being the spiritual leader, and taking the kids places. The list went on and on, and I was exhausted just listening. Those were all requests from his wife. I asked him if he had promised to do all those things, and he said yes.

"Do you want to do all those things now?" I asked.

"Not really, but I have to," he replied.

"What do you mean, 'you have to'?"

He said, "Well, if I don't, she will get mad and say that I don't love her, and that if I did, I would take better care of her."

I was beginning to get the picture. "You mean that you basically promise to do anything she wants? How in the world can you make more money and at the same time spend all of your spare time working in and around the house?"

"Well, I can't seem to be able to. I really do have the intention to do it when I promise, for I know it makes her happy. But I can't seem to get around to everything in a way that pleases her," Jim said with tears in his eyes.

"Have you ever considered thinking about what may be reasonable to promise her and what isn't?"

"What do you mean?" he said.

"It seems that for her to be happy, she is going to need three or four husbands, and you are only one," I told him.

"But she gets very unhappy with me if I don't do what she wants, and she says I don't love her." He was looking more puzzled the more we talked.

"Have you ever considered that her unhappiness with your limitations on what you can do is her problem? I think she needs to deal with that reality. If I were you, I would give her a choice. I would say, 'Honey, I love you, and I want to work hard for your happiness. I have ten hours this month that I will do work for you around the house. How would you like me to use them?"

"Oh, she would hit the roof if I said that!" he burst out.

"Why?"

"Well, she would think that ten hours would never be enough," he said emphatically.

"Enough for what?" I asked.

"Enough to accomplish everything she wants done."

"That is precisely my point," I told him. "She gets angry because she can't have everything she wants, and you feel responsible for that. If you don't change the perception that you are responsible for her anger, you will never accomplish what you promise. You will never be able to say no honestly."

I went on to explain to him that in reality, he was already saying no. He was saying it with his behavior, even though with his mouth he was saying yes. The problem was not that he was irresponsible, as he imagined; the problem was that he was lying. He was saying yes when he really meant no, and then he was *following up on what he really meant.*

Whenever there is a crossover in boundaries, and one person becomes responsible for the other's feelings and happiness, there is an inability to be free from that person and, as a result, an inability to love properly. Guilty compliance is never love; it is slavery.

My guess is that most problems causing people to seek counseling have at some level a crossover in boundaries. The Fall so destroyed our sense of responsibility that we are all confused about who is responsible for what, and we try to make others responsible for us and we take responsibility for them. The Bible sends a clear message that we are to be responsible "to" others, not "for" them. This is an important distinction.

If Jim were being responsible "to" his wife, he would sit down with her and say something like, "Honey, let's look at some of our goals as a couple and a family, and our goals as individuals, and then see how we can help each other meet those. Let's look at our time and resources to meet those and figure out how we are going to spend them." In that kind of discussion, it would become clear that there were very few limits on her wants and very few of his wants in the picture.

If he were to continue to be responsible to her, he would not passive-aggressively procrastinate (resist passively), but would say, "I understand that you want all of those things right now, but I can't do that. That would mean that the kids and I don't get any of the things that we want to see happen, and that's not fair. I'm sorry that is upsetting to you, but I want us to all work together."

If she has any awareness about her, she will be able to see her self-centeredness and realize that she has been controlling the family with her feelings. If not, she may get angrier, and the only thing that will help will be for him to be very firm. If she pouts, the family needs to learn to say things like, "Mom, we love you, but we don't want to be around you when you are pouting. Come into the den when you feel better."

This sounds like the family is dealing with a two-year-old, and in some ways it is. People who control others by their feelings of anger or sadness or whatever are in a very immature stage of development. It works for them, however, because others feel responsible for their behavior and give in to the demands of their feelings.

At twenty-four years old, Steve was suicidally depressed. He was still living at home, but was using drugs and was unable to stay in school. Since he came from a "good Christian family," his parents were very upset about his problems that tarnished their image in the church, and they didn't like that at all. As a result, they brought him to therapy.

As we explored the problem, it became apparent that the parents were having serious marital problems, but they were not facing them responsibly. Instead, they brought Steve into the conflict and spoke through him. In other ways, each parent confided in him about the other person instead of dealing with the feelings directly.

Steve, the last of seven children, was unable to grow up and live responsibly, as he wanted to do, for one main reason. His mother told him that she could never stand to be left alone with his father; if Steve left home, she was fairly certain they would get divorced. Then, she said, she would commit suicide, and it "would be Steve's fault." The guilt—over not being able to move out and become an adult against the other option of moving out and then being responsible for his mother's divorce and suicide—gave him no choice. He felt that he would be bad either way, so the only thing he could do was commit suicide. That is the only way he would not be guilty, so he tried a car wreck.

Luckily, afterward there was another option. He could learn that he was not responsible for his parents' feelings toward each other or for his mother's depression if she got divorced. It took him much work to realize that, but slowly he was getting somewhere. I will never forget one day in a family session when he told his mother that he had decided to move out and return to school.

He said, "Mom, I've been thinking, and I think it's time for me to finish school. I want to be able to get a job."

"But the family needs you here. Why, your father and I are still . . ."

"No, Mom," he interrupted. "What you and Dad do is up to you. I'm twenty-four, and I'm going to get on with my life."

Instantly she began to cry. Steve responded by saying, "Mom, you can turn off the tears because they aren't going to work anymore. Every time I have tried to do something for myself, you begin to cry, and I change my mind. I'm not going to do that anymore. If you are sad about my leaving home, and you and Dad are going to fight, you will have to work it out."

Steve learned what his mother never learned: each person is responsible for his or her own feelings. When we cross those boundaries and try to change the way someone feels, we have lost the steering wheel to our own car. It is as if the car in the next lane can steer us by blowing its horn. At that point, we are out of control.

Taking responsibility for feelings means they can be utilized to solve problems. Earlier I mentioned a woman who took responsibility for her depression when she was abandoned, and she began to solve problems and accomplish things.

Feelings can also be used to make relationships better if we are responsible for them. For example, when I am sinned against, my feelings of anger can lead me to problem resolution. My anger tells me that something is wrong. I can use those feelings to tell me that someone has done something wrong to me and that I need to resolve the problem. This is to obey Jesus' command in Matthew 18:15: "If your brother sins against you, go and tell him his fault between you and him alone. If he hears you, you have gained your brother." Or to obey Moses' command in Leviticus 19:17: "You shall not hate your brother in your heart. You shall surely rebuke your neighbor, and not bear sin because of him."

In these two examples, the responsibility for dealing with the feelings lies with the one having them. Moses points out that you have two choices. Either you reprove the one you are angry with, or you allow the feeling to turn into bitterness and hatred. When you go to that person and work it out, the anger can be resolved, and the relationship improves. Each person is better for it. But if we do not deal with our feelings after having been sinned against, then it turns into hatred and goes nowhere. The command speaks clearly to the responsibility when it says, "You shall . . . not bear sin because of him." He is responsible for his behavior, and you are responsible for dealing with your feelings about his behavior and, to the best of your ability, trying to gain your brother.

The issue of confrontation can be confusing. I can see Jim's wife taking a course on confrontation and then "confronting" him with her anger toward him for "all he is not doing." She does not realize that by not obeying her wishes, he is not sinning against her, and she really has no right to confront. If she did not have those wishes, she would not be angry. When we are truly sinned against, there is a concrete offense by the other, apart from our wishes and feelings.

Jesus made that clear in the story of the boss who paid the workers exactly what he agreed to, but some workers were angry because they wanted more (Matt. 20:1–15). Jesus eliminated the boundary confusion over who was responsible for the anger. He said that no wrong had been done to the displeased workers, who should deal with their envy. However, if the boss had not paid the men what he agreed to, there would be a sin against them, and that would be true whether or not the men were angry.

Taking responsibility for our feelings is essential to maturity. We are to deal with our feelings, either by confronting the one who has sinned against us and forgiving, or by giving up our expectations causing the anger. Then our lives can progress as God intended. If we require others to take that responsibility, then there is all sorts of confusion.

Jesus asked individuals to be responsible for their own feelings, as separate people, and also not to take responsibility for someone else. In some cases, the advice sounded brutal, but He always presented hard decisions, ones that many people did not like. When one disciple said that he needed to go and bury his father, Jesus replied, "Follow Me, and let the dead bury their own dead" (Matt. 8:22). I am sure that the man's family did not like what he did. Another said, "Lord, I will follow You, but let me first go and bid them farewell who are at my house." But Jesus responded, "No one, having put his hand to the plow, and looking back, is fit for the kingdom of God" (Luke 9:61-62).

In each case, Jesus called them to make choices that other people would not like. He was saying, in effect, those at home have their own responsibility to deal with, but "You follow Me." We know that Jesus' intent is not to split families; it is to bring them together. In 1 Timothy 5:4, people are commanded to "show piety at home and to repay their parents; for this is good and acceptable before God." But each person needs to be in control of those decisions and submit them to the Lord. If they are made on the basis of what others like or dislike, they can never be made accurately.

It is often painful to take responsibility for our feelings. But Jesus draws clear boundaries around our task. Another example is found at the end of the gospel of John, when Jesus prophesied that Peter would be crucified. Peter looked at John and asked, "Lord, what about this man?" Jesus replied, "If I will that he remain till I come, what is that to you? You follow Me" (John 21:21-22). Jesus was saying to Peter, "That is not your concern. What I decide to do with John is between him and Me. You deal with what is yours."

Most of us don't like it when others get a different deal from ours, and we stop coping with what is ours and begin to envy others. Envy is a difficult emotion to take responsibility for because its very focus is on the other. It's as if envy deceives us into thinking that because someone else has something, we have less. Or because we have something, someone else has less. If we are without, the fact of what someone else has or doesn't have is not our problem. We must take responsibility for our "being without" and seek God's solution to it. James says, "You . . . covet and cannot obtain. You fight and war. Yet you do not have because you do not ask" (4:2). He puts the responsibility for feeling without and envious squarely on our shoulders, where it belongs.

Attitudes

When we look further at crossed boundaries, we see that often we do not own our attitudes; instead, we take responsibility for the attitudes of others. Sandy took responsibility for her mother's attitude of what Sandy "should" do with her time. Yet Sandy neglected an attitude that said, "I should do whatever Mother wants." She believed that was causing her problems, *not* her mother's "should."

People often complain about how this person or that person is "putting expectations" on them, as if an expectation is something you can Velcro to someone's brain. That does indeed happen in childhood when we internalize the expectations of parents, but part of becoming an adult is figuring out what our attitudes and expectations are going to be apart from parents and others. When we take responsibility for them, we can be free from the expectations others place on us.

Whenever we feel victimized by another's expectations, we have to find the attitude within that is allowing us to feel pressured by that expectation. In Jim's case, his wife's expectations, her attitudes of what he "should" do, were her problem, not his. His problem was his attitude of "I should do what she wants." If his attitude were something like "I should take into consideration what she wants and then choose what I want to give," he would not be passive-aggressive with her. He would be straightforward, and for the first time, she could take responsibility for her life. However, as long as he continued to enable her to keep her attitudes by his taking responsibility for them, they were stuck.

He did change his attitudes, though, and stopped enabling hers. Gradually, she realized that her attitudes toward what a husband should be were not in accord with reality, and she was forced to either change them or be frustrated. That is precisely what reality does for us. It gets us in touch with our confused ways of looking at the world and forces us to handle them. If, on the other hand, someone is protecting us from our attitudes by taking responsibility for them, we never grow. That, again, is the essence of crossed boundaries: owning what is not ours or not owning what is ours.

Whenever we feel pressured to do something, it is our problem and not the problem of the one who pressures us. If we did not have something inside to make us feel "pressured" (which means that we agree with their attitude instead of our own), then there would be no pressure. We must get in touch with how we get hooked and not blame others.

I remember one woman who came into therapy with extreme anger toward her family and all of their "expectations." I agreed with her that her family's expectations were wrong and that I understood her anger. She was very comforted that I agreed with her on that point. But when I suggested that they were not going to change and that she had to free herself from them by changing her attitudes toward them, she would get angry with me, saying, "You're just like them. You don't understand, either." She felt that if I did not agree with her victim stance, I didn't care.

I assured her that she had indeed been victimized growing up, but now she had to stop victimizing herself by freeing herself from her expectations of them.

She couldn't understand that and said, "I don't have any expectations of them; they are the ones with the 'shoulds.'"

"On the contrary," I said, "you're just like them. They say that *you* should be a certain way. And you say that *they* should be a certain way, or you will feel pressured. In other words, it's up to them to set you free so that you won't feel pressured. You're saying that they 'should not have any shoulds,' and that is the same thing they are doing." I tried for a long time to help her see that until she took responsibility for her internal "shoulds," she would never be free. She didn't want to do that and instead continued to say that they "should not expect those things of me. I will always have to feel pressured by them until they let up." Since I wouldn't agree with her that it would be necessary for her family to change in order for her to get well, we hit a stalemate.

She felt that if I were on her side I would agree that her misery was their fault and not hers. I agreed with her that they had deeply injured her and were the *source* of much of her pain, but I asserted that they were not the ones *continuing it in the present*. She was an adult who could select new attitudes about life separate from theirs. But she felt that I was "being on their side" and that I was not understanding, so she quit coming for therapy. I tried to help her comprehend that because I was on her side, I wanted her to take the power back that she had given them over her life. I wanted her to get free from their expectations, and the only way was to change herself. But she still believed that they had to change their attitudes first.

I saw her about three years later, and she was still stuck, still blaming. She was griping about how her family did this and that, totally neglecting her ability to change her attitudes about her need for them to be different. Since they were not different, neither was she. That is the essence of a lack of separateness.

Robert sought therapy because of a series of lost jobs. Enormously talented and intelligent, he had some interesting attitudes. He had been raised by a doting mother and a harsh, critical father. It seems that every time the father required something of him, it was too harsh to comply with. Then his mother felt sorry for him and did his work.

His mother required very little from him in terms of responsibility. In fact, over the years she trained him to think that the world should take care of him, for he was "special." She told him that "meaningless" jobs were for less gifted people than he was and that he was entitled to much more.

So, Robert learned to share her attitude: "I am special and therefore entitled to special treatment. The world owes me considerations that others don't get." What was once his mother's attitude toward him had become his own attitude. He thought he was entitled.

When he entered the business world, he found that his bosses and coworkers did not share his attitude. Theirs said, "I expect work from someone I pay!" and you can guess what Robert's track record was like as those attitudes clashed.

The situation was further complicated by Robert's wife. She reinforced his thinking, but when the creditors were knocking at the door, they forced her to change some of hers.

Robert's therapy consisted of getting in touch with the reality that his attitudes were causing his problems, not those "jerks" at work.

He had to take responsibility for his views of work and the world that were causing his troubles. In addition, his wife had to learn that she was enabling him to keep those views.

Slowly, he began to change how he saw things. As a result, he got along with people better and was able to work more steadily. But if he had not taken responsibility, owned his attitudes, he could never have changed. He would have continued to go from job to job. As Jesus says, "First take the log out of your own eye, and then you will see clearly to take the speck out of your brother's eye" (Matt. 7:5 NASB). Robert couldn't see others clearly because he was blaming them for the problems caused by his own attitudes. By taking the log out, he could see them clearly.

Behaviors

Crossed boundaries in the arena of behaviors is a crucial dynamic for healthy living. Our sense of being able to own our behavior is critical for having a sense of power over our lives and a sense of self-control. We have talked about the importance of the law of sowing and reaping and how it is the most trustworthy law of behavior. We can trust it to bring us satisfaction or misery. If we sow to life, we will reap life; if we sow to death, we will reap death.

However, the law of sowing and reaping is a bit like the law of gravity: it can be suspended. The consequences can be taken away if there is a buffer. If I drop a glass, the law of gravity will pull it to the floor and break it, *unless* I tie a rope around the glass from the ceiling. Then I have taken away the consequences of the gravity by holding up the glass.

The law of sowing and reaping can be suspended, also, if someone is willing to take responsibility for another's behaviors. For example, the law of sowing and reaping says that if a man does not work, he will not eat, unless someone suspends the law and gives him a handout. This enables him to exist apart from the consequences of his actions, and the law of sowing and reaping does not take effect. But he loses out on the security of knowing that his actions have consequences, the law of cause and effect, and thus begins to feel utterly powerless and dependent on the "enabler," or the person covering for him.

This story is classic in an alcoholic home. Someone is drinking and behaving in a way that should have natural consequences, but the enabler, usually the spouse, keeps the consequences from happening. She calls the boss and tells him that her husband is sick. She tells the neighbors that the child fell playing instead of the truth that her husband, in a drunken stupor, fell on the child. In other words, he is shielded from the consequences of his behavior; reality does not grow him up and force him to change. Alcoholism is an irresponsible lifestyle, and without someone to buffer it, it cannot go on.

Whenever anyone is not allowed to own behavior, that is, suffer the consequences, there are crossed boundaries. Someone else must take up the slack to prevent the irresponsible person from suffering. And that is a totally unbiblical thing to do, to shield someone from the consequences of personal behavior. God gave us gravity so that we could learn to walk. He gave us wages so that we could learn to work and on and on. If limits are not placed on our behavior in the form of consequences, we are out of control.

Some people as they are growing up learn that they can do almost anything they please, and someone will cover for them or bail them out. They think that will continue in adult life, and they are usually able to find someone to carry on the tradition. The problem is, it is at the expense of that person and everyone around. This is the classic enabling syndrome: you do the behavior, and I'll pay the price.

A successful man came to see me to "straighten out" his daughter. She was thirty-five years old, not working, and taking massive amounts of drugs, he said. I asked where she was, and he said she wouldn't come with him to the appointment.

"What does she do with her time?" I asked.

"Well, she spends most of it at the club, playing tennis," he said somewhat angrily. "I can't understand how someone so smart would waste time like that."

"How does she afford it?" I wondered aloud. "That's a pretty expensive place. If she doesn't work and spends money on drugs, she must have a supply somewhere."

"She is living off a trust fund I set up for her. She has plenty of money. The money's not the problem. It's her wasteful life that bothers me."

"Well," I offered, "I think that the money is at least part of the problem."

"How's that?" he asked.

"You're a smart man, Harold," I said. "What would your clients do if you didn't deliver?"

"They would go to another firm," he said. "I would be out of business. What does that have to do with my daughter?"

"Well, it seems to me that she's getting paid pretty well for 'not delivering.' In fact, I wouldn't mind having her job. You're allowing her to waste her life away. There is no chance for her until you cut her off," I replied, hoping that he would see the connection.

As we continued to talk, I learned that Harold had a special fondness for his daughter, for she was from a previous marriage in which his wife had died. He had remained close to the daughter because it was a way of staying close to his first wife. He could never bring himself to place consequences on her for fear that she would not stay close to him. He had been bailing her out ever since college where she overspent her budget and wrecked cars, only to get a check in the mail to cover the expenses or to get a new car. She had never learned the law of cause and effect, and she was out of control.

"What would she do if I didn't give her money?" he asked. "I would be afraid she would not live very well."

"Well, that would be up to her. If she decided to use her very expensive education, she could do quite well. She would also have to go into drug treatment and get her act together. But the way it's set up now, she doesn't have to do any of those things. She has the best of both worlds. She can be lazy and have lots of money. Exactly the deal I've always wanted. Haven't you?"

Harold smiled. He saw how ridiculous the whole situation was. He was a bright man who had made a fortune by requiring responsible behavior of himself and others. But when his love for his daughter crossed his boundaries, he lost reality. The crossed boundaries worked like this: she loafs, he pays; she snorts, he pays; she sleeps, he pays. He wouldn't work that way in any other area of life, yet in the relationship that was most important to him, he was enabling irresponsible behavior, much to her detriment. Proverbs says that "he who spares his rod hates his son, but he who loves him disciplines him promptly" (13:24). If she had had the discipline of consequences earlier, she probably would not be in the mess she was in. But it was difficult for him to require responsibility of her, and that left her out of control.

Many times someone's love for another makes it difficult to place consequences on behavior. This is most often true in abusive marriages. There should always be a limit on abuse, and there should be consequences. The spouse should say, "I will not allow that behavior, and until you are able to control it, I will be staying at ———'s house." But because of crossed boundaries, that behavior is often enabled to continue for years, with no consequences, and someone else pays the price. The spouse pays for the behavior with depression, or the children with all sorts of pain. But the abuser never has to take responsibility for his or her behavior because someone else does. This tendency is a participation in evil, and one must refuse it if there is hope for change.

Thoughts

Crossed boundaries in the area of thoughts are similar to those in attitudes and feelings. I will not repeat those here, but suffice it to say that the same principles apply to our thinking: we must own what is ours and take responsibility for it; we must allow others to own what is theirs and let them be responsible for it.

Our thoughts have much bearing on emotional growth. Although I disagree with the notion that *all* emotional disturbance comes from thinking, it still plays a vital part, and we must take responsibility for it. (In reality, our emotions affect our thinking more than the other way around, for feeling is a primary process and thinking secondary. But this is not a book on theories of psychology. Let's leave it that *they affect each other,* and both must be owned.)

Our thinking affects the way that we respond to people and situations. We discussed in the section on attachment, for example, that distorted thoughts can make us move away from relationship. Someone may think, *He would never like me anyway, so I won't call.* That is an example of thinking oneself into isolation. We must check those thoughts and practice thinking more along the lines of reality.

In that same way, we cannot be responsible for the thoughts of others. If others think good or bad about us, that is their property, and we must allow it. We can try to affect it, but we cannot control it. Many people spend undue energy worrying about what others think of them, which is something they cannot control anyway. We must allow others to think what they will and give them that freedom, for that is reality. We can't change their thoughts anyway. Ask Jesus.

People thought some pretty crazy things about Him, and He allowed it.

Whenever we exercise our choices in life to follow God, there are those who will think we are wrong, just as they will have feelings about it. We should listen to their thinking and evaluate it. But if we are convinced in our hearts that we are doing what is right, we must allow them to think whatever they want. That is their freedom.

When Harold cut his daughter off from her finances, she thought he was being mean. When the alcoholic's wife intervenes in his life, he thinks she is a traitor. When the parent grounds the teenager, the youth thinks he is an old fuddy-duddy. Whenever we do anything, people have opinions about it, and that is good. It is not good if we do not allow them to own those and try to cross boundaries and change them.

As Jim began to talk to his wife differently, she thought he was selfish because he would no longer do what she wanted. She described him as an immature adolescent, running from responsibility. Little did she realize that she was not taking responsibility for her frustration. Nevertheless, she thought he was a bad guy. He had to allow her to think that and not try to change her thoughts, either by changing his behavior or by talking her out of them. He just had to accept it, and then they had a chance.

You must not fear people's condemnation. Many people will think you are "bad" for not taking responsibility for their lives. To be responsible, you must allow them to think negatively of you. Remember what they thought of Jesus: "The Son of Man came eating and drinking, and they say, 'Look, a glutton and a winebibber, a friend of tax collectors and sinners!'" (Matt. 11:19). People will always have opinions based on who they are at any given moment.

I remember one meeting with a man who told me that it would be God's will for a child to suffer from psychological and emotional pain if Scripture could not be applied to his problem. The situation was a hypothetical one that I drew to find out his thinking on counseling, and I described a neglected infant whose undeveloped mind could not handle language skills. I told him that a developmental psychologist could work with the child to help him relate to the world better and end his suffering. The man said that the Bible did not allow for psychological intervention, so it was God's will for the child to suffer. This example is similar to what the Pharisees did when they tried to use theology to excuse them from love. They tried to tell Jesus that the law did not allow healing on the Sabbath, but He said it was always lawful to do good. We must take responsibility for what we think. It usually has some meaning about the nature of the heart.

We must own our thinking that prevents relationship, such as the distortions mentioned earlier and also the way that we judge others. Condemning thoughts toward others indicate we are thinking in non-loving ways, and those always hurt us. We must own our critical thinking and confess it, allowing God to change the way we think. This would also be true of self-condemnation. Self-condemning thoughts are clearly unbiblical, for the Bible asserts that "there is therefore no condemnation to those who are in Christ Jesus" (Rom. 8:1). We have to take dominion over and responsibility for those thoughts. They have no rightful place on our property.

This is true of all distortions, prejudices, and generalizations that lock us into some unbiblical corner. Jesus said that there are those who teach "as doctrines the commandments of men" (Matt. 15:9). These sorts of prisons keep people's souls bound. A theology that does not allow for a God-given need, such as love, freedom, or responsibility is distorted and must be changed. Boundaries get crossed in thinking when people try to put those thoughts onto others, thus putting them in prison. This sort of boundary crossing can wreck someone's spiritual and emotional life. We will discuss this more in the section on authority.

Abilities

Earlier we examined accepting and owning our abilities and gave some examples of crossed boundaries. Basically, they come in two forms: looking to others' property and trying to own what is theirs, and having others decide what is one's property. We should never compare ourselves to others, for God made us different, separate. To do so is to be out of accord with reality for several reasons. Paul urges, "For just as we have many members in one body and all the members do not have the same function. . . . And since we have gifts that differ according to the grace given to us, let each exercise them accordingly" (Rom. 12:4, 6 NASB).

We must stay within our own boundaries, realizing our own inventory. An eye is not a hand, nor do they have the same history. Crossing boundaries in this area leaves one with false pride or false guilt.

An eye may look at a hand and declare, "I can see so much better than that hand! Aren't I great!" or "I can't pick up anything like that hand can! I'm so stupid!" Both appraisals are inaccurate.

For other reasons, a hand cannot compare itself to another hand. One hand can come to the table saying, "Look at how weak I am. I can't pick up things as well as that hand." It negates the fact that it has been in a car wreck and is going through a process of rehabilitation. Or the other hand feels proud for being so strong, denying the fact that it has had a relatively easy life without much injury, so it wonders, "What's wrong with that other hand? It should get its act together!" Both aspects of crossed boundaries are wrong.

The second form occurs when someone decides on the abilities of another. For example, a parent may want a child to be an intellectual when he is an athlete or vice versa. Enormous pain is associated with not being one's true self in relation to loved ones. If loved ones cannot appreciate and value the real talents, the individual is likely to conform to their expectations and deny the real abilities.

The Bible says to "train up a child in the way he should go" (Prov. 22:6), not "train up a child in the way you want him to go." This distinction is crucial in a child's development. We must value the abilities of the true self. Crossing someone's boundaries by telling him or her what the abilities should be is dangerous and negates God's design for that person.

Choices

Probably no area of crossed boundaries is as significant as this one. Boundaries involve responsibility, and the basis of responsibility is choice. God has put into the spirit, soul, mind, and body of every human the ability to choose. When that ability is taken away, something less than human remains and therefore less than the likeness of God. Crossed boundaries in this area take place whenever we make others' choices for them or whenever we think they are responsible for making our choices for us.

Nothing strikes at the heart of God quite like making others' choices for them. The Old Testament is full of situations in which His people were taken into slavery and their freedom was stolen. His cry was always, "Let My people go!" (Exod. 5:1) or "Is this not the fast that I have chosen: to loose the bonds of wickedness, to undo the heavy burdens, to let the oppressed go free, and that you break every yoke?'' (Isa. 58:6). God wants His people free of heart so they can make choices to love Him as they will. He is against people who bind them and sin that binds them. He has always been a releaser of the captive.

Whenever we try to bind others by taking away their choices, we have reduced them to slavery. We say, "My will is the only one that counts here!" And we force them, either actively or passively, to do what we want them to do. This is a terrible evil.

There are many ways to take away someone's choices. One of the most common is through guilt messages. A parent who says, "How could you do this to me?"—when the child is not actually doing anything "to him"—binds the child's choices. The parent basically says, "You cannot make a choice and still have my love. If you make that choice, I will withdraw my love from you." Then the child must choose between love or freedom, and that is a cruel dilemma. Love and freedom must always go together; when they are split, the person is without a real choice.

Burt was the twenty-five-year-old son of Christian parents. From his childhood, they made most of his spiritual choices for him. He was not allowed to question, doubt, or make up his own mind about God. When he chose friends not to their liking, they bad-mouthed them and tried to control his choices of friends, even well into his teens. He basically had to choose between being a person with his own choices and following God, because of the way they had set up his life.

If he moved toward God, the choice never seemed like his own; it seemed like theirs. He could have his own choices only by choosing against what they liked, and that meant God. Deep down inside, he really wanted God, but it meant a total loss of autonomy for himself.

When he left home, he went wild. He started to drink more and party more to the point of feeling that he was gaining more control over his life by "losing control." Paul understood about such things; he said that the law increases sin. But Burt's parents could not understand that. They were unable to take the stance of the prodigal's father who said, in effect, "I love you, and I disagree with your values. But they are your free choice, and I will set you free to pursue your choices. But remember this, I love you very much, and you are always free to come back. I will never say, 'I told you so.' I will only welcome you and rejoice that you have chosen what is good."

We had a family meeting with Burt's siblings, parents, and grand-parents. I tried to get them to understand that he was a free adult who could make whatever choices he wanted. God had allowed him that freedom, to choose evil, and they must, also. It was the only way that he would ever be able to choose God and have it be his decision. Suffice it to say, they did not like that idea. They continued to try to get him to be like them and to place guilt on him when he was not. Thus, the cycle continued. He kept moving way from their control in order to make his own choices. One day, I believe, he will gain enough distance to experience what the prodigal did. He will learn that a pigsty is not a nice place to sleep, and he will choose God's way. But he probably will not do that until his choice can be his own.

Usually crossed boundaries are not so blatant. They do not involve having to choose an entire lifestyle. They have more to do with being bound in guilt over smaller decisions. For example, when Sandy wanted to choose to spend Thanksgiving with her friends, she was considered ungrateful. She was "bad." That is a very strong way of producing an indecisive person. If the choice muscle is bound with vines of guilt, it doesn't work very well.

Or look at Jim. Whenever he wanted to choose to spend some time not doing work for his wife, she withdrew love from him. That was bondage, not freedom. There can be no intimacy where someone is not free to choose separateness without guilt.

Or think about Steve's dilemma. If he chose to be an adult and leave home, his mother would say that he didn't love her enough to stay and that she would commit suicide. That is hardly having a choice. She had crossed his boundaries by trying to control his choices through manipulation. He had nowhere to go to feel free and loving at the same time.

Trying to take people's choices away from them is done in count-less other ways, also. When you say no to someone's request, you may get the silent treatment for a period of time. You have a choice, but you become unloved. You become bad. Or you become intensely angry. This is not freedom at all.

Or you may have heard, "If you love me, you will do this or that." Jesus is the only One who can say that, for He is the only One who knows the best for us. And He never uses it as a power move. He uses it descriptively; it is just a fact. If a bond servant loves someone enough to sign up for *voluntary* service, it is true that the person will perform it. This is not a manipulative statement on His part (John 14:15). It is just a statement of fact.

However, when used in human relationships, it is most often a crossing of boundaries to take away someone's free choice of *how* to love. To say, "If you love me, you will not go bowling," is not true; it is an attempt to say, "If you love me, you will do anything I want and have no choices of your own unless I like them." Those sorts of statements should be confronted with a clearing up of the boundaries: "That is not true. I love you, *and* I will choose how I will spend this evening. You cannot decide whether or not I love you. That is my choice."

This seems to be one aspect of what is behind God's statement: "You shall not put the Lord your God to the test" (Luke 4:12 NASB). It denies God's freedom to be His own person and to love us any way that He wants. Think of the times each of us feels that "if God really loved me, He would . . ." He says, "I love you, and I will not . . ." He cannot be manipulated. But we are free to make requests of Him, and some He will choose to grant, and some He will not. That is a real relationship. But He loves us nevertheless, and the extent that we love Him will determine the extent that we allow Him to be God and *still love Him*. (Ask Job about that one!) We can still be angry about His choices or anyone else's. However, we must realize that the anger is our problem, not theirs. Think of the difference it would make to Sandy if her mother said, "Well, I don't like it that you won't be home for Thanksgiving. I get angry about that, not because you are bad, but because I'm not getting what I want. I don't want to deny the fact that I'm angry, but I don't want to blame it on you, either."

That sort of responsibility ownership is integral to allowing someone to be free to make choices. It says, in effect, "I don't want you to go bowling tonight. I get sad and angry at the idea. But it really is your choice to make, and I don't blame you for it. It's my problem." Thus, each person can empathize with the losses that choices bring and at the same time make choices. That is how a good relationship works. The individual says, "Oh, I'm sorry you aren't coming for dinner. I'll miss you," instead of "That figures. You always do whatever you want anyway!"

Invariably, people who cross boundaries and try to take away others' choices call the others selfish. For instance, Jim's wife would say that he was selfish for saying no to doing the work she wanted.

She didn't see how selfish it was to say what another person must do! She considered him selfish for doing something for himself, yet she wanted to have control of her life as well as his. That is true selfishness: self-centeredness. The Bible never says that doing things for ourselves is bad; it assumes that we need to do some things for ourselves. However, it speaks harshly against living *only* for ourselves. That is being self-centered, and that is evil. As Paul writes, we are to look out for others' interests as well as our own: "Let each of you look out not only for his own interests, but also for the interests of others" (Phil. 2:4).

Within controlling relationships, there is a self-centeredness that does not look out for others' interests. Sandy's mother, Jim's wife, and the bowler's spouse were well aware of their own interests. There is nothing wrong with that. The evil came when they did not look out for the interests of the other as well. That is true self-centeredness— no one else's wishes matter.

Anytime we bind someone's choices by guilt or manipulation, that is not love; it is slavery. Remember, "whenever you tie a chain around another person's ankle, it will invariably end up around your neck."

The second way we cross boundaries is by thinking others are responsible for our choices. We talked about this earlier, but let's review.

If Sandy gave in to the guilt and went to her mother's home for the holiday, she would be making a choice. Granted, not one freely given, but a choice. She would be giving her time to her mother out of her own free will. But she would probably blame her mother for "making" her come through guilt manipulation. "You manipulated me into coming here," she might be tempted to say. There is truth in that, but we can never be manipulated without our permission. The truth is that if Sandy goes home for the holidays, that's her choice, and if she doesn't like it, that's her problem.

This is the fruit of passive-aggressive people. Not taking responsibility for their choices, they blame someone else for making them do it. Many examples are found in Scripture, and God always reminds them of their responsibility. Recall what the boss said to the servants in the parable of the vineyard workers hired at different hours. He said, in effect, "You chose to take the job; don't yell at me."

Or these people agree to do things that they don't really want to do and then gripe about it. "I get sick and tired of everything you make me do!" they may say. The reply should be, "Then why don't you please tell me when you don't want to do it?" I know some people who have been so hurt by passive-aggressive givers that they are afraid to make requests of anyone, for fear of being resented. It becomes very difficult for some to receive after having been given to by people who really resented their giving.

As adults, we can never blame others for what we choose to do. If they try to make us feel guilty for a choice, we must choose our attitudes about that and realize that guilt is a result of our attitudes, not their manipulation. If someone tries to manipulate me, and I have an attitude that manipulation is evil, I will not feel guilty for saying no. Instead, I will think, *My, aren't you being controlling?* But if I believe that I should keep her happy, I'll think, *I should do what she wants, and I'm guilty if I don't.* My attitude makes me guilty, not the guilt messages.

If we aren't responsible for our choices, controlling others can have a field day with us. They can set our course for a day, an evening, a weekend, or even a lifetime. We are to determine our giving and our course as we work out our salvation with God.

In sum, then, of crossed boundaries in choices, we need to let others have their choices, and we need to take responsibility for ours.

Desires

Basically, desires are like feelings and any other element lying within our boundaries. We must own ours—and ours only. We must realize that they are our responsibility and not someone else's.

Jim's wife had a desire for a nice yard. That was her desire, not his. Therefore, she is responsible for it. She can certainly ask him to give it to her, and he may. But she is still responsible for it. If he doesn't give it, and she still wants it, she must take responsibility for getting it. If she doesn't get it, that is her problem, also.

If we fail to understand that our desires are our responsibility to deal with, we blame others for our deprivation. Remember the woman who was abandoned by her husband and took responsibility for her wants. She got an education and achieved her goals. If she did not see those as her responsibility, she would be blaming life for cheating her. This is the victim mentality that declares, "The world is responsible for me," and never does anything to better the quality of life. Paul writes, "For each one shall bear his own load" (Gal. 6:5). This point is interesting in view of what he writes three verses before that: "Bear one another's burdens, and so fulfill the law of Christ." He is referring to the coming together of individual responsibility and sharing with one another that we discussed earlier. Both are present in the Bible. In the Old Testament, people were commanded to leave food for the poor, the gleaners, but the poor were required to pick it.

And just as we must own our desires, we must not own others' desires. Jim must not own his wife's if it is not his. He must realize that an immaculate yard is her desire, not his. He then can choose to grant that request or not, but he is not responsible for it.

He will be able to choose what he wants to give and what he does not if he understands that she is responsible for her wants. He can decide that doing the yard work is a way in which he wants to love her and do it. Then he doesn't feel controlled into it and resist it.

Owning our desires breeds responsibility and love. We can lovingly give to others their requests, for we know that we don't have to in order for them to love us. We can be motivated to get what we want if the world does not drop it on our plate. Then we are not bitter for what we do not have; we are curious as to how we can achieve it.

It refocuses our attention away from obligation and guilt to love and sharing. If we do not believe that we have to run from obligation, for example, we can approach others and find their needs that we purpose to meet. As long as we have a choice, we will give. Through realizing the freedom that God gives us, we are motivated to give out of freedom and gratitude.

Limits

Crossed boundaries is the same in terms of limits. We decide what limits we will set on ourselves, and let others be responsible for the limits they set on themselves. We must set certain limitations on time, money, or anything. If we extend them too far, it's our fault. At the same time, we cannot determine someone else's limits.

In the alcoholic home, if someone chooses not to limit his behavior in drinking, that is his responsibility. However, the wife can set limits on how she will be affected by it. She can say, "I will limit my exposure to your behavior. If you continue to drink, I will move out until you get sober." She cannot stop him from drinking, but she can stop herself from being affected by it.

This is what I mean about setting one's own limits and not someone else's. She could try for years to get him to limit his drinking, but only he can do that. But she can limit her exposure to it, and he may choose to do something about his own problem.

We cannot stop someone from being abusive, but we can stop exposing ourselves or our kids to the abuse. That is to limit oneself. It is to realize that "I must take responsibility for limiting my exposure to this abuse." That can happen in several ways. "I can call the police, and they will limit my exposure. I can call the elders, and they will come over when he gets abusive. I can leave and go to Anne's"—all are examples I have heard from women when they realized that they lived with someone without limits on behavior. When they drew their own line instead of hoping that he would, things changed.

If we cannot set those limits by ourselves, we are wise to enlist the help of others. That is still taking responsibility. If we call the police and ask them to limit our exposure, that is a responsible move. If we call a friend every time we feel out of control in some area and ask for prayer, or counsel, that is taking responsibility for lack of limits. This pattern has worked for people with compulsive behaviors for years. They find themselves without limits, so they take responsibility for getting help in setting them.

Our limits define what we will allow and what we will not allow "onto our farm." The fence around my farm keeps good things in and bad things out. It guards my possessions and keeps the thieves and wolves off my farm. This is a very important aspect of what limits do.

We must be oriented to long-suffering and forgiveness to have relationships work. But there is a point at which long-suffering enables evil behavior to continue, and limits must be set. Each of us has different limits in different areas, and we must take responsibility for those individually. Some that I have heard are listed here:

- "I will no longer allow myself to be with you when you are drunk. If you choose to drink, I will leave until you can stop."
- "I will no longer allow the children to be abused that way. If you do that again, I will take some action."
- "I will no longer be talked to that way. I will go into the other

room until you can stop yelling at me and have a mutual conversation."

- "I will no longer bail you out of financial difficulty. If you choose to overspend again, you will pay the consequences."
- "I will not lend you my —— again. Every time you have used ——, something gets broken. Please buy your own."

These examples illustrate ways of establishing one's limits of what one will allow and what one will not, which is essential in every relationship and is the basis for mutual respect and love. In no way does this imply that we will not forgive or continue to love and work on conflict. It does mean that we will require responsible behavior on the other's part, for only then can the conflict be worked through.

I am not saying that we should require perfection, we should overlook multitudes of things, as the Scripture affirms in many places, for "love will cover a multitude of sins" (1 Pet. 4:8).

But limits must be set when there are dangerous repetitive patterns of evil. If we do not necessarily like some trait or habit of a friend or spouse, that is one thing, and it is not destructive. But some things are destructive, and allowing them to continue does not help the person or the love between us. The evil must be limited and bound.

This theme is consistent throughout the Bible, and we are commanded to set limits on what we will tolerate:

> If your brother sins against you, go and tell him his fault between you and him alone. If he hears you, you have gained your brother. But if he will not hear, take with you one or two more, that "by the mouth of two or three witnesses every word may be established." And if he refuses to hear them, tell it to the church. But if he refuses even to hear the church, let him be to you like a heathen and a tax collector. Assuredly, I say to you, whatever you bind on earth will be bound in heaven, and whatever you loose on earth will be loosed in heaven (Matt. 18:15–18).

In this passage, Jesus tells us to limit the effects of evil. He even describes it in terms of a boundary: "Whatever you bind . . . will be bound." We bind evil by not allowing it to dominate our homes and relationships. If we are truly dealing with responsible persons, we

SYMPTOMS OF INABILITY
TO CREATE BOUNDARIES

Blaming others
Codependency
Depression
Difficulties with being alone
Disorganization and lack of direction
Extreme dependency
Feelings of being let down
Feelings of obligation
Generalized anxiety
Identity confusion
Impulsiveness
Inability to say no
Isolation
Masochism
Overresponsibility and guilt
Panic
Passive-aggressive behavior
Procrastination and inability to follow through
Resentment
Substance abuse and eating disorders
Thought problems and obsessive-compulsive
    problems
Underresponsibility
Victim mentality

will "win them." But sometimes stronger boundaries must be set to bind the evil, especially in the areas of abuse. Allowed to continue, these problems have long-term effects on the family. I have heard many hurting adults express the wish that one of their parents had put some limits on the effect of the abusive parent in the home. Their lives would have been much different if that had happened. Instead, they watched the abusive behavior dominate for years and years. Unbridled evil does not subside on its own; it grows. It gets "loosed" in the spiritual arena and does not lessen without being limited.

Just as we must set limits on what we will allow others to do to us, we must set limits on ourselves so that we can live responsibly. We must limit our body, feelings, attitudes, behaviors, thoughts, abilities, choices, and desires appropriately.

Because some people have overly strict limits on all of those things, they never find their capacities. Others have very few limits and overextend themselves in all of those areas. Maturity is a process of properly realizing our real limits. For example, some people never realize any anger. They limit their realization of anger to nonexistence, and they miss out on the message their anger is trying to tell them. Others may never limit the feeling of anger; therefore, they reach the point of not being able to find out what is driving it.

It is good not to limit our desires to the point of making ourselves miserable. The Bible speaks about that in several ways (Col. 2:20–23). The limits need to be broad enough so that we can enjoy God's blessings. But if there are no limits, our desires take over life and reality. There needs to be appropriate limits on every aspect of ourselves, and that is what it means to have good fences, or boundaries.

Fences also enable the exchange of good and bad. On a farm, I would have a gate in the fence that allowed the delivery truck to bring groceries and supplies in and the trash truck to take the garbage out. Flexible boundaries, or fences with gates, let good things in and allow others to come into our space and hearts for the sake of love. On the other hand, we sometimes have trash that we need to express through confession. Spiritual fences permit an exchange of good and bad within the soul.

Leviticus 19:17 speaks of this exchange: "You shall not hate your brother in your heart. You shall surely rebuke your neighbor, and not bear sin because of him." When we reprove those we love, we are "taking the trash out," not letting it turn into hatred or bitterness.

In the same way, the gate allows us to take some of the good that we have on our farm and give it to others. We can take some milk and vegetables to our neighbor. The gate allows us to open up to the world and share what we have in a loving way. Many people are so closed off with rigid fences that there is no gate for love to be given or received. It is a sad thing to hold onto all of one's good. It tends to spoil if kept too long.

In many regards, then, our limits tell us much about where we end and someone else begins. We can know what we want versus what someone else wants, and who is responsible for what. The same is true about the other attributes. We can also figure out what we will allow on our property and what we will not, so that evil will not take over our house. We can bring good in and out as well as take out the trash in confession. Realizing our property line spiritually is basic to responsibility, freedom, and love.

Symptoms of Inability to Create Boundaries

If we don't realize what we own and what we don't, we will experience some of several symptoms.

Inability to Say No

As we have talked about, saying no is the most basic boundary function. An inability to say no leaves a person open to all sorts of control, intrusion, and abuse. When someone cannot say no, his or her boundaries are easily crossed.

Depression

Many people experience depression because they haven't set good boundaries. The lack of boundaries often sets them up for being mistreated, and a lot of pain follows.

Others are depressed because of anger turned inward. If they aren't in touch with their choices, they think that others are controlling them. They become resentful, perhaps even bitter.

Panic

Panic disorders most often fall in this category. Many people feel panic because they seem to have no control over what happens to them or what they end up doing. It is scary to have others in control of one's life and choices. That is a prescription for panic disorder.

Resentment

Many people resent what they are doing because it was not done out of a purpose of the heart (2 Cor. 9:7). Too often, they comply with others' wishes and do what they really do not purpose to do, then resent it later. This is an example of the martyr syndrome, where giving is not really giving.

Passive-Aggressive Behavior

When we do not set our limits and let our " 'Yes' be 'Yes' and [our] 'No,' 'No' " (James 5:12), we tend to set our limits passively. Many struggling with uncompleted promises to others are really being passive-aggressive; they express the aggression of saying no in a passive way.

Codependency

If we do not comprehend who is responsible for what, then as we discussed earlier, we become codependent and enable evil. This symptom always indicates a confusion in boundaries.

Identity Confusion

Identity comes from owning who we are and realizing all of our attributes. People who are not owning what falls within their boundaries, and are being separate from others, are unable to tell what is them and what is someone else. There is a developmental need to know who we are apart from others.

Difficulties with Being Alone

Some people have not established adequate boundaries so that they are able to have a self apart from others. They fear being alone, for they will not be with anyone, that is, there is no one inside. They do not have the internal structure to contain the love they have for and from others. They always have to be with someone in order to survive. In these instances, there is not a lack of bonding; there is no internal structure to hold the bonding inside. It is like pouring water into a cup with no bottom. The more they get, the more they need, but they are unable to hold onto it. Limits are needed to help them form some structure internally.

Masochism

This inability to set limits on others' abusive behavior is a vicious cycle because the pain causes more need, which makes it harder to set limits on other persons. They need others so much that they can't limit them. A support network is integral to learning to set limits on abuse.

Victim Mentality

According to this way of thinking, individuals consider themselves victims of circumstances and other people, never taking responsibility for themselves. They use phrases like, "I had to . . . ," "I have no choice . . . ," "Everything happens to me." Any sort of responsibility is denied, especially in the area of choices.

Blaming Others

Blaming is similar to victim thinking; responsibility for pain and change is always directed toward someone else. There is no doubt that others cause us pain, but when we get into the "blame game," we make others responsible for dealing with our pain, and that keeps us stuck. People who stay in the blame stage never change, for no responsibility is taken.

Overresponsibility and Guilt

People without clear boundaries feel responsible for what is not theirs, such as others' feelings and disappointments. They feel guilty for not being what others want them to be and not doing what others want them to do. They feel that they are bad for not carrying through on "their" responsibility: to make others happy.

Underresponsibility

Often people who are overresponsible for others do not carry their own load (Gal. 6:5), for they are too busy carrying the load of others. In this typical codependent behavior, people feel so responsible for others that they do not deal with their own pain and lives.

Feelings of Obligation

Paul mentions in 2 Corinthians 9:7 that people have these feelings when they are not choosing what they will give and what they will not give. They are compelled to give to others; they are not free and in control of themselves.

Feelings of Being Let Down

Since many are so good at taking care of others, they feel that others are obligated to take care of them. But they are let down when this doesn't happen. They perceive others to be unloving and uncaring if they aren't taking responsibility for them.

Isolation

A person experiencing boundary confusion and distortion and lack of freedom will often avoid relationship in order to feel a sense of boundaries. For many people, getting close means losing their boundaries and ownership of themselves. It is so frightening and conflictual that relationship is eliminated as an option, and they choose a world of isolation.

Extreme Dependency

People who have not gotten a feeling of ownership of their lives believe they cannot function responsibly on their own. Often depending upon someone else to negotiate the world of responsibility for them, they tend to have a fused identity with others. They are very fearful of separateness.

Disorganization and Lack of Direction

People who have no clear definition of themselves often lack direction and purpose, for they cannot choose their goals, likes, and dislikes. They get easily sidetracked by whatever anyone says to them.

Substance Abuse and Eating Disorders

Many people turn to food or substances either to dull the pain or to have some control, as in the case of anorexia or bulimia. More often than not, boundaries are a strong issue in the resolution of addictions. Usually, when boundaries are cleared up, self-control functions better as they begin to have a clear sense of their own person. This is especially true in bulimia, as issues of separateness are resolved. The ambivalence that is expressed in food is resolved as the ambivalence of relationship is cleared up through boundary definition.

Procrastination and Inability to Follow Through

Often these problems are related to a lack of clear boundaries. Individuals don't feel they are the ones choosing. They say yes when they mean no, and then they express their real goal through procrastination. In the parable in Matthew 21:28–31, the procrastinating son was not honest about his "no" as was the other son. If the other son could be honest about "no," he could be honest about "yes."

Impulsiveness

Impulsiveness invariably has a boundary component because the person lacks internal structure. Whatever is thought is done, and there is limited ability to say no to the self. As boundaries are cleared up and self-control is a fruit of saying no, the person gains control of the impulses.

Generalized Anxiety

Some people struggle with a vague sort of tension and anxiety sometimes related to boundaries. This internal lack of structure makes for an inability to process and contain feelings as well as external demands. While this often cannot be pointed toward one particular conflict or problem, the anxiety is still felt. Instead of working on some "issue," the person needs to firm up identity by creating stronger boundaries.

Thought Problems and Obsessive-Compulsive Problems

Thinking is primarily an aggressive part of our personality as well as boundary setting. If people cannot set clear boundaries, the aggression not used in that way "turns against them" in the form of painful distorted thinking or compulsions that they "must" perform to be safe. These painful realities can be resolved by strengthening the ability to set and keep boundaries, thus providing the internal structure that can stand against attacking thoughts and say no to compulsions. By their very nature, compulsions indicate a lack of freedom, and that is why developing boundaries and the ability to say no to others creates the freedom needed to work through a compulsive problem.

Barriers to Creating Boundaries

Injury and distortions can get in the way of our creating boundaries. Following are some examples that illustrate how this happens.

Injury

As in every other aspect of spiritual functioning, injury affects our ability to set boundaries. All of us have suffered in this area because we have been raised in a world that is severely mixed up as to where one person ends and another begins. We grow up not understanding what we own and what we don't, what we are responsible for and what we are not.

Injuries can be understood in relation to what is needed to realize one's sense of property. If we have not been allowed to own our bodies, feelings, attitudes, behaviors, thoughts, abilities, choices, wants, and limits, we are injured to that degree. If that happens, or more accurately, *as* that happens, we will have boundary disturbances to that degree. In addition, we have to take into consideration our wishes to avoid responsibility. Injuries always make taking responsibility more difficult, as we naturally resist doing so anyway.

You may have been raised in a way that did not allow you to own your choices, and you felt responsible for the choices of others; that is a specific injury to your realization of boundaries. Sandy grew up with a mother who did that. She had to go through a process of "reclaiming" what was hers, namely, her choices, and giving back to her mother what was the mother's, namely, the mother's choices and responsibility.

Each person has to consider the specific way in which boundaries were not allowed to grow. Abuse, control, guilt manipulation, and other sorts of injuries result in crossed boundaries inside us. There is the added injury of not being able to have boundaries as a result of the injury. In other words, we often do not have the abilities to set boundaries because of injury and, as a result, are injured all the more. It is no wonder that a loving God could say, "But when He saw the multitudes, He was moved with compassion for them, because they were weary and scattered, like sheep having no shepherd" (Matt.

9:36). God realizes how lost we really are, and His wish is to help rebuild the boundaries and sense of identity that we lost at the Fall.

Distortions in Our View of Others

As a result of these injuries and our fallenness, we have many distortions of God's reality as far as boundaries are concerned. Just like the distortions in the area of bonding, we need to clear up our distortions about responsibility. Again, they fall into three categories. Everyone has particular ways of distorting others, themselves, and God.

"They will hate me for saying no." If we have learned that we are responsible for others' disappointments, we will fear resentment and hatred for owning what is ours. We will imagine that other people will always reject us for setting limits on what we will and will not do for them. In actuality, research and life experience show that people who can say no are the best liked people by far.

"People will leave me for having my own boundaries." Many are raised where love was withdrawn as they began to own their lives and create a separate self. They suppose that they will always be left if they own themselves. Again, this supposition is the opposite of the truth.

"People are controlling and want to manipulate me." Lacking a good sense of will and choice means having a great fear of manipulation and control. Such people are always on the lookout for how others are going to control them, and they fear getting involved. Good boundaries give one a sense of not being able to be manipulated and controlled.

"Others will resent my assertiveness and requests." Often people have been raised in settings in which direct expression of wants was resented or considered selfish. They have learned to be passive about them for fear of resentment and judgment from others. They are afraid of being seen as pushy by their loved ones. On the contrary, direct people have the clearest and best relationships. It is difficult to feel close to passive persons, for we have to guess what they want.

"They will leave me if I don't keep them happy." People who have learned that they are responsible for others' feelings fear loss if they don't take responsibility for others' happiness. This may have been a reality in their lives, as well as the other distortions, but the real distortion is when that is generalized to everyone.

"Others are responsible for me." In the same way that others feel that way toward us, we tend to cross their boundaries as well. We tend to see others as responsible for our feelings, attitudes, and choices, and do not view them as free people with their own lives.

"People are selfish if they do not do what I want." We may not realize how our sense of crossed boundaries is projected onto others, and we judge them for their freedom.

"People are unloving if they say no to me." Often, if we have a split between love and limits, we take others' no as rejection and feel unloved. This is a distortion of them and a lack of respect for how they choose to love us. We tend to see them as mean if they have limits.

"People expect me to be compliant to their wishes." Often we do not realize how much freedom others give us to own our lives. If we grew up in a controlling situation, we may be burdened by the distortion that others will expect us to have no personal freedom.

"Others are responsible for my behaviors." If we were enabled in the area of behavior, we tend to perceive others as responsible for our behavior and consequences. Thus, we may not realize the law of cause and effect in our lives and have a wish to always be bailed out. I know one secretary who has a sign on her desk that reads, "Poor planning on your part does not constitute an emergency on my part." In essence, she is saying she is not responsible for someone else's behavior.

Distortions in Our View of Ourselves

"I am bad for having boundaries." Probably the biggest problem to work through in terms of boundaries is the guilt involved in realizing freedom to own one's life. Many people have been taught that they are selfish and bad for not being responsible for others' feelings, behaviors, and choices, which keeps codependent behavior going. People with boundary problems invariably feel bad when they are honest about their limits and wishes because they have an inordinate sense of responsibility for others. Their lack of freedom leads to feelings of badness.

"I am selfish for owning my life." The people who make this remark have been told, "You are selfish if you do not give me what is yours." But when people are vulnerable to control, they feel that they are selfish for deciding to do with their property what they wish. In reality, that is the only way we can ever get to true love, for then giving is out of freedom.

"My wants are not important." This statement denies one's life in an unbiblical way. We are told in the Bible to deny ourselves, but this is only real if we own ourselves. People who do not own their lives cannot give their lives away, for they aren't theirs to give! We must take responsibility for our wants and take care of them, and then we can be good stewards of our lives, giving to others as well.

"My wants are the only ones that are important." This is the distortion in the other direction. When we do not have boundaries on ourselves, we take over the lives of others, not seeing them as separate people. The real meaning of selfishness—the denial of others as people in their own right with needs and feelings—is a lack of respect for others' lives.

"I must have everything I want." This distortion of the self is very destructive, for it puts us out of control. We need boundaries on our wants so that we can give to others as well as tolerate deprivation. Not getting things is often good for us; it builds boundaries and limits and structure. It is like saying no to some demands of children. They learn to contain themselves and others.

"I am responsible for others." We have seen the ways in which this belief keeps others in an immature position. The truth is that we need to be responsible *to* others, not *for* them. We have a real responsibility to others in need. However, we must require responsibility on the part of those who are able. To not do that is to enable them to remain immature.

"I must do whatever anyone wants of me." This feeling comes from being enslaved to or owned by another. If we feel this way, we cannot purpose in our giving, and we are being irresponsible. God has given us finite amounts of whatever we have to give, and we must purpose that giving. If we let others dictate our purpose for us, we are not answering to God.

"Whatever goes wrong is my fault." People with boundary problems have an inordinate sense of fault. They feel responsible if someone driving to their house has a wreck. They feel responsible if they can draw any connection to the behavior of others, and they blame themselves. This is particularly true in parenting. Parents may blame themselves entirely for their children's failure. They deny the responsibility of others and really leave children impotent. It says that children cannot have any power over their own lives, that parents have it all.

"Nothing is my fault." This statement indicates the failure to own responsibility in whatever we do. It is not realizing what is on our property line and not taking responsibility for our actions. Blaming is a classic example as well as not owning our part in another's pain. Some parents will not own their part in their children's struggles, which is just as wrong as taking all the blame. It is possible to make another stumble (Matt. 18:6).

Distortions in Our View of God

"God doesn't want me to own my life." Many people with boundary problems think that the commandments for us to give our lives to God and to deny ourselves are commandments not to exist. That is incorrect. We *must* own our lives before we can give them to God, or they are not ours to give. The Bible and experience show that we must realize all the components of being a person so that we can submit to God as bond servants. A bond servant is a freed slave who owns his life and voluntarily gives it to a master.

God wants a relationship with us, and that requires two people. When Jesus was in the Garden of Gethsemane, He submitted to the will of the Father, but he was acutely aware of His own wishes. "Let this cup pass" was an expression of His wants that He later surrendered to the Father. He was owning and expressing His wishes. A similar relationship has been accomplished by all the great saints of the Bible, from Job to David. God wants us to be real people and own what is ours. Only then can we choose to give it away.

"God doesn't want me to have anything of my own." Many with boundary problems feel guilty about having wishes, desires, and property. The Bible is replete with examples of God telling us to ask so that He can bless us and share what we have. Some believe God frowns upon their having their desires met. This heresy can be shown to be the opposite of what God wants. He wants to bless us, but we are to see Him as the focus, not our blessings: "Command those who are rich in this present age not to be haughty, nor to trust in uncertain riches but in the living God, *who gives us richly all things to enjoy. Let them do good, that they be rich in good works, ready to give*"

(1 Tim. 6:17-18, emphasis added). God has richly supplied us with blessings to enjoy and to share. A guilty asceticism is not biblical. It is a distortion of God the blessing giver.

"God wants me to have everything I want." Other people suppose that their wish is God's command and that He has no limits to His giving. This idea is equally unbiblical, for God often says no to us, and He does not owe us any explanation as to why. Jesus said to the worker that He was free to do what He wanted with what was His (Matt. 20:15). Some of the "name it and claim it" thinking makes God into a servant of our wishes and denies His boundaries and choices. He often says no, but that doesn't mean that we do not have enough faith. Ask Jesus in the Garden.

"God thinks I am selfish when I say no to others." On the contrary, God says to give only as we purpose in our hearts. He loves for us to share and to give out of freedom, not compulsion. He is all for our sense of boundaries and freedom, for He created them. As a result, we can turn into real givers, not compliant givers.

In addition, we help Him to mature them when we say no to others' irresponsibility. Paul comments, "And if anyone does not obey our word in this epistle, note that person and do not keep company with him, that he may be ashamed. Yet do not count him as an enemy, but admonish him as a brother" (2 Thess. 3:14-15). When we say no to enabling behavior, we serve as God's hand of discipline in others' lives.

"God wants me to allow others to do whatever they want to me or to others." This is a similar distortion. God says many times for us to rebuke others. Not to do so is to split grace and truth and to enable them to remain immature (Lev. 19:17; Prov. 27:5-6; Matt. 18:15-18; 1 Cor. 5:1-5, 9-13; 2 Cor. 2:5-11; Gal. 6:1; Eph. 4:25-26; and many others).

"God doesn't want me to pursue what I want." This statement denies the reality that two people are in the relationship. Many people feel guilty about owning their talents and goals. God says that we are to work with Him on such matters, and He will guide us, opening and closing doors: "A man's heart plans his way, but the LORD directs his steps" (Prov. 16:9). "Delight yourself also in the LORD, and He shall give you the desires of your heart. Commit your way to the LORD, trust also in Him, and He shall bring it to pass" (Ps. 37:4-5).

"God is totally sovereign and in control; therefore, I have no responsibility." This is a boundary problem because it denies our ownership in our lives. Many people do not realize how much responsibility and freedom God gives us to manage our lives. God restricts His boundaries so that we have our own wills and choices. We are responsible for them and will one day give an account for them.

"God is a 'hands-off' God and is not involved in my life." This boundary problem works in the other direction. It is not allowing God the reality of the degree of ownership of His power that He really has. He is very active in our growth and is working to bring it about. Both have responsibility in the growth process: "Work out your own salvation with fear and trembling; for it is God who works in you both to will and to do for His good pleasure" (Phil. 2:12–13).

"If God says no to me, He doesn't love me." God is free to limit His giving for His purposes and ours. It isn't unloving for God to say no, even to our healing. He knows that sometimes we need to work out things for our healing instead of something He could do. For example, if I am depressed because I do not attach to others, God's healing of my depression would prohibit me from becoming loved. That is one example of when He may say no for my benefit. We, like Job, must trust His "no" and His timing. It does not mean a lack of love.

"God is forgiving and has no response to my sin." This is a denial of God's limits. He will not allow evil to take over. He wants a clean farm, and since He has invited us to live there, He want us to take our shoes off if they have mud on them! He will discipline us for our own good. He is interested in our developing righteousness because it isn't healthy for us to remain immature.

"God is all limits and no love." Such comments are far from true. God has many compassionate feelings and much forgiveness, and we must allow Him to own them.

Skills Needed to
Create Boundaries

Now that we've seen the importance of discovering our boundaries and responsibility to own our lives, let's look at some skills that are helpful in the endeavor. You'll probably want to think of others, too.

SKILLS NEEDED TO CREATE BOUNDARIES

Accept others
Arrive at negative definitions
Be honest
Become active, not reactive
Challenge distortions
Choose values
Define the self
Develop persistence
Develop the "no" muscle
Display self-control
Gain awareness
Realize separateness
Refuse to play victim
Set limits
Stop blaming others

Gain Awareness

Since we're talking about ownership of what is ours, we must begin to be aware of ourselves. Thus, we must become aware of our bodies, feelings, attitudes, behaviors, thoughts, abilities, choices, wants, and limits. This skill is essential to take responsibility for one's life.

Enlisting others in this task is helpful. We need feedback from others to discover ourselves, for we do not often see what we have disowned. They can help us to become aware of all of those functions as they give feedback about them.

Define the Self

Just as we have seen God define Himself, we ought to assert ourselves. We can begin to say what we feel, what we like, what we want, what we will do, what we think, and so on. In this way we carve out an identity and declare, "This is who I am."

Arrive at Negative Definitions

We must also say who we are not. It is helpful to say what is "not me" as well as what is me. We must say what we do not agree with, do not like, and will not do. Many times, people with boundary problems do not stand against anything. They take everything in, but that is a very destructive tendency. God calls us to hate some things.

Develop the "No" Muscle

The child learns to set boundaries by saying no. Many people who have eliminated that word from their vocabulary need to develop that ability. It is like a muscle that needs to be strengthened. Begin with little tasks, such as saying no to going to a certain restaurant that you do not want to go to, and work your way up to bigger barbells. This is probably the most important task for some people in creating boundaries, especially to parents' wishes.

Stop Blaming Others

This step in setting boundaries is a major move out of bondage and on toward health. It is empowering to take responsibility for the pain that one owns. Stop blaming others for the trouble and deal with it.

Refuse to Play Victim

As an adult, you have choices. Take responsibility for them and own them. If you are giving something, you at some level are making a choice to do it; stop acting as if others make you give to them. If you are working somewhere that you do not like, take responsibility for finding something else. If you are criticized by a friend, take responsibility for the fact that you agree to meet with him or her. You are responsible for what you choose to do. You can change your life by refusing to play victim.

Develop Persistence

We are commanded to develop perseverance, which has a role in establishing boundaries. Goal-oriented behavior is a purposeful task that creates discipline and responsibility. This will go a long way in structuring one's personality.

Become Active, Not Reactive

People with boundary problems often think of themselves not as initiators, but as reactors. They make choices by passively responding to others. We need to choose to love and give, not just love and give when it is required. We need to choose to work and accomplish, not just when it is required. A structure to the personality and a sense of "I will" develop in this way.

Set Limits

An essential skill is to set limits on abusive behavior by others. Stop enabling others to be self-centered and irresponsible. Put some limits on the ways that their sin affects you, such as substance abuse or physical abuse. In addition, there are more subtle ones, such as criticism and blaming, that you may be enabling by not setting limits.

Also, realize the limits of what you have to give to others in terms of time, money, and energy. If you sow sparingly, you will reap sparingly, but if you sow more than you have, you will be bankrupt. Get with God and others to find what is reasonable for you at this time.

Choose Values

Define who you want to be and where you want to go. As Joshua said, we must choose whom we are going to serve. We must decide actively what our values are going to be and work to purpose our goals. This may be very different from what other Christians tell you your values should be, but they are not inerrant. Each one must take responsibility for personal choices.

Display Self-Control

This process of setting limits on your wishes begins to structure the personality. If, though, you have too many limits on your wishes, you have controlled yourself out of having a self. There must be a balance between the person and the control.

Accept Others

As others define their person to us, we must learn to love and accept them for who they are. If we do not, we are intruding on their boundaries and taking control of something that is not ours—their person. If we want to feel accepted, we must accept. With this is an acceptance of their limits and their "no." If we resent others for saying no to us, we will be conflicted about our own "no" and will be controlling them. We need to love people when they say no and relish in their freedom.

Realize Separateness

With the ones you love, develop some separate time and interests. Realize that separateness is a good thing that will add to your relationship. Otherwise you are a clone. This is also true in terms of realizing your differences from them. Counting the ways you are different as well as alike will help your sense of identity.

Be Honest

The Bible tells us to be honest with one another. Many times people will not be honest because of the fear of loss of intimacy and togetherness. In reality, honesty will bring you closer together, for it will increase your boundaries. The more you realize your separateness, the closer you can get. Tell your loved ones what is really on your mind, and tell others what you really think, for that is the foundation of love.

Challenge Distortions

Jesus taught that the truth sets us free, and as in the area of bonding, we need to see the truth of God's reality in the area of boundaries. If we identify our distortions and act in accordance with the truth, we learn new ways of being, and thus render a different kind of fruit. This is hard work, requiring the help of friends and God's Spirit to lead us into the truth about ourselves and about His world.

Inventory of Progress
Toward Creating Boundaries

As we learned in the area of bonding, an inventory provides a way of seeing where we have come from, where we are now, and where we can go in the future. Most boundaries have been hurt some way in the past, and it is helpful for us to see how that happened, so we can give up old patterns and strengthen our weaknesses. In addition, because we tend to continue past patterns into the present, those need to be recognized and confessed. This process will lead us to a commitment for the future. Let's look at each one individually.

The Past

First, we are to forsake old patterns and confess them if they are not of God. We have all been guilty of crossed boundaries in various ways, and we need to confess our sin of not owning our lives. Discerning old patterns helps us to break the bondage of the past and turn in a new direction.

Second, we need to know if others have crossed our boundaries and injured them. We need to forgive those who have sinned against us in that way. If we do not, we will be stuck in that pattern. As we identify certain patterns that belonged to a particular relationship, we can begin to give them up as belonging to relationships of the past and not of the present. This effort diminishes our distortions. It breaks some sort of bondage with that person when the sin is confessed, even by us (Neh. 9:2). And we can see what has been lacking in our past relationships and performance so that we can have direction for the future. Here are some questions to think about.

1. With whom in the past was I able to discover and keep my boundaries? What qualities of the relationship supported my boundaries?

2. Who crossed my boundaries in the past? How did they do that? What qualities of the relationship were hurtful?

3. What convictions and distortions did I develop in those relationships that need to be challenged and replaced with God's precepts? How would I describe my philosophy of boundaries as I learned it in those significant relationships?

4. Have I been able to forgive those who hurt my sense of boundaries? Have I called what they did to me sin and let them be responsible for it? (If not, I may be taking responsibility for what is not mine before God and feeling guilt that does not belong to me. I must confess the truth about their sin so that I can forgive them and get on with life. Unforgiveness is a chain that binds me to that person. I must let go of it and ask God to help me do that.)

5. Have there been instances in the past when I failed to keep my boundaries? Have I allowed others to cross my boundaries when I was old enough as an adult not to allow that? Have I tried to make others be responsible for aspects of myself?

6. Have I invaded someone else's boundaries and crossed them? Can I see a pattern that needs to be confessed and turned from? Do I need to make restitution with someone?

7. What parts of my fences and boundaries did I take outside time, and when did that happen?

The Present

The past tells us what sort of forgiveness and lackings need to be taken care of, and the present tells us where we are repeating the past. We need to evaluate the present to be sure that we are wisely conducting ourselves.

1. With whom do I have a good relationship at present in which boundaries are not crossed? What components of that relationship allow for mutual responsibility of all the aspects of ownership? How can I increase those elements? How can I respect their boundaries more?

2. With whom do I now experience crossed boundaries and a lack of boundaries and limits? Why? What elements make it that way, and what will it take to change those?

3. How am I allowing the aspects of boundary problems in those present relationships to reinforce my original beliefs about boundaries? How are those present relationships reinjuring my sense of boundaries?

4. What distortions are dominating me in the present in relation to boundaries and limits?

5. Are there times when I am better at setting and realizing boundaries than at others? Why?

6. What exercises am I doing to bring my boundaries back into time and get practice so that they can develop?

7. To which people do I have difficulty saying no? Why?

8. Whose "no" do I not respect and try to override?

9. Whose boundaries am I overriding in other aspects? Why?

10. What of the above do I need to confess to God and others and receive forgiveness for? What of the above do I need to confront others for in order to resolve a present, ongoing issue?

The Future

As in every other area of life, the continuation of the past and present guarantees a like future. Devising plans to make some things different will get us back into "good time" and give us practice in getting somewhere productive.

1. As I evaluate the future in terms of the problems I see in boundaries, what am I going to change? How?

2. Knowing that it takes relationship and truth to change, whose help am I going to get for my plan?

3. In which specific ways am I going to challenge my distortions and barriers?

4. What are some specific practice activities that I can undertake to strengthen my sense of boundaries?

5. What difficulties do I envision when I begin to create boundaries? How will I negotiate those difficulties?

6. Who will I get to share and pray with me and support my plan?

7. What specific areas of crossed boundaries with others am I going to confront?

8. How do I expect them to react when I confront them? How will I deal with that?

Conclusion

In looking at the issue of boundaries, we cannot escape one main point: responsibility. Our boundaries basically define our sense of responsibility for us. They tell us what our lives consist of and what we are responsible for. We have seen one way of looking at those things in terms of the aspects of body, feelings, attitudes, behaviors, thoughts, abilities, choices, desires, and limits.

If we stopped there and stayed on our own farms within carefully guarded fences, we would live a very safe, but very unbiblical, existence. We would fall short of love, the goal of life. And we would not fulfill the law of Christ.

The biblical concept of agape love involves loving others and being willing to lay down one's life for others. In this sort of love, one truly finds one's self, for the real self was created for loving. However, it is impossible to give away what we do not own, and boundaries are our way of becoming aware of the self that we can then choose to give away. We must own our lives before we can give them away. This is the essence of freedom, and there is no love without freedom. When we give before we are free and truly own ourselves, we have fallen short of bond servanthood and into slavery. Realize what you own, and then share yourself with others.

Stephen

At the beginning of the book, you met Stephen, who had trouble with his sense of boundaries. That is why he was so scattered and spread out, able to get very little done. If you remember, he was resentful of others, irresponsible, and burned out.

When Stephen came into counseling, he felt badly about himself, for he knew that others were unhappy with him. The church staff was disappointed, and his wife was perpetually let down by his inability to follow through.

At the same time, though, he had strong feelings of being victimized by their demands and being unappreciated by those he served. He tried to make everyone happy, but all he got in return was complaints.

In therapy, Stephen began to sort out his sense of boundaries. He first figured out what he was giving out of compulsion and obligation and learned to purpose in his heart. This was true in terms of time, energy, money, and love. He got back in control of himself and stopped giving as a response to feeling responsible for others.

It is probably clear that a big part of this effort was learning to say no, which was extremely difficult for Stephen. Whenever others would be disappointed by his "no," he would be tempted to give in begrudgingly and lose his boundaries. But as time went on, he got more control of himself and gave to others what he chose to. This change caused considerable upset in his marriage in the beginning, for his wife was used to being in control of him, at least ostensibly, and she fought him as he tried to gain control of himself. However, he continued to regain ownership and self-control, and he became a more defined person. He began to do what he had said he would do for her, and he established a track record of following through. And his wife became more secure in trusting him to follow through.

In a like manner, he said no at work and defined himself more. He offered his thoughts and opinions, and became more and more aware of what he could offer. He found more of what God had created him to be and then shared it with others. There were some rocky times, but his sense of purpose eventually returned. Others began to realize that they were working with someone who was well defined.

Another fruit was his sense of goal setting and purpose. It helped him to be more of an initiator and less of a responder. He could start things and follow them through to completion. He was encouraged by his progress and by his discovery of what he really enjoyed. Owning more and more of himself, and giving up more and more of what wasn't him, was part of the process.

Stephen had to confront many distortions he had developed over the years. They mainly came from his beliefs that he was responsible for others' lives and feelings. His father had died at an early age, so Stephen had felt responsible for his mother from that time on. A somewhat controlling and self-centered person, she taught him the rules of crossed boundaries very well.

As a result, he continued those rules into his present life, and he lost control and responsibility for himself. In a real sense, he was reliving the relationship with his mother with everyone he knew. He had to do a lot of work on confessing her sins and his own ways of responding to her in order to learn the patterns and be free of them. Over time, he was able to accomplish that task.

After this program of tending to the tree, his fruit changed. He did not work on the symptoms, or the bad fruit of burnout, fatigue, and feeling victimized, because those were not the problems. His sense of boundaries needed to be built, the image of God within him. As he faced that developmental issue, the symptoms, or fruit of his life changed, and Stephen became a better defined and more responsible person.

CHAPTER FIVE

How to Resolve Good and Bad

Wherever you are as you read this, you will notice that both good and bad are present. If you are inside your house, there is probably beauty in your decor and furnishings. If you look outside, you can probably view the natural beauty all around you; in some areas it can be breathtaking. At the same time, you'll probably be aware of smudges on the walls and a few scratches on the furniture. The house does not function wholly as it should, for some of the floors are not level, and one closet door sticks when it rains. Outside, there is trash on the street, and the air is dirtier than it was a few years ago.

If someone is with you, you can see the unmistakable awe and wonder of the person God created. The senses of seeing and hearing function together so that reading the book and hearing the music can be relaxing. Physical grace and beauty may characterize the person. And consider the talents manifested in your relationship. The individual has added love to your life and astounded you at times with creative bursts of energy. But something else is true. The person has let you down, gotten unfairly angry with you, or been very self-centered, not thinking about your needs at all. At other times critical tones and words have taken a toll on your self-esteem. As much as you love that person, you are aware of the imperfections.

Then, for the hardest task of all, look in the mirror and reflect on the last few days. You can probably see the attractiveness of the unique features God has created. It may be in your smile or in an expression. You may like the sincerity of your eyes or their color. You remember the thoughtful way you listened to a friend in need; you really cared and did not in any way fake your concern. You were loving. Then you took that extra time to give to your child, or another friend, who experienced a disappointment. Or the guy in the supermarket you refused to trade insults with; instead you wondered what hurt motivated him to attack. The special project you have been working on looks as if it is really going to work; you are talented indeed. If you are a student, you are proud of that test you passed; your hard work paid off. But you notice some other things. There are some wrinkles and blotches on your skin; it is not flawless. As you think of certain situations, there are expressions that give away the resentment and sarcasm you would love to hurl at "you know who." Some memories surface of your overlooking needs of those close to you because you were just too lazy to sacrifice a bit of yourself. And then with that guy on the freeway—no one would ever know you behind the wheel if they had seen you in the choir. So you have shortcomings as well.

The truth about the whole picture is this: our world is good and bad. The people around us are good and bad. We are good and bad. What's an idealist to do?

The Bible's Picture of Good and Bad

As we have learned, the world was not always this way. There was a very real time on planet earth when everything was "all good." God painted a picture on the canvas of reality, and the reality of His picture was perfection. The creation was without blemish, and man was part of that perfect creation. He was without what the Bible calls sin.

Perhaps you have been close to a realization of what perfection must be like. You can see it sometimes as you gaze at a gorgeous sunset. It is evident in some people's physical beauty or physique. Particular musical performances challenge you to find a mistake. Some star athletes surprise you with perfect performances of grace and beauty. Moments of intimacy between those who love each other bring heaven close to earth.

At times like those we have little problem imagining the ideal world, others, and self. We can get lost in the fantasy of what a creation must have been like without the knowledge of good and evil. We were created for that sort of world. We were never to live where we live now; that was a mistake. It's as if we were delivered to the wrong address. God created us for perfection, but we find ourselves living somewhere else. We've gotten off the plane in the wrong city!

We were not prepared to live in an imperfect world. The way human beings were put together, we were not to have to deal with the effects of the Fall. There were to be no cavities in teeth, no thorns and thistles to puncture soft feet. We were not to have to protect ourselves against one another, either; our spirits are much too tender to live in a world with hurtful people. The plan was for perfect relationship with perfect people; instead, the people we know invariably hurt us in some way. They may lie or be unfaithful, or they may just be mean. Our defenseless spirits take that sort of injury pretty hard.

We were not prepared to be imperfect selves, either. There is not enough grace inside to anesthesize us against the pain of our badness. It is horrible enough to feel the sin itself, but the guilt of the sin is even worse. We were not ready for that. In addition, we were not wired to metabolize the pain of existence, all the sadness, the anger, the anxiety.

And then there are the realities of the spiritual conditions after the Fall: hatred and separation instead of love and connection; envy of others instead of appreciation and gratitude; sadness and anger over the grief of loss; panic and worry over loss of control; shame and self-hatred over the loss of our ideals; anxiety and guilt as we anticipate failure; and finally, utter fear and terror of God. All of these realities are issues of good and bad, and to be emotionally and spiritually successful, we must be able to deal with them. If we cannot cope with the coexistence of good and bad, we have a hard time living in this world.

We tend to swing back and forth from seeing things as either all good or all bad and cannot have a consistent relationship with ourselves, others, or the world around us. People will sometimes go from friend to friend, or spouse to spouse, or church to church, or job to job, for this reason. They think everything is OK, but as soon as badness appears, they are unable to deal with it. They demand perfection; whatever is not perfect is "all bad" and therefore rejected.

Perhaps you have had a relationship in which you thought everything was OK, but then you made a mistake. The person turned totally against you and treated you as if you were the devil himself. Such a person is unable to accept badness in others.

Or maybe you thought that you were doing well in some area, but when you failed, you felt enormous hatred for yourself. You considered yourself a total failure.

Or maybe you were excited about a new purchase. And then it got scratched and became worthless. Imperfection means it's all bad.

Or you prepared a special meal for guests, and it looked wonderful. But the cake flopped and ruined the whole evening for you.

These are all problems of resolving the issue of good and bad, and if we are to negotiate life appropriately, we must find a way to live in a world of both. Let's look at some sources of these problems.

The Ideal Self

Several implications are involved in the fact that there was a time when man was perfect. We can imagine what we were meant to be; each of us can imagine what a perfect "me" would be like. Think for a second about the perfect you. Think about the possibility of doing perfectly everything you have the potential to do. When you let yourself think about that consciously, you can see to some degree the tension between what you can imagine and what is real, the true self.

Within all of us is some realization of the difference between the ideal self (the imagined perfection) and the real self (the one that truly is). If these two are in a battle, we cannot function very well without conflict. We tend to be at war between what we wish were true, and what really is true. This sets up a conflict between the real and the ideal that hinders functioning. We will talk about the conflict a little later, but for now let's look at the ideal self.

The ideal self is the one you can imagine and want to be. If you think about your particular abilities, you can imagine their perfection. For instance, I am a golfer. There are days when I can hit a few shots that approach the way I would ideally hit every shot. The swing feels as if it can get no better, and the ball flies exactly like I want it to. I can imagine the ideal drive on every hole and strive for it. In fact, that striving helped me develop a pretty good game over the years. The ideal self is the imagined ideal me who hits every shot the way it is supposed to be hit. It is a wonderful fantasy and a wonderful goal.

Let's say your abilities incline you toward becoming an attorney. On some days the understanding of the law and cases seems to open up before you. You write and think so that you weigh every possibility and interpret the law clearly. At the same time, you dream of defending your client in court in a way that the competition hasn't a chance. You build such an airtight case that it cannot be challenged, and your presence in the courtroom is a holy protection for your defendant. You tap into talents and potentials that you did not even know you had.

Or let's say you're a teacher. As you interact with your pupils, you create a bridge between them and the subject matter that allows them to march into greater understanding than you thought possible. You are able to discern instantly the need of the moment and work them through their blocks to knowledge. You dream of creative ways that will aid future classes to make leaps over conventional expectations of learning.

Or you're a parent. You imagine what it would be like to know every need of your child and respond appropriately every time. You see yourself as the model your child admires and copies. You envision a wonderful relationship between the two of you.

If you are in business, you can see the success of your company as you ideally imagine it to be. You can think of new branches opening all over the nation, and the information and expertise that you amass through your experience.

The list goes on and on, both in the achievement arena and in the personal one. We have ideal wishes about several aspects of who we are. They are the lost potentials of the image of God within, but they can be imagined, and we do that both consciously and unconsciously. It may be what an ideal woman would be like if you are a woman. It may be what an ideal man would be like if you are a man. It may be an ideal intellect, talent, attribute, or whatever, but in every area of our existence, we can imagine the ideal, and we long for it. Paul summarizes the problem:

> For the creation was subjected to futility, not willingly, but because of Him who subjected it in hope; because the creation itself also will be delivered from the bondage of corruption into the glorious liberty of the children of God. *For we know that the whole creation groans and labors with birth pangs together until now. Not only that, but we also have the firstfruits of the Spirit, even we ourselves groan within ourselves, eagerly waiting for the adoption, in this hope, the redemption of our body.* For we were saved in this hope, but hope that is seen is not hope; for why does one still hope for what he

sees? But if we hope for what we do not see, we wait eagerly for it with perseverance (Rom. 8:20–25, emphasis added).

The eagerness to have the lost ideal recovered is built into the very nature of who we are or, more accurately, who we were and who we will be one day. In the meantime, however, we find ourselves only wishing for the ideal, unable to possess it.

The Real Self

We talked earlier about the importance of the real self and its involvement in grace and time. It is what we truly are. The real self is not ideal, no matter how much we wish it were. The reality is that our real self has fallen, and the ideal has been lost. We are beset with weakness and fallenness; we are in many ways broken and not what we would like to be. Paul puts it this way: "But I am carnal, sold under sin" (Rom. 7:14). In addition to our sinful aspects, we are weak, and oftentimes we represent our weakness as if it were bad. We do not perceive that it is acceptable to have that part of the real self.

In addition to sinfulness and weakness, brokenness is an aspect of the real self. We have been injured in many ways, and the real self houses all of the evidences of those injuries. The pain, the brokenness, and the emotional underdevelopment that we all possess to one degree or another are parts of who we really are, not who we wish we were. We must realize that the brokenness and the immaturity are parts of the real self, even if they don't fit our ideal.

It is easy to see why we would naturally value the ideal self more than the real. It works better, looks better, functions better, needs less maintenance. In short, it is a better model than the real thing. The problem is this: *it is a fantasy and therefore cannot be embraced or related to.* When we try to fool ourselves or others into believing it is real, we are out of relationship, truth, and time.

Therefore, exploring the relationship between the ideal self and the real self is imperative. If we have them set in a conflict, there is going to be a perpetual war inside. Whenever the real self becomes apparent, the ideal self will judge it and try to make it hide. We are not truly "there" when we are hiding, and that takes us out of relationship with God and others.

By demanding perfection from ourselves, we are not living in reality. The real self is not perfect, and that is a reality we all must come to grips with. Many people *say* they realize that, but their attitudes and actions say otherwise. They reveal that no imperfection should live in them.

The Relationship Between the Ideal and the Real

We have seen how the ideal self has certain content for everyone, and it is different for everyone. We all have our particular ideal wishes. In addition, we have seen how the real self is always different from the ideal. That is normal, and in some ways good, for we need to have goals. But an inherent problem in the relationship between the ideal and the real is in its emotional nature. The ideal is used to judge the real as unacceptable and, as a result, brings forth condemnation and wrath at the real. This sets up an adversarial relationship between the two, and like all adversaries, they get further and further apart. The enmity between them creates a divided self.

Richard entered the hospital to receive therapy for uncontrollable thoughts that were very frightening to him. At times, he had mental pictures of beating his wife up. At other times, he had angry fantasies toward his children. He tried and tried to get them out of his head, but they always returned, even more strongly. He prayed and read his Bible, but he was still unable to keep them out of his mind.

When he talked about them, he always prefaced them with remarks such as, "I know I shouldn't have those thoughts, but . . . ," or "It's really awful that I think this, but . . . ," or "I can't believe I picture this, but . . ." In other words, he always made a statement of what would be ideal, that is, the ideal Richard wouldn't have those thoughts. But he really did have them, and they were reality.

His problem developed into what is called an obsessive-compulsive disorder. He tried certain compulsions to rid himself of the thoughts, but they returned. He decided that he was hopelessly evil, and he felt awful.

But during his hospital stay, he learned that he was very angry with his wife for many things he had never told her about. He thought that he shouldn't have any angry feelings, so he denied and repressed all of his anger. In addition, he was angry with himself over his childlikeness, believing that he shouldn't have any childlike feelings. As he judged and hated the childlike part of himself, he hated the childlikeness of his children at times.

The problem was not that he had angry or childlike feelings. Both are a part of life. The problem was that they were unacceptable to him; his ideal self had decided that they shouldn't be a part of him. Therefore, they were beginning to control him. The "badness" that had been denied was coming out in destructive ways through obsessional thoughts.

As Richard began to understand the demands of his ideal self and to accept his real self the way that God does, he was able to work through his anger toward himself and his wife. Gradually, the obsessions went away.

This split between the ideal and the real, which has caused many people many problems, is a major reason that Christians struggle. There is such a demand for the ideal within the church that many people don't believe they can be human and still be Christian. That is an incredible belief when we realize that they came to Christ in the first place because they were sinners in need of forgiveness. Whatever happened to that reality?

The important aspect of the relationship, then, between the ideal and the real is the emotional tone. If there is a legal tone, one of condemnation and wrath toward what is real, then there is a house divided. The ideal will judge and condemn the real into nonexistence. The result will be shame, guilt, hiding, denial, splitting, and all sorts of other defenses to attack the real self. Whatever is not allowed and accepted in grace will be under judgment and condemnation, and that means trouble.

However, if the emotional tone is of love and acceptance of the real, there is hope for transformation. By accepting the parts of themselves that they do not consider ideal, people can be loved and healed. They can grow in ways they never imagined. Acceptance is the answer to the dilemma of the ideal versus the real.

Paul's struggle provides a good example: "For what I am doing, I do not understand. For what I will to do, that I do not practice; but what I hate, that I do. If, then, I do what I will not to do, I agree with the law that it is good. But now, it is no longer I who do it, but sin that dwells in me. . . . For the good that I will to do, I do not do; but the evil I will not to do, that I practice" (Rom. 7:15-19). He wishes for one thing but finds the painful reality of another. The natural tendency is to try harder, but Paul has an answer to that.

His answer is acceptance: "There is therefore now no condemnation to those who are in Christ Jesus" (Rom. 8:1). The answer to his struggle is the realization that the demands of the ideal have been met and that he is no longer condemned for not being perfect. God sent His Son "that the righteous requirement of the law might be fulfilled in us" (v. 4). This requirement of the law is the demanding nature of the ideal, the wrath that we are under when we relate to a perfection-istic standard that judges and condemns us when we are less than ideal.

When we can reach a point of "no condemnation" for the true self, we can confess what is wrong and be in relationship just as it is, with no pressure to be ideal in any way. We can achieve incredible growth and spiritual power.

The nature of the relationship, then, between the ideal and the real needs to be one of grace. That means unconditional love and accep-tance. If that is true, there is no internal war, no fight between the ideal and the real, and a good relationship can begin to flourish.

The relationship should hold onto the ideal and at the same time lovingly accept the real. Then the real can be encouraged to grow toward the ideal. Solomon puts it this way:

> Do not be overly righteous,
> Nor be overly wise:
> Why should you destroy yourself?
> Do not be overly wicked,
> Nor be foolish:
> Why should you die before your time?
> *It is good that you grasp this,*
> *And also not remove your hand from the other;*
> *For he who fears God will escape them all* (Eccles. 7:17–18,
>   emphasis added).

Demanding the ideal of oneself will ruin one's life. We all know perfectionists who do not enjoy life in the least. It is even drudgery to be around them! On the other hand, letting go of standards and ideals will get one killed. The God-fearing person brings forth both aspects of the self, the good and the bad, and thus has peace. In such a state—where the standards are accepted and cherished as goals and the present reality is accepted as a loved true self—there is peace and growth. This view of the self is consistent with God's view. He says we are incredibly wonderful, extremely sinful, beset with all sorts of weakness, and overflowing with talents. Think of all of that at one time! It's a real exercise in the task of resolving good and bad. Let's look at some "conflicting" statements:

> What is man that You are mindful of him, and the son of man that You visit him? For You have made him a little lower than the angels, and you have crowned him with glory and honor. You have made him to have dominion over the works of Your hands; You have put all things under his feet (Ps. 8:4–6).

> There is none righteous, no, not one (Rom. 3:10).

> For He knows our frame; He remembers that we are dust (Ps. 103:14).

> Do not neglect the gift that is in you (1 Tim. 4:14).

The Bible teaches two themes. The first is that man, created in the image of God, has incredible value. The second is that man is sinful and broken. There is the standard of the ideal, and there is the real. Both are true, and both need to be reconciled into a grace-giving relationship with God and others.

Ideal Content

The ideal self is composed of three things. The first is the lost perfect image-bearingness as we were created, that is, what a perfect human being would be like. The second is the requirements of the law of God—we have some idea of what is right and wrong. The third is what is *thought* to be ideal, even though it was never part of the ideal human God created. For example, God created man to have needs for relationship with other humans: "It is not good that man should be alone" (Gen. 2:18). But some people believe that the ideal self does not need other humans.

Some people have created an ideal self that does not have any sexual feelings. Others' ideal self does not feel angry or sad. But we know that all those feelings are parts of the being created in the image of God.

To other people, the ideal self does not need to express itself in creative work or task accomplishment. Yet, as God created man, He gave him dominion over the earth before the Fall. Such people think they should be happy not having any goals of their own that express God's talents in them.

The ideal self primarily comes from our upbringing. Whatever the family valued tends to get internalized into the ideal, and whatever is not "up to snuff" is judged as bad, whether or not it really is. Many people feel bad about really good things, but those things were not accepted in their family. Those aspects of the true self are judged by the ideal as being just as bad as murder. One common example in our culture is needy feelings within men. Men are told to be strong; expressing feelings of sadness is considered bad, even though it is not. The ideal self is not necessarily inerrant! It is a system of internalized values from our upbringing as well as our wishes for ourselves. Whatever is true and is not acceptable to the ideal gets judged and done away with in some form or another.

Before Patrick came into therapy, he had seen about fifteen or twenty doctors for his "disease." He had been to various emergency rooms, thinking he was having a heart attack or a stroke. Convinced he had cancer, he went to several specialists. But no one could find any physical illness. Finally, his internist told him to seek psychological help.

Pat could in no way accept the fact that there was nothing wrong with him. There was a good reason for that: he was right. There was something desperately wrong, but it wasn't physical. It was emotional. Pat was a very high functioning man who headed a major corporation. His goal in life had always been to rise above everything with his intellect, and he had done very well at that. However, he had negated several aspects of himself that did not fit into his ideal self, and as a result, he was suffering.

Pat's ideal self was like his father, a "strong man" who never showed emotions. He grew up thinking that to be a man meant to be like him as well as to be as different from his mother as possible, who was "an emotional wreck," as he described her. He denied any weakness because he judged it "bad," which in reality meant that it was not part of his ideal self.

Over time he began to have various phobias and fears, mostly of physical illness. His "weaknesses" came out as physical illness because physical illness was acceptable to the ideal. Therefore, he could be physically ill as long as he was not emotionally weak or sad.

As he began to work in therapy, he reclaimed parts of his real self that were not ideal to him. Yet, they were not bad per se, just bad to him. In fact, those feelings were a very real part of human existence, and as he reclaimed them, he became much more human. Another side benefit was that his fears and phobias went away. He no longer ran from emergency room to emergency room, fearing that he was dying.

Another common example of the content of the ideal self becoming distorted occurs when the drive to separate and set boundaries is regarded as bad. Many people have had to repress their natural tendency to set limits on others because it was unacceptable within their family. Remember Sandy, for example. Her ideal self would do whatever her mother wanted, even if it was incorrect. Her own wishes would be judged as bad, and as a result they would have to be done away with in some fashion.

Where Does It Go?

If the good and the bad function as enemies, where do the different aspects go? Let's look at some of the possibilities for handling this conflict.

Denial of the True

By denial, some handle the content of the true self that is not acceptable to the ideal. Richard denied the fact that he was angry with his wife because anger was judged and condemned. He also denied his childlike feelings, seeing them as condemnable as well. Sandy denied her drive to separate and acted as if it wasn't there. As a result, she experienced powerlessness.

Other people deny other feelings if they are not part of the ideal self. Among people who have been taught that emotions are not acceptable, sadness is denied when there is a loss. Not experiencing sadness invariably leads to depression, for that is God's way of dealing with hurt and loss. I remember one woman who, in the midst of a divorce of a twenty-year marriage, was planning vacations and parties. She said that there was no pain whatsoever over the separation. She totally denied it.

In many ways the Bible speaks to the tendency we have to deny our badness, and sometimes it speaks harshly, for it addresses the sin of pride. Listen to Jesus' words to the Pharisees: "Woe to you, scribes and Pharisees, hypocrites! For you clean the outside of the cup and dish, but inside they are full of extortion and self-indulgence. Blind Pharisee, first cleanse the inside of the cup and dish, that the outside of them may be clean also. . . . For you are like whitewashed tombs which indeed appear beautiful outwardly, but inside are full of dead men's bones and all uncleanness" (Matt. 23:25–27).

There is a strong thread in the Scriptures to not deny the internal bad.

Denial of the Good

Another way of dealing with the conflict of good and bad is denying the good. These people feel so burdened by ideal demands that they do away with standards altogether. They live in the badness, without any realization that doing that is bad. *Or,* they tend to deny the good parts of their loved ones or themselves. All they can see is the bad, and many wonderful qualities are lost and denied. When good is denied, it robs them of enjoying the other person as well as themselves. We feel all bad or feel that they are all bad.

Attack and Judgment of the True

This is the most common form of coping with badness. It is the "normal" conscience that judges and condemns. It sees the fault and says things like, "I'm so stupid, or worthless, or bad." It is a condemning, hurtful attack at the real self. It is what the Bible calls the "sorrow of the world" that leads to death: "For godly sorrow produces repentance leading to salvation, not to be regretted; but the sorrow of the world produces death" (2 Cor. 7:10). Godly sorrow is sadness over the badness that turns to repentance. The worldly way of dealing with badness is through attack and condemnation. Judas and Peter illustrated this difference. Judas attacked himself and committed suicide. Peter felt sorry for denying Jesus and turned around through the acceptance that Jesus gave him. Acceptance has that effect on us; judgment never cured anything.

Acceptance

This biblical alternative is called grace and truth. Neither the ideal nor the truth of the badness is denied. The bad is accepted and forgiven; at the same time the standard is advanced as an unrealized goal that we strive toward in an atmosphere of full acceptance, a "standing in grace." This strategy does not split the good and the bad, but utilizes both at the same time.

The Conflict as It Relates to Others

Just as we relate to the less than ideal aspects of ourselves, so do we relate to others. We all have an ideal "other" picture in our heads of an ideal spouse, friend, parent, or child. When the real "other" shows himself or herself and we are unable to resolve issues of good and bad, we must react in unusual ways to handle it. But intimacy is impossible in such situations.

The picture of what the ideal other "should be" is different for all of us, but we all have one. For some, it may be someone who never is angry or selfish. For others, it may be someone who never tells a lie. For still others, it may be someone who is not weak or dependent. Whatever the ideal demand, it tends to force one into a style of relating that makes things impossible to work through. Everyone has different things about others that are difficult to accept.

But Scripture commands us to deal with others and ourselves in the same way, the way of forgiveness and acceptance: "And be kind to one another, tenderhearted, forgiving one another, even as God in Christ forgave you" (Eph. 4:32). Let's consider the problems of coping with the badness of others.

Denial of the True

This alternative makes someone all good and denies the bad. It is like idolatry, for it denies the humanness of the other.

Ruth came into therapy because of depression. She continually put herself down for petty matters, but I couldn't find out what was bothering her. It seemed to me that she was under a terrible burden, but whenever I asked about her life, she said that things were OK.

Finally, I met her husband, and I understood. In nice terms, the guy was a jerk. But she had represented him to me in totally idealized terms. For years she had denied his badness and had been the brunt of his sin. He was critical and demanding, and he put her down at every turn. It was no wonder that she was depressed, for she denied his badness; thus, they were unable to resolve their problems. She was stomaching all of them; she was all bad and he was all good.

Denial of the Good

We can split the good and the bad in ourselves and get out of touch with the good, and we can do that to others as well. John was twenty-six and recently married. He came to see me to help him "with his marriage," he said. He described how critical and demanding his new wife was and how "she never does anything around the house." The picture he painted was awful. He also said that since their marriage, she "had let herself go" and was not attractive anymore because of her weight. I requested that he bring her to his next visit so I could more accurately evaluate the relationship.

When I saw her, I was amazed that she was the one he had been talking about. She was as thin as a rail and as responsible as anyone could hope to be. In reality, he placed incredibly perfectionistic demands on her and made her all bad. And she tried to please him even more, a strategy that never works with a perfectionist. Her performance was very good, just not perfect. But he could not tolerate the fact that she was not ideal.

Attack and Judgment of the True

Many people can see both the good and the bad, but they attack the badness in others. Phil was a very loving husband. He was aware of his wife's good points and supported her faithfully. He praised her when she did well, and he let her know how much he appreciated her.

But whenever she made a significant mistake, he would judge and criticize her. He would get angry, yell at her, and say very mean things. He would say things that were guilt provoking and imply that she should be ashamed of whatever it was that he didn't like.

It wasn't that he denied either the good or the bad, but his attitude toward the bad was harsh and critical. He was judgmental and without grace when he spoke the truth to her.

Acceptance

Again, acceptance is the biblical way. Paul explains how to accomplish this: "And be kind to one another, tenderhearted, forgiving one another, even as God in Christ forgave you" (Eph. 4:32). And, "Looking carefully lest anyone fall short of the grace of God; lest any root of bitterness springing up cause trouble, and by this many become defiled" (Heb. 12:15). Or, "Brethren, if a man is overtaken in any trespass, you who are spiritual restore such a one in a spirit of gentleness, considering yourself lest you also be tempted" (Gal. 6:1).

In all these passages, the combination of grace and truth is apparent. The truth is faced and dealt with, but there is acceptance, not rejection, and kindness, not wrath. Proverbs 17:9 says, "He who covers a transgression seeks love, but he who repeats a matter separates friends." There is always to be an attitude of grace that tries to deal with severe transgressions, but never lets go of the value of love and forgiveness.

So What's the Big Deal?

If failing to resolve issues of good and bad is so destructive, why don't we just do it? What's the big deal about acknowledging the existence of both? Why don't we just accept the bad and value the good?

To understand this process, we have to remember the nature of the Fall. We were never intended to handle the coexistence of good and bad. God tried to protect us from it. But we sinned anyway and found ourselves in a tough spot. *We are born without grace, and it takes an internalization of grace to accept the bad without rejecting the relationship. That is difficult for people without grace, and that ability has to be learned.*

According to the Bible, we are born unconnected, and we must be invited into relationship. As that happens, we internalize love and forgiveness. There is a scriptural principle that we love and forgive because we have been loved and forgiven. A woman "who was a sinner" ministered to Jesus and gave Him "fragrant oil." Because she was a sinner, a Pharisee said that He shouldn't be around her. Jesus responded that "her sins, which are many, are forgiven, for she loved much. But to whom little is forgiven, the same loves little" (Luke 7:47).

It is the same theme that we learned about love, that we love because He first loved us. We forgive as He has forgiven us. "And be kind to one another, tenderhearted, forgiving one another, even as God in Christ forgave you" (Eph. 4:32). We do not come into the world as forgivers, for we have not been forgiven. The Bible teaches that to the extent we have been forgiven, we will forgive. We must realize our own forgiveness in order to forgive and not split people off as "all bad," thus losing our connection with them.

A Developmental Perspective

When a child comes into the world, he is unconnected and unforgiven. As a result, he is unforgiving. Grace and truth, or love and limits, are split apart. He loves if he is happy; he hates if he is distressed. These two states form two very distinct categories in his head: the good guys and the bad guys as well as the good me and the bad me. Good and bad are totally separated, for there is a deep fear that the bad will wipe out the good.

This way of experiencing and thinking is pervasive for a child. If he is given to, the world is a good place, mommy is a good mommy, and he feels happy. You can see this on a child's face when he is particularly satisfied. He seems to be saying, "All is well." A child shows no shades of gray; things are just all good when he gets what he wants.

On the other side, when he is frustrated, everybody is bad, mommy is a bad mommy, and the world is a bad place to live. He cannot put it together that the same mommy who is three minutes late for feeding is the one who comforted him and made life wonderful the night before! There is a total inability to put those two together. At that moment she is all bad.

When she finally comes and contains all of his "accusations," and gives him what he wants, she is all good again. No one in the world would be able to convince him that she is not perfect at that moment.

Over time, when she continues to minister to his needs and this love is internalized, he slowly realizes that she is not all good or all bad. There has been enough goodness to withstand the frustration. He learns that it is the same person who loves him as well as frustrates him. The same mother who plays with him sometimes makes him wait to play. If there is enough good, he reaches a point of being able to tolerate the bad.

However, if there is not enough good and enough forgiveness of his "accusations," the good and the bad never come together. He continues splitting his world into good guys and bad guys, loving people who gratify him and hating people who don't. He loves jobs that gratify him and leaves jobs that don't. He loves his wife as long as she gratifies him and leaves her as soon as she doesn't. It is easy to see this splitting in an adult "child."

On the other hand, a child who is never frustrated can become unforgiving. If getting the good and the bad together depends on a dance between frustration and gratification, but one is never frustrated, one never learns to forgive the frustrating "other" or the frustrating world or the frustrating God. We all have seen pampered people who make the world all bad as soon as they have to wait five minutes in a line for a movie. They have an inability to put good and bad together as well.

In either case, when good and bad are not tolerated together, one tends to see people as good if they are gratifying and bad if they are not. There is no ability to forgive the "good guy" who also makes mistakes.

Later in development, as the child becomes more mobile, the ideal self comes into play. He feels as if he can do anything, and there is a period when he feels grandiose and superhuman with his newfound "power." He can talk, explore, and run, not yet having enough experiences of falling down. The ideal is at its height, and there is a strong wish to be seen as ideal. This is the elated period of "Look at me, Mommy!"

Gradually, however, the grandiose ideal self should give way to reality. He learns that falling down is a part of life and that he is not as great as he wishes he were. When the frailties are understood and loved by others, he learns to accept them into his picture of himself and to value the real self that is not perfect. He acquires what Paul calls "sound judgment" in thinking about himself (Rom. 12:3 NASB). He learns not to see himself so grandiosely, and he values the real self with its frailties, as well as forgives and accepts the real self of others with their limitations. He realizes good and bad at a different level from self-gratification.

Then, later, as he is able to get into real performance, he learns not only that he is good and bad, but that he succeeds and fails as well. He works on the nature of the relationship between expectations and real performance. This aspect was mentioned earlier about the possibility of developing an attacking and judging relationship to the real. The bad relationship happens when the failures and sin are not forgiven lovingly, but are harshly attacked and judged. In the normal scenario, the failures should be brought into the open, discussed, and forgiven. This is the biblical way.

His parents need to accept the failures in the same way that God does. He does not deny them, nor does He browbeat the child for them. He convicts him, which means to show him the truth, but He gives him tender love and compassion for them as well, for "the goodness of God leads you to repentance" (Rom. 2:4). The kindness and compassion, not judgment and condemnation, of God tenderly lead him to deal with failure and badness. I like the way it is put in Galatians 6:1: "Restore such a one in a spirit of gentleness, considering yourself lest you also be tempted." If that were everyone's parenting style, very few people would feel that their failures were too big to handle or that they were the only ones who ever failed.

If the failures are handled with anger and attack, as well as judgment, condemnation, and withholding of love, that is the nature of the relationship between the ideal and the real that will be internalized. It leads to a whole host of problems.

But if things go well, the good and the bad on the performance level are resolved so that ideals can be kept as goals and failures can be forgiven. This is a coming together of grace and truth. The truth and the ideal are held onto, and the real being is loved and forgiven. This leads to a coexistence of good and bad in a real world that leads to greater and greater love and sanctification.

Love and Acceptance

The role of love must be recognized because that is basically the solution and resolution to all problems of good and bad. When we were in the Garden of Eden, perfectly loved and accepted, the resolution of good and bad was not an issue. When we lost the love, that became the paramount issue. In our lives now, if there is enough love with limits, or grace and truth, we experience the way that God relates to us and learn a standing in grace (Rom. 5:2) whereby judgment and condemnation do not enter the picture. Instead, we experience badness and failure as a sad thing, for it causes us to miss out on loving someone. Guilt and condemnation do not belong in the equation.

When sin, or failure, is present, we are more concerned about the one we hurt if we are not worried about condemnation. This is "godly sorrow" (2 Cor. 7:10) and also the sorrow that Peter experienced when he denied Christ, as opposed to the guilt that Judas experienced because of a lack of love.

I talked earlier about why someone wouldn't hit a person in the face with a baseball bat. The reason of "I would be a bad person" or "That is a bad thing to do" is not a Christian one. Since condemnation and "bad me" are out of the picture for the Christian, the real reason is based on love: "Because that would hurt you." That is what Jesus meant when He said that the whole law could be summed up in the law of love. When we see our failures and sin as a lack of love, instead of "badness," we have moved to a more mature way of perceiving issues of good and bad.

This is true of ourselves as well. If we can see that failure, or sin, is an issue of hurting ourselves instead of indicating that we are "bad," we can get out of the slavery of the law of sin and death. Only when we get a picture of the self-destructive nature of our sin can we change. Guilt manipulation does not work; it only makes us sin all the more: "The law entered that the offense might abound. But where sin abounded, grace abounded much more" (Rom. 5:20).

The simple truth of the gospel is this: only grace sets us free. "Who will deliver me from this body of death?" Paul asks when he is struggling in the sin cycle (Rom. 7:24). He goes on to say that "There is therefore now no condemnation to those who are in Christ Jesus" (Rom. 8:1). Only when one is no longer condemned for the bad can it be released. He also points out that because we have been set free from that law, we can walk after the Spirit. But if someone still sees badness as something that incurs condemnation and guilt, the sin cycle will continue.

This cycle is evident in addictions or compulsive behavior. There is a feeling that if persons engage in the act, they are terrible and unlovable. Then they act it out, feel enormous guilt, repent, and act it out again.

Lee checked into the hospital for depression that was secondary to overwhelming guilt for sexual addiction. His cycle went this way. Feeling lonely, he would get the desire to be with a prostitute. He believed he was totally bad for wanting to do that, but did it anyway. Afterward, it took him weeks and weeks to shake off the guilt. In the meantime, because of the guilt, he would feel more and more unlovable, and he would withdraw more. That would increase his "need," and the compulsion would return, to release the tension, pain, and loneliness. He would then visit another prostitute, and the guilt cycle would return.

When he talked about his addiction in a group, he found that he was not condemned. People were not surprised by his "badness." When it presented itself, he was loved. He tried to resist that love and acceptance, and to hide from it, but it gradually got through. He learned that "no condemnation" was a state that he could not lose, and that he would not be condemned if he sinned again. He was learning that his standing did not change with his performance.

Lee also learned that his "badness" and guilt were not the issues at all; they had been taken care of at the Cross. The real issue was the way he was living and selling himself short of real love. That was killing him. But he could not get to the reality of the destructiveness of his sin until he could get out of the guilt cycle.

Guilt takes us away from the real problem, which is unrighteousness. For Christians, the badness has been taken away because we are accepted "in the Beloved" (Eph. 1:6). The real issue is the sin, not whether or not we are "bad." The "badness" is what God took care of so that we could deal with the problems. We are not to be on a cycle of going from feeling like we are good to feeling like we are bad when we sin. We are supposed to be in a constant position of being loved. The writer of Hebrews goes to great pains to point out that the issue of guilty versus not guilty has been dealt with: "For by one offering He has *perfected forever* those who are being sanctified. . . . [The Lord says,] 'Their sins and their lawless deeds I will remember no more.' . . . And having a High Priest over the house of God, let us draw near with a true heart in full assurance of faith, having our hearts sprinkled from an evil conscience and our bodies washed with pure water" (10:14–17, 21–22, emphasis added).

Many Christians think they go from a forgiven state to a guilty state and back to a forgiven state, and they never feel secure in their acceptance. They do not acknowledge that Jesus, "because He continues forever, has an unchangeable priesthood. Therefore He is also able to *save to the uttermost* those who come to God through Him, since He always *lives to make intercession for them*" (Heb. 7:24–25, emphasis added). Jesus has made us acceptable once and for all, and this is not something that we lose, slipping into a "bad" state with God.

Whenever we hurt someone, God, or ourselves, that will grieve us if we do not focus on the guilt involved. That grief, called godly sorrow, will move us to take care of the one being hurt, and not to punish ourselves or anyone else. This is the essence of a love-based morality instead of a fear- and punishment-based morality prescribed by the law.

This "no condemnation" is a powerful thing that transforms lives. When people can get to a point of not feeling condemned, no matter what they do, they are well on the way to being more and more loving, for "he who is forgiven much, loves much." The nature of the relationship between the ideal and the real needs to be one of correction toward a goal of love instead of one of anger and attack toward the real self who fails.

Getting to That State

The state of "no condemnation" is what God intends for us. But how do we get there emotionally?

When we examined the emotional nature of our relationship between the ideal and the real, we discovered that in a relationship of loving acceptance and correction toward a loving goal, we tend to relate to our failures with empathy and correction, with motivation toward God's goals of love. But if the nature of the relationship is one of good-bad splitting, anger, condemnation, and punishment, we have little development of love.

Nature-Nurture

There are two sources of the wrong relationship between the real and the ideal—nature and nurture. We are all born with a sin nature. For one thing, that means we have a wish to be "like God" (Gen. 3:5; Isa. 14:13-14). It is in our nature to want to be more than we are. This is part of the reason the ideal self is so lofty. Also, we are born under the law, and "the law brings about wrath" (Rom. 4:15). Therefore, we are born with a fallen conscience that punishes us "wrathfully" for not being perfect and failing in any way. James says it this way: "For whoever shall keep the whole law, and yet stumble in one point, he is guilty of all" (2:10).

It is in our nature to have a wrathful conscience that lets us know in anger when we or someone else is not perfect. We have talked about that process, which occurs even in infancy.

In addition, we are raised by imperfect people who relate to us imperfectly, and they often act "wrathfully" toward us when we fail, thus reinforcing the conscience we have as unregenerate beings. Their critical natures tend to be internalized into a self-evaluating system that we call conscience, and it speaks to us much in the same way that our parents did. If they were loving and accepting, our conscience is loving and accepting. If they were harsh and critical, our conscience is harsh and critical.

The Way

However, we can be forgiven out of that unloved state. Therefore, we have hope. Forgiveness is something that can be learned in relationships of grace. That is the function of the body of Christ. We are to accept and love one another in spite of our failures, and to gently correct one another toward a goal of love: "As the elect of God, holy and beloved, put on tender mercies, kindness, humility, meekness, longsuffering; bearing with one another, and forgiving one another, if anyone has a complaint against another; even as Christ forgave, so you also must do" (Col. 3:12–13).

These sorts of forgiving relationships within the body can cure the developmental problems of good and bad, but there must be some important ingredients. There must be a revealing of the real self, first of all, through a process called confession.

Confession

We are told, "Confess your trespasses to one another, and pray for one another, that you may be healed" (James 5:16). Christians primarily think of confession in their relationship with God. But this is only half of it. A lot of our pain comes from our inability to feel loved and forgiven, and this pain was borne out of our human relationships. As a result, *there has to be acceptance within human relationships.* If we are in the process of confessing to one another, our offenses to them as well as all others, our relationship to the ideal changes. We internalize the acceptance we feel from others and the nature of our conscience changes; it becomes more loving.

At the same time, the badness that was in the darkness (1 John 1:5) comes into the light, and God transforms it. Confession is the only way that our problems with good and bad can be transformed. What was buried in the darkness comes into the light and gets loved, both by God and by others.

Because the Fall separated us from God, ourselves, and others, aspects of ourselves are hidden "in the darkness." We hide them from God, ourselves, and others. So, they get worse. They are outside relationship, and they are getting darker and darker. In addition, the part of ourselves connected to attitudes and deeds is separated from grace, truth, and time, and therefore is not growing.

When we confess to God, that buried part comes into relationship with Him, and He can cleanse it and heal it. When we confess to others, it gets human acceptance and restores the split and isolation we have on the human level. Our sense of self-acceptance is transformed.

First John 1:5–10 summarizes these points:

> This is the message which we have heard from Him and declare to you, that God is light and in Him is no darkness at all. If we say that we have fellowship with Him, and walk in darkness, we lie and do not practice the truth. But if we walk in the light as He is in the light, we have fellowship with one another, and the blood of Jesus Christ His Son cleanses us from all sin. If we say that we have no sin, we deceive ourselves, and the truth is not in us. If we confess our sins, He is faithful and just to forgive us our sins and to cleanse us from all unrighteousness. If we say that we have not sinned, we make Him a liar, and His word is not in us.

Some important truths emerge here. First, God is in the light, and nothing is covered up and dark in Him. Second, if we have things in the darkness, we do not have fellowship with Him; that aspect of ourselves is not in relationship with Him. Third, if we are in the light and we confess, that aspect of ourselves is in relationship with God and is being cleansed. Fourth, we all have those aspects; that is, we all have sin.

This picture clearly depicts the confession process. Because we have darkness in us, we need to come into the light. When we do this, God cleans that part and makes it new. Jesus said, "If then your whole body is full of light, having no part dark, the whole body will be full of light, as when the bright shining of a lamp gives you light"

(Luke 11:36). When God's light uncovers the dark parts within us, we experience healing and cleansing. By taking whatever is in the darkness and bringing it into the light, both to God and to others, we resolve the basic separation that occurred at the Fall.

Many people have a problem with confessing to others. They think of all sorts of excuses, *but that directly contradicts the Word*, which says to confess to one another, period. Anything short of confession is pride. Generally speaking, we do not want to reveal the real self because we want to appear to be perfect, or all good.

Of course, we are not to confess to just anyone; that is dangerous. We need to confess to those who love us and can offer us the grace of God as His incarnational ambassadors. That will transform our split between good and bad, for he who has been forgiven much loves much. When whatever is in the darkness comes into the light, it gets transformed.

Many people think of such superficial things to confess—not setting aside quiet times, being impatient, swearing—instead of the cancers that kill the soul. Jesus offers one list that would be a good start: "evil thoughts, adulteries, fornications, murders, thefts, covetousness, wickedness, deceit, lewdness, an evil eye, blasphemy, pride, foolishness" (Mark 7:21–22). If we confessed those tendencies to God and others, and felt absolutely no condemnation for them, there would be an integration of the personality. Hiding those aspects of ourselves causes certain parts to go into the darkness and have a life of their own. This is how the roller-coaster Christian experience often happens. A whole host of hatred and grief is covered up, and it comes out in all sorts of psychological problems and dysfunctions. If those aspects of the self were confessed and loved, they would be transformed and integrated.

The problem is, the "should" always gets in the way and divides us into two people: the real and the ideal. Jesus abolished the "enmity, that is, the law of commandments contained in ordinances" (Eph. 2:15). The reference is to Israel, but it applies equally to the personality. When the enmity, the commandments, the "shoulds," are abolished in their power, He can "create in Himself one new man from the two, thus making peace." When the condemnation of the "should" is gone, and there is grace for whatever is in the darkness, the aspects of the self that have been hidden can be confessed and forgiven.

This process of realizing our forgiveness through confession of the real self to others in grace and truth is the key to healing the personality. What is in the darkness is integrated, and the nature of the relationship between the ideal and the real is changed. As the condemnation goes out of that relationship, there is greater and greater peace, and the person becomes less and less divided between the two. The ideal can become a goal instead of a demand, and the true can be loved along the way.

Al came into the hospital because of explosive rage. At unexpected intervals, he just exploded at anyone who made a mistake. The anger that poured forth scared everyone, especially his children.

As he began to confess, he said that he had hatred for his father that he felt a Christian "shouldn't" have. By denying it, he had become two people: the Christian "nice" guy and the man seething with hatred. He learned that the Bible did not condemn him for his feelings of hatred, and he was able to confess them to others and to God and find that there were real reasons for their presence. He gained empathetic understanding for his injuries that had caused the rage and forgiveness for wanting to get back at his father. He was free to confess in an atmosphere of no condemnation, and the "dark parts" began to heal and be forgiven. This process is different from catharsis. The light touches the dark wounded places and does away with the "ordinances" that force the "unacceptable" aspects into hiding.

Eventually, he began to have much more acceptance and forgiveness for others when they failed. The way that his father had sinned against him was being transformed through the process of confession. He was confessing his unacceptable hatred and being forgiven for it.

Forgiving Others

The first part in confession is in our forgiveness; the second part is in our forgiveness of others. Jesus said that "if you do not forgive men their trespasses, neither will your Father forgive your trespasses" (Matt. 6:15). Since we are forgiven in terms of salvation when we accept Christ, this has to mean our realization of our forgiveness, the binds that we are held under when we don't forgive.

Matthew 18:29 offers a clue. The man who was forgiven a great debt says to God, "Have patience with me, and I will pay you all."

He then goes out and demands repayment from people who owe him very little. The key is in that statement of "I will pay." In effect, he never received grace. He was still trying to repay God, so he demanded repayment from others as well. Usually people are unforgiving because they have never truly received grace for themselves. They are still trying to repay God and earn their ideal standing. They are still on the law system with God.

On the other hand, there are those who have received grace and still want repayment from others. To be healed, we must forgive the debts that others owe us. If we don't, we are tying ourselves to the abuse they gave us through unforgiveness. A grudge is a handcuff to the one who hurt us, and it must be cut through forgiveness. To let someone off the hook for what he has done to you is to be freed from the abusive relationship. The bitterness will connect us to them unconsciously forever. There must be a severing through forgiveness, and then an acceptance of them as God has accepted us. When this happens, we are free to integrate our "bad" parts and unforgiven aspects. We cannot have any part of us loved and loving others if it is tied to a revenge relationship with others. Hatred must be confessed and forsaken.

Integration of Other Aspects of the Bad

So far we have looked at the confession process in terms of confessing the "sin" and the "real" bad. But other negative experiences and feelings must be integrated. This would include the whole arena of dealing with negative emotions.

Many people learn to conceal their negative feelings of sadness, anger, and fear. As a result, they are unable to cope with good and bad, for the bad feelings never get processed. As a result, there can be all sorts of problems, such as fearing relationship, as well as having symptoms of depression and anxiety. They must recognize that negative feelings are valid and must be dealt with so they won't cause problems.

Anger

Anger is our most basic negative emotion, for it tells us that something is wrong. It is our tendency to want to always protect the good that we don't want to lose. That is why anger is not sinful. It is a signal that we are in some sort of danger, either to ourselves or to something that matters to us.

When people are taught not to be in touch with their anger, *they are taught to be out of touch with what matters to them.* The anger tells them that something they value is at stake, and that is certainly a good thing to know.

Paul asserts, "Be angry, and do not sin; do not let the sun go down on your wrath, nor give place to the devil" (Eph. 4:26). The anger is good to feel, for it tells us of the danger and shows us what needs protecting. But we are not to sin in our attempt to resolve the problem. That would mean to resolve it in some unloving way, which would ultimately hurt us as well as the other.

Major consequences for denying angry feelings range all the way from psychophysiological disorders, such as headaches and ulcers, to character disorders, such as passive-aggressive traits, to inability to work and to serious depression and panic. Any way you look at it, denying anger will not work, and it keeps one from solving problems.

Denying anger may turn into bitterness, and that opens us up for a critical and unforgiving spirit: "[Look] carefully lest anyone fall short of the grace of God; lest any root of bitterness springing up cause trouble, and by this many become defiled" (Heb. 12:15). The statement in Ephesians about giving place to the devil is related, for in bitterness, Satan gains a stronghold in the personality and can control the person.

Anger must be owned and examined to find its source. As this happens, one can find out what is being protected. It may be one's vulnerability that was injured or one's will that was controlled. Perhaps one is under condemnation from someone and needs to get out from under that sort of perfectionism. Whatever the source, the anger can indicate that there is a problem, and it should never be denied.

On the other hand, the anger may protect pride, omnipotence, control, or perfectionism. Maybe someone feels angry because the control of another is being lost. That anger is there to protect something bad, and that wish must be given up. But if that anger were denied, one could not get to the source. Anger is helpful, for it is a sign that something is being protected, either good or bad.

Sadness

Sadness is our next basic emotion, for it tells us about hurt and loss. We live in a world where we get hurt and lose things. We need it to help us grieve and let go. If we repress and deny sadness, there is inevitable depression. Unresolved sadness always leads to depression and often to other symptoms.

Solomon proclaims, "Sorrow is better than laughter, for by a sad countenance the heart is made better. The heart of the wise is in the house of mourning" (Eccles. 7:3–4). Psalm 30:5 says, "Weeping may endure for a night, but joy comes in the morning." Sadness is always the way to joy, because sadness says that there is a hurt of some kind that needs to be processed, and usually it involves a loss.

When people deny their sad feelings, they "harden" the heart, and that is to lose touch with the tender grace-giving aspects of the image of God. The New American Standard Bible describes the hardness as being "callous" (Eph. 4:18–19); other versions render it as "being past feeling" (NKJV) and "having lost all sensitivity" (NIV). They become unable to love and be tender, and to feel grief over their sin. This state leads them to become insensitive persons.

In addition, it leads to all sorts of symptoms. Depression, physiological problems, substance abuse, eating disorders, and the inability to get close to others can result from unresolved sadness.

Susan was in her midtwenties when she began to have panic attacks. She would wake up in the middle of the night fearing that she was dying. If she saw anything on television about death or heard about death in any way, she ceased to function. The panic and dread of death overwhelmed her. She was referred to me when the panic rendered her unable to work.

"I feel ashamed that I am so afraid to die," she said in the first meeting. "I know that since I am a Christian, I shouldn't be so afraid. My friends keep telling me to memorize verses on death, but it doesn't help." I will never forget the confusion and hopelessness that she showed over the problem, for her friends' answers hadn't worked, and she didn't know what else to do.

She had grown up very isolated in her family, with the exception of feeling some love from her sister, who was a few years older than she was. Her parents were nonrelational people. When Susan was fifteen, she got up one morning and tried to get her sister out of bed, to no avail. Her sister had died during the night.

Understandably, her grief was enormous. But her father told the family that day, "There will be no more discussion of this. We must all be strong. Let's forget the past and go on." That was the way the death was handled.

As it turned out, Susan had many unresolved grief feelings about her sister. She was very sad that she was gone, and because she didn't work through the grief, she still had a very deep wish to be with her sister, her only source of love. The wish was registering in her conscious mind as a fear; in reality, it was what she wanted, to be with her sister.

We began to talk about that loss, and she went into the long-awaited sadness and grief. She was able to talk out all of the feelings she had been denying for so many years. Over a period of months, she went through a normal grief cycle, letting go of her sister. That should have happened when she was fifteen, but because the family had a rule against sadness and weakness, it was delayed.

She lost her fear of dying as well as the vague depression she had experienced off and on for years. She also regained some loving parts of herself. The loving part that was sad and buried, away from time, was again available to her to grow and nurture. In addition, her sexual feelings returned, which she had not been able to feel, either. Whenever a trauma is not worked through, the developmental stage present at that age gets affected. In her teens, it was love and sexuality. By processing her pain, she regained herself. There was joy after sadness.

When we lose our ability to feel sad, we lose our tenderness. It is a major aspect of the image of God that must be protected at all costs. If we can't feel sad, we get coldhearted.

One man had a history of sinus problems. When exploring his feelings, he got in touch with incredible amounts of repressed sadness. For months and months he grieved many losses incurred in previous years, learning that he had a sad, tender part that had been lost.

As he worked through his sadness, his sinus problems disappeared along with what he had described as a lifelong state of tension. In addition, he regained his sensitivity and was able to empathize with his wife and kids for the first time. His coldheartedness had been redeemed, as God had found his sad aspect.

Fear

Fear is another negative emotion that we are taught to deny. But fear conveys to us that there is danger. It may be an unreasonable danger, but the danger is there nevertheless, and we must be aware of it to work through it.

The Bible often tells us to "fear not," for God will protect us. We are to place our trust in God and His provision. It is an essential choice to make. However, if we aren't even aware of the fear, we can't make that choice; thus, we stay even further away from God.

Others who deny their fear turn into cold, insensitive people who are generally proud and combative. If they do not trust in God, the only other option is to be combative and trust in their own ability to win in every situation. They get out of touch with their humble position in the universe. Fear and lack of control over much of life lead to the heavenly Father, and they must be in touch with their fears to get to a position of need. For example, if someone is out of touch with her fears of abandonment, she will be out of touch with her need for the other person and treat him insensitively. This happens often in marriage when one partner is not in touch with the fear of being left. There is a "taking for granted" of the other.

Fear gets us in touch with our very real vulnerability, and for that reason, it gets us in touch with our need for others and God. Many times people treat others insensitively because they are warding off their fears of being vulnerable.

Symptoms of Inability to Resolve Good and Bad

Let's consider some symptoms that occur when we can't deal with good and bad in our world.

Perfectionism

Perfectionism is the tendency to demand perfection of self, others, and the world. Everything must be without flaw, or it is not good. We can see this in work, relationships, hobbies, and feelings. It is the demand for a pre-Fall existence and the rejection of anything not ideal, person or otherwise.

Idealism

This romantic version of perfectionism is an inability to see the bad that is really there. Everything is "made perfect" in the eyes of the beholder. It can get many people into some very bad situations, for the bad is denied from the outset and later comes up and gets them.

Inability to Tolerate Badness

This is the rejection of anything "not holy." The pharisaical per-

SYMPTOMS OF INABILITY TO RESOLVE GOOD AND BAD

Affective problems
All bad me
All good me
Anxiety and panic
Broken relationships
Eating disorders and substance abuse
Guilt
Idealism
Inability to tolerate badness
Inability to tolerate negative feelings
Inability to tolerate weakness
Narcissism
Perfectionism
Rage
Self-image problems
Sexual addiction

sonality is averse to human badness. In this "holier than thou" syndrome, badness cannot be tolerated, much less accepted.

Inability to Tolerate Weakness

The weakness that is part of humanness is rejected because it isn't ideal. Based in the wish to be Godlike, this symptom is a very cruel sort of splitting. It leads to all sorts of relational difficulties and hates vulnerability and inability of any sort. It is a very prideful stance, for we all are weak, and in that weakness, God's strength is made manifest.

Inability to Tolerate Negative Feelings

This avoidance of any negative emotion can be seen in numerous ways, but the result is a moving away from uncomfortable feelings. They are often denied altogether.

Affective Problems

Problems such as depression and excessive moodiness can result from the inability to handle negative feelings. If sadness, anger, and such cannot be processed, they will invariably cause a mood problem.

Self-Image Problems

The only way to have a workable self-image is to have the real self loved. If someone cannot deal with good and bad, the less than ideal parts of the self cannot be brought into relationship and accepted. If this happens, the self-image cannot be sound, for there is too much fear.

Anxiety and Panic

These symptoms come from the possible discovery of any negative. The anxiety can come from the internal threat of the negative feeling coming into consciousness or from someone else becoming aware of a negative aspect of the self. I have seen some people have a panic attack because they had a spot on their clothes.

Eating Disorders and Substance Abuse

These can be ways of dealing with unresolved negative emotions. If negative emotions cannot be processed, these disorders can result. People eat or use substances to numb the painful negative emotions.

Narcissism

In this disorder a person is preoccupied with the self and the idealized image. There is so much focus on the self, and the image that one portrays, that the real self is lost. As a result, life is a series of events organized to support the idealized image. Subsequently, love is out of the picture. Self-admiration is all that counts.

Guilt

If the real self cannot come into a confession relationship with God and others, the critical conscience can never be resolved, and the state of "no condemnation" can never be reached from an emotional level. Consequently, guilt plagues the person. Issues of personal goodness and badness take up a lot of attention instead of the love relationship with Christ and others.

Sexual Addiction

Many people who compulsively act out sexually are running from lost ideals and from unprocessed pain. They are looking for sexual idealism or trying to use sex as a way to deal with pain of some sort.

Broken Relationships

A series of broken relationships—with people, jobs, careers, spouses—signals a severe problem. In the beginning, something looks good, but when the negative aspects appear, the relationship is broken off, or the job is quit, or the career is changed, or there is another divorce. Good *and* bad in one person or one situation cannot be perceived. Only good *or* bad is accepted.

Rage

People who split good and bad have excessive problems with rage. Their frustration tolerance is minimal, and when something bad happens, they recognize nothing good to mitigate their feelings. The person they are dealing with has suddenly turned into their worst enemy, and the emotion is all negative. There is no love to temper the anger.

All Bad Me

Sometimes people believe they are "all bad." They can't perceive their strengths as well as their weaknesses.

All Good Me

A general defensiveness toward owning any fault characterizes many people. They may assent to the fact that they are "sinners," but they rarely admit a specific fault in issues as they arise.

Barriers to Resolving Good and Bad

Just as in the other issues, the barriers that block us from resolving good and bad tend to fall into the same categories of distortions in the view of self, others, and God.

Distortions in Our View of Ourselves

"I am really not worth loving." Unable to risk the real self to accepting others, people may still think that they are unlovable, a belief they built in childhood. They don't realize that "lovability" largely rests on the ability of the one doing the loving, not on their merit. One man in a group said, "I don't deserve their love." I told him he was right; none of us deserve love that comes our way, for we don't earn love. It is just given to us. Approval can be earned, but love can't.

"My badness is worse than anyone else's." This belief is common among people who have not had many experiences of opening up to fellow strugglers. They have not found the community of strugglers that the Bible describes. They think they are the only ones with the feelings that Jesus mentioned in Mark 7. They feel as if everyone else is somehow less fallen than they.

"I have feelings that are unacceptable." This problem is similar to the one above, but is more on the feeling level. It revolves around less than ideal feelings, such as feelings of neediness, sadness, sex, and/or weakness. These things are human, and not sinful, but have been judged as bad by the ideal.

"I should be better than I am." Many people underestimate the

Fall. They have not yet seen how deeply the Fall has affected us, and somehow they think they should have missed it.

"I am ideal." Rarely stated so blatantly, this comment is often believed. The persons think that they really are special, and that normal sorts of badness do not really apply to them. They are somehow above that.

"I am unforgivable." Often people think they have committed some unpardonable sin. To them, their badness exceeds that of the human race and the limits of God's forgiveness. They do not know that the only way they can be unforgivable is not to want forgiveness.

"I can't stand an imperfect world." This disturbance keeps many people slaves to perfectionism. They cannot be happy with a world that is less than ideal. They become so disappointed that they reject whatever appears as less than ideal.

"I have no strengths or talents." Some feel that they have been born without any goodness whatsoever. The Bible teaches that we are fallen, but that we all have strengths and talents. But some fears and distortions convince individuals that they have none.

Distortions in Our View of Others

"They will dislike me for my badness." People who struggle with good and bad have learned that their badness will be hated or disliked. They view others as rejecting parents, quick to judge and not love them. Because this fear keeps them from opening up, it cannot be disproven without new experiences. For this reason, confession to others is important.

"They will attack me for my weakness." Some assume that their vulnerability will bring down the heavy hand of the law. It's as if there is some presence ready to pounce on their weaknesses and judge them the way their parents did.

"They don't have feelings like this." Often people will idealize others to the point of perfection. Then they fear that they will be "less than" others. Learning that others are sinners, too, makes life easier.

"They will leave me if they find out . . ." A fear of abandonment underlies many attempts to be perfect. There is a deep belief in the shakiness of the connection so that a mistake or flaw will sever it. Actually, opening up about weaknesses cements relationships and bonding. Keeping them hidden keeps the connection weak. This happens in a lot of marriages.

"They will not like me if I am not all bad." Some people develop the all-bad position as a defense against the envy of others. They try to hide their strengths from other people, fearing that they can be liked only without good parts, without talents.

"They will respect my Christian walk only if I am perfect." This comment summarizes a major heresy. Christ is supposed to be the focus of the respect. There is nothing less attractive than a Pharisee, and we need to show others that Jesus is the Savior of imperfect people like us so that they can be led to grace instead of spiritual narcissism. That is why the Bible lists so many failures as spiritual leaders, to show the grace and strength of God.

Distortions in Our View of God

"God expects me to be all good." Nothing could be further from the truth, but no distortion is experienced more than this one. God has said repeatedly that we are sinners, and He expects us to fall over and over again. He knows our frame, says the psalmist (Ps. 103:14). We must comprehend the way in which God sees us, both to be humbled away from our perfectionism and to be awestruck by His grace.

"God accepts me when I am good and rejects me when I am bad. Then He will accept me again when I am good." This roller-coaster view of God does not realize the once and for all aspect of the salvation God provided. We truly are in a safe standing with Him; therefore, we can reveal our weaknesses.

"God is shocked at times by me." Some people cringe at what they come up with in thought or deed. The truth is that God knew it all before we were even born. He knew that sin or that weakness, and He still loved and saved us. Nothing can shock Him.

"God will reject me if I do . . ." The Bible teaches that the Christian can never be rejected. Some people have been so conditionally loved that they cannot imagine another person who will "by no means cast [them] out" (John 6:37). As a result, they fear losing their relationship with God.

"God is keeping track of my badness." Although it is true that God is watching us and keeping some sort of record of our lives, it is not for the purpose of punishment. He has put our sins as far away as the east is from the west. Christ will appear again "for salvation without reference to sin, to those who eagerly await Him" (Heb. 9:28 NASB).

"God thinks immaturity is bad." People forget that God understands the growth process, and that it takes time. He does not excuse things; He takes them into account. He regards us as a father regards a child. We are growing, and He does not expect perfection. Remember the story about Jesus' predicting Peter's failure and recovery. He knew it was coming. Immaturity is not a moral question. Young is not bad; it is young.

"God cannot understand my struggle." People sometimes think that because God is God, He cannot understand human badness and weakness. That is the purpose of Jesus' becoming man. He is a High

SKILLS NEEDED TO
RESOLVE GOOD AND BAD

Become aware of strengths and weaknesses
Challenge distortions
Confess
Do not discard others
Expect faults from the creation
Expect real badness and weakness
*Monitor the relationship between the ideal
  and the real*
Offer forgiveness
Practice loving the less than ideal
Pray
Process and value negative feelings
Rework the ideal

Priest who can "sympathize with our weaknesses" (Heb. 4:15). He has felt everything that we can ever feel, yet He is without sin.

These distortions form the prison of the real self. It has always been a trick of Satan and his demons to have us believe a lie, and he steals lives through these lies and distortions. It is imperative that we confront the lies and see where they came from, rebuking them in the mighty name of Jesus.

All of these lies were learned in the context of relationship, and it is in the context of relationship that they will be unlearned. We internalize how we are treated, and we must put ourselves into situations where God's ways are learned instead of the old ways of relating. Again, as in the other stages, this is not done without risk, and there will be pain. However, real healing and spiritual power are to be found if one can get into a confessing, safe relationship where the darkness can be made light, and the dark parts can find forgiveness and acceptance.

Skills Needed to
Resolve Good and Bad

Growth does not come without effort. Many skills must be learned and practiced so that the good and the bad can be resolved. A list of some of them is shown on the facing page.

Confess

This skill is probably the most important, for resolution rests upon forgiveness. As one confesses the real self with its badness and weakness, it is integrated with the ideals. The fear and judgment occur less frequently, and one gains more and more self-acceptance. This forgiveness from God and others leads to being more loving.

Pray

Ask God to shine His light into your soul and reveal anything that you are unaware of, and claim His forgiveness for it. David prayed in this way when he said,

> Search me, O God, and know my heart;
> Try me, and know my anxieties;

And see if there is any wicked way in me,
And lead me in the way everlasting (Ps. 139:23–24).

Rework the Ideal

Much of the content of our ideal self is false; it is not what an ideal person would be. Check out what needs to be eliminated from your picture of an ideal you. There may need to be some eliminations from the list. Such ideals come from your family or the culture, not from God.

Challenge Distortions

Challenge the distortions about God, self, and others. These strongly held beliefs don't give way easily, but in new relationships, they can be unlearned. We need to specifically study the Scriptures to see what they say about our ideal, our reality, and what God and salvation are really like.

Offer Forgiveness

When someone's badness presents itself and injures us, we must be aware of the forgiveness we have received from God and give it to others. If we are really aware of what we have received, it is easier to forgive. Try to understand the facts of what you have been forgiven if you are having trouble forgiving someone else. Jesus said, "He who is without sin among you, let him throw a stone . . . first" (John 8:7).

Monitor the Relationship Between the Ideal and the Real

How do you respond to the less than ideal? Do you deny it? Do you deny the good? Do you attack and judge? Do you accept and forgive? Many people are stunned to find out how attacking they are toward themselves and others.

Practice Loving the Less than Ideal

Learning to accept badness and weakness brings about healing in the split of the good and the bad. If we stay connected to others when they are less than ideal, we value real relationship and stop demanding idealism. In this way, our attachment increases, and our ability to love grows. The less than ideal begins to matter more than the ideal, for we have a real relationship.

Do Not Discard Others When They Are Less Than Perfect

If you have gone from friend to friend, spouse to spouse, church to church, because you find some little flaw and make them all bad, stay where you are and work out the problem. Actively see the good as well as the bad, and love the whole person. Make reality your friend instead of your enemy.

Process and Value Negative Feelings

When we are committed to reality, the good and the bad, negative feelings are viewed as part of life. If we get less afraid of them, we can process them as they arise and avoid problems, such as the symptoms listed above. Most problems with negative feelings come from a phobia about them. They really are not as bad as the fear makes them out to be. They will not kill you, but the avoidance of them can.

Expect Real Badness and Weakness from Everyone You Know

I am not saying to turn into a pessimist. I am saying to be a realist. Everyone you know, including yourself, has good and bad, strengths and weaknesses. Therefore, expect to see them in action. When the faults come about, embrace them and love them so that you can overcome your splits between good and bad and feel closer to others.

Expect Faults from the Creation

Because the world is real, not ideal, everything will eventually break down. Every holiday you plan can potentially get rained out. Every plant you grow will have some dead leaves. Expect some things to go wrong, and you will not be surprised. Then you will be able to value that less than ideal car, house, or city. It may not be ideal, but it's probably good enough.

Become Aware of Strengths and Weaknesses

Try to be aware of your good and bad parts. Consistently evaluate yourself and realize both strengths and weaknesses. This can help you to see yourself more accurately.

An Inventory of Progress
Toward Resolving Good and Bad

As in the other areas, an inventory is useful in the task of learning to deal with good and bad. We need to see the unresolved bad in the past, present, and future and take steps to resolve those tendencies not to deal with issues of good and bad. This can be the essence of the power of forgiveness in our lives.

The Past

We need to examine specific patterns of dealing with good and bad in our lives. If there are those who have taught us that we are all good or all bad, we need to reevaluate and forsake those perceptions. In terms of the injury that judgment and hatred of our badness caused, we need to forgive those who injured us. Here are some questions to help in that process.

1. *To whom in the past did I feel safe to confess my badness or weakness and have it accepted? What qualities of that relationship made me feel safe to be less than ideal?*

2. *Who denied my badness in the past and destructively saw me as without fault or weakness? Why did I allow this?*

3. *Who denied my good parts and saw me as all bad? How did I respond?*

4. *Whose badness in the past did I deny? Have I seen it yet? Have I faced how bad they actually were, or do I take responsibility for their badness or weaknesses?*

5. *Have I forgiven them?*

6. *Whose goodness did I deny? Do I still believe they are all bad? Have I forgiven them?*

7. *When have I in the past tried to appear all good or ideal? How did this affect my relationships? What would I do differently now?*

8. *When did I hide weakness from accepting people? Why?*

9. *When in the past did I not take into account my good? What were the results?*

10. *Is there someone I have not forgiven? Am I still holding that person in an unforgiven state? Can I see how this is hurting me?*

11. *Is there anything from the past that I need forgiveness for that I have not confessed to God and someone who loves me? What keeps me from allowing that into the light?*

The Present

Take a prayerful inventory of the present to see if there are issues of good and bad you are avoiding.

1. With whom do I have a safe confessional process now? Do I show them my badness and weakness? All of it? What helps me do that in the relationship?

2. Who denies my badness at present and makes me all good? How is this destructive? Why do I allow it?

3. Who denies my good parts at present and makes me all bad? Why did I allow that?

4. Which persons do I consider to be all good and deny their badness at present? Why?

5. Which persons do I see as all bad and deny their good parts? Why?

6. Who in the present have I not forgiven? Why?

7. How and where am I hiding weakness and badness in the present? Why? How is it hurting me?

8. How am I expending energy to appear ideal to others? Why?

The Future

If some things do not change in the future, you will repeat your past. Consider the plans you can make to become more of your true self with others and see more of their true nature as well.

1. Whose badness do I need to confront? When and how?

2. Whose goodness do I need to appreciate? How will I let them know?

3. With whom can I share my real self? How will I let them know about my badness and weakness?

4. How will I take my good parts out of hiding?

5. What aspects of my ideal self will I get in line with a true ideal as God sees it?

6. How will I work on my relationship between the ideal and the real? How will I make it more forgiving?

7. What are some present imperfections in others and in situations that I can work on accepting and loving?

Conclusion

In looking at the problem of living in a world of good and bad, we can see one overwhelming theme: grace. The grace of God is the beginning of the resolution of the problem as He comes to embrace a fallen world with open arms. He does not deny the bad and act as if nothing is wrong with man and the creation. He never denies badness, but He takes care of it through the forgiveness of the Cross.

At the same time, He does not deny the goodness of His creation and its value to Him. His unending love moves Him to hang onto fallen people and try to work things through. He does not get rid of us when He notices the badness and the immaturity.

How wonderful it would be if we could all relate to one another in such a real way! We could acknowledge the badness as it revealed itself, correcting and reproving one another to our betterment. At the same time, it would be done in a spirit of love and acceptance that communicated no threat of condemnation for the less than perfect. We could be safe with one another. We are called to see to it that no one falls "short of the grace of God" (Heb. 12:15).

We need to have that same attitude toward ourselves and not "set aside the grace of God" (Gal. 2:21). If our relationship between our ideal and our real is one of grace, we will grow. How comfortable we would be with who we really are if we had this attitude. And relationships could become much closer, too.

The ideal is a good thing, for it is God's goal for all of us. But it is not present reality, and we need to accept what is true. The ideal itself, however, can be full of error, and we need to look at the way that we have constructed our ideal self. Is it really an ideal that God would see as a real ideal, or is it based on one of Satan's lies?

In our lives and circumstances, we need grace and truth. This world is good and bad, and the rain falls on both the just and the unjust. We need to expect trouble as well as good things and respond accordingly: "The LORD gave, and the LORD has taken away" (Job 1:21). Trouble and trials are guaranteed, so they should not surprise us. If we take the attitude that bad things "shouldn't happen to me," we will stay in an unforgiving position toward life itself.

If we are in a position of "no condemnation," we do not have to be afraid. If we are standing in grace for ourselves and others, we do not have to be afraid of our badness or others' badness, either. We will be led to a greater and greater ability to move toward others and ourselves with open arms of acceptance. This is to fulfill the law of God: "If you really fulfill the royal law according to the Scripture, 'You shall love your neighbor as yourself,' you do well" (James 2:8).

Ted

Earlier, we saw how Ted was set up for a breakdown in his thirties. He had come from a home where there was a lot of pain. There were many sadnesses and hurts that he had never been able to show anyone, and the ways that he had been treated had not left him feeling secure about failure.

His parents had many problems, and they tried to cover them up with an idealism about themselves and success. They tried to appear as if they had the perfect home, and they criticized any aspect of Ted or the other children that did not fit their perfect image. There was a lot of pressure for everyone to be ideal in school, sports, manners, and everything else.

In addition, the father was a "strong domineering man," who attacked weakness in Ted or anyone else. He did not like for anyone to show sad or needy feelings, and as a result, Ted's ideal self had no hurt, sadness, or weakness. He could not feel safe about showing those aspects of himself to others; consequently, he learned to hide them from himself.

Furthermore, the breaking up of the home had devastated him. He loved both parents and did not want for them to split up. He was filled with anger, sadness, and confusion as to whom he belonged to. He had needed for years to show someone how hurt he really was over the treatment he had received as well as the divorce.

Instead of being able to do that, he had continued using his parents' solution to life's badnesses: become more ideal. He had constructed an ideal self that would rival the best of them, and had accomplished more in a short life than many accomplish in a long one. However, it did not erase the bad. The pain and isolation of his real self remained, and the ideal only covered them up.

This approach worked for a while, but when the ideal was threatened with business failure and marital problems, he had nowhere to turn. Not feeling accepted for his real self, he could not imagine that all his friends would still love him when his business failed and he was no longer everybody's ideal. He did not know love apart from admiration.

Luckily for Ted, others could conceive of it. His friends rallied around him and began to show him in his hospital stay that he was loved for his real self. They convinced him that they had seen his real self all along, and that he had not really had anyone close to him fooled.

He was with others who showed weak and hurt parts of themselves and talked about their failures. He learned that failure was not the end of the world, and that love was not built on success. He began to open up about his hurts, and about his fears that no one would love him as he really was.

His friends and the other patients were great. They received his weakness and failure and loved him back to health over time. He slowly gave up the pursuit of the ideal self as a demanding task, and instead showed people his real self with all its hurts, sinfulness, weakness, and immaturity. This became a liberating theme for him over time, and later he started some support groups in his church and business.

Ted did not give up the pursuit of excellence; he put it into perspective. His fuel became love instead of admiration, and from a loved position of his real self, he continued to push for the ideals of his faith and business. He learned that if he failed, it was not the end of the world, and that if he succeeded, he was no more lovable than before. Thus, he could appreciate his work and enjoy the real people in his life more. When he found love, he didn't need the ideal.

CHAPTER SIX

How to Achieve Adulthood

My friend had one of those looks on her face that people sometimes have when they discover the truly profound. This was no exception. She said something I'll never forget: "You know, life is upside down."

"What do you mean?" I asked.

"We should be adults first and then become children. It's too hard the other way around."

Becoming an Adult Authority

Everyone who has ever lived has encountered a particular problem: *being born a little person in a big person's world and being given the task of becoming a big person over time.* We are all born children under adult authority, and over time we are to become authorities ourselves and be in charge of our lives. This task, as my friend observed, is not easy.

This section will explore the problem of coming out from under a one-down relationship to the adult world and assuming one's role as an adult equal with other adults. It is the assumption of the authority position of life, an important part of the image of God.

Authority has several aspects: power or right to command or act; ability to officiate with this power; influence resulting from knowledge and/or prestige; and expertise. In terms of functioning in the image of God, we need to have command over our lives and domain that God has given us, officiate a role or office when asked, influence out of real ownership of something, have expertise, and submit to the authority of God and others without conflict.

Think of growing up as involving all of those things and you can see why growing up is such a hard thing to do! Many forces and circumstances interfere with the process; nevertheless, we must accomplish the task to function successfully as real image bearers. If we do not attain that position of adulthood, there is significant psychological and emotional distress associated with staying a child in the adult years.

Adults who have not yet become "big people" feel one down to their contemporaries. Or they defensively take the position of being one up on everyone else. In either case, the developmental task of establishing equality with other adults is imperative if guilt, anxiety, depression, sexual dysfunction, talent development, and spiritual bond servanthood are to be worked through. The developmental process is one of starting life from a position of "one-down" to the adult world, and gradually growing in stature and wisdom (see Luke 2:52) to the point of being an adult in an adult's world.

This process takes more and more power and responsibility as we are mature enough to handle them. We are to finally identify with the adult role enough to be able to do adult sorts of things without conflict, including development of career, sexuality, mutual friendship, peerness with others, direction, opinions, independence, talents, roles, thought processes, and principle thinking. It also means that we can establish a sense of competency over life and what we are responsible to do.

This process of starting as little people and becoming equal with big people begins with bonding, having boundaries and separateness, and resolving good and bad, but ultimately has to do with *coming out from under the one-down relationship that a child has to parents and other adults and coming into an equal standing as an adult on his or her own.* This is the final step of development so that one can exercise the gifts and responsibilities that God has given. It takes a big leap to come into adulthood, but we are supposed to become equal with other adults. Then we can all be siblings underneath the fatherhood of God. It takes us out of the parental relationship with other adults, which is a sickness.

Jesus calls men out of the one-down relationship to other humans with a respect for the role of authority at the same time:

The scribes and the Pharisees sit in Moses' seat. Therefore whatever they tell you to observe, that observe and do, but do not do according to their works; for they say, and do not do. For they bind heavy burdens, hard to bear, and lay them on men's shoulders; but they themselves will not move them with one of their fingers. . . . But you do not be called "Rabbi"; for One is your Teacher, the Christ, and you are all brethren. Do not call anyone on earth your father; for One is your Father, He who is in heaven. And do not be called teachers; for One is your Teacher, the Christ (Matt. 23:2–4, 8–10).

He says to do what Moses commanded, but not to consider other men somehow above us. Do not see them as fathers, for God is the Father of Christian adults, and adults are all brothers. Do not see others as the leader, for Christ is the leader. There is a call to mutual equality of believers, as siblings, which does not do away with the offices others hold, for we are to respect the offices of the church. We are to think of other people as equal siblings with us under God, even if they have an office. *To submit to them is to submit to God, not to men.*

People who believe others are above them as people are still relating from a child's position of being under a person, not under God. This belief makes the difference in one's ability to follow God and to seek God's approval instead of what people want. People who are stuck in the stage of "people pleasing" cannot take the authority over life that God commands: "Nevertheless even among the rulers many believed in Him, but because of the Pharisees they did not confess Him, lest they should be put out of the synagogue; for they loved the praise of men more than the praise of God" (John 12:42–43). The believers could not exercise their faith because of their need for approval from human authority.

Compare this to the statement about Jesus in Mark 12:14: "Teacher, we know that You are true, and care about no one; for You do not regard the person of men, but teach the way of God in truth." Jesus, a man as well as God, did not have the fear of men and the need for their approval as parent figures. As a result, He could speak the truth to them and let them worry about whether or not they liked it. He says to fear only God and His approval: "And do not fear those who kill the body but cannot kill the soul. But rather fear Him who is able to destroy both soul and body in hell" (Matt. 10:28).

Elsewhere He remarks, "Woe to you, when all men speak well of you, for so did their fathers to the false prophets" (Luke 6:26). There has to be some sort of people pleasing going on when everyone speaks well of you! You have to be speaking from both sides of your mouth. People pleasing can keep one from seeing what is true from God, as Jesus said to the Pharisees: "How can you believe, who receive honor from one another, and do not seek the honor that comes from the only God?" (John 5:44). Think of how much of people's theology and philosophy of life comes from trying to please their teachers instead of seeing truth.

Paul also talked about getting out of the "approval of men" trap: "But as we have been approved by God to be entrusted with the gospel, even so we speak, not as pleasing men, but God who tests our hearts" (1 Thess. 2:4). Both Paul and Jesus realized that to do the authoritative work of adulthood, one could not seek the approval of other adults, for that turns one into a child. Children cannot do adults' jobs!

We will look at the specifics of the developmental process shortly and how that happens, but for now, let's understand the overall picture of becoming and being an authority. Authority concerns the question of "Who's in charge?" and it is a process for one to get in charge of one's life under God. If you think of it in terms of being in charge, it is easy to see why it is a process; we have to grow into it.

You can probably think of people who seem to have charge over their lives and function as adults. They are aware of their opinions, think through things for themselves, make decisions, do not depend on the approval of others for survival, and have an area or a few areas of real expertise. One gets an authoritative sense from being around them. They seem like adults.

On the other hand, you know adults who seem wishy-washy, look for other people to tell them what to think and believe, blindly follow whatever the last "authority figure" has said, and are easily swayed by the thoughts and opinions of others. Others seem to have power over them and can make them change direction with a word. Others can have too strong an influence over their identity, leaving them with strong feelings of guilt and anxiety.

These are all issues of becoming one's own adult, or taking authority over one's life so that one can submit to the authority of God by choice. Let's look at the biblical basis for authority.

The Biblical Theme
of Authority

The Bible's first statement is this: "In the beginning God created the heavens and the earth." It goes on to tell the story of how God made a great creation and then entrusted it to man to govern and rule. In short, He placed man in a position of authority over the creation and expected him to function in that position. Then God said, "Let Us make man in Our image, according to Our likeness; let them have dominion over the fish of the sea, over the birds of the air, and over the cattle, over all the earth and over every creeping thing that creeps on the earth" (Gen. 1:26). God also said to "be fruitful and multiply; fill the earth and subdue it" (Gen. 1:28).

God made a big move to give man such a position. This position of authority was so lofty that inherent in it was the ability to determine the entire course of the creation. God had really given man freedom to be a real authority over the creation. He allowed functional autonomy, that is, the granting of position with real power and responsibility and real consequences.

Listen to the incredible delegation of power: "Out of the ground the LORD God formed every beast of the field and every bird of the air, and brought them to Adam to see what he would call them. And whatever Adam called each living creature, that was its name" (Gen. 2:19). God trusted man and depended on him to do a job. He was to fill the earth and subdue it, to move out and manage.

What a lofty position man had. There was only one condition. That position of authority was in submission to a higher authority: *God.* Man was told to do all that was delegated to him freely, but he was to stay within the parameters God gave him. He was not to go past his authority and usurp the authority of God by eating "of the tree of the knowledge of good and evil" (2:17). God warned him what would happen if he tried to function past his given authority and questioned the authority of God: he would die.

This is the model. God has granted to man a lofty position of rulership and authority, of adulthood and responsibility, of freedom to be in charge of certain things. Also involved is submission to the authority of God, and that includes the positions of authority that God has put in place, as we shall see later. What is important in the beginning, however, is to see *how much trust and responsibility God grants to man to be in charge.* Your life really counts! There were—and are—three very real aspects to this "being in charge": authority, responsibility, and accountability.

We can see the reality of this trust in the nature of the Fall. When man blew it, something *really* happened. We are all suffering for man's movement out from under the authority of God, and a blowing of his authority over the creation. When man does not take the responsibility to manage as God has ordained, there are serious consequences, and we all can feel those consequences daily. We feel the collective consequences of the Fall and also the individual consequences as we fail to take authority over our lives and areas of domain that God has given us individually. When we act like children in our adult responsibilities, we run into trouble. Adam and Eve listened to whomever came along, and did what a serpent said without even questioning, and there were disastrous results.

Maybe you can feel individual consequences for the failure to take authority over the domain that God has given you to manage. Maybe your finances are a wreck, or you don't know what you believe about certain doctrines, or your children are out of control, or your talents are undeveloped. Whatever the area, when you do not exercise this function of being in charge of whatever God has given you to do, there is a "fall" from the position that God has given, and there are serious results. This is not punishment from God; it is a validation of the trust and responsibility He has given to man. The problem is that we fail to see that, and fail to take our lives as something precious that He has granted great freedom and responsibility for. Whenever we do that we suffer, because the amount of trust He has extended to us is real, with real power.

This is the position that God first gave to us. After the fall of Adam, we were no longer in a free position to take authority over life. We became slaves, with sin having authority over us: "But God be thanked that though you were slaves of sin . . ." (Rom. 6:17). The entire book of Romans is dedicated to the theme of how we lost our freedom and became slaves of sin and how, through grace, we are returned to freedom and can be servants of righteousness (6:18).

Redemption is a reversal of the effects of the Fall, and a return to the freedom and authority that we had in the beginning. Only now, we are united with the new Adam, who is Jesus, and it is impossible for Him to rebel against God! "The first man Adam became a living being" (1 Cor. 15:45). Therefore, to be united with Jesus is to be restored to a real position of authority and submission that cannot fail. Our task of regaining our authority over life, then, is directly related to how much we walk "in Him" (Col. 2:6; 1 John 2:4–6). He cannot fail in His task as the second Adam, and as we identify with Him, become like Him, we fail less and less in our taking authority over our domain.

Authority has existed from the beginning, as God is the ultimate authority over all. It is certainly part of the image of God to be authoritative, and if we are to be image bearers, we are to be authorities. We are to have the sorts of things that our definition spoke of: power or right to command, officiate, and influence out of knowledge or skill and expertise.

We can see in the Old Testament that God placed many people in rulership: "Choose wise, understanding, and knowledgeable men from among your tribes, and I will make them heads over you" (Deut. 1:13). He always wanted his kings and leaders to walk with Him, however, and to lead His people to Him and His ways. There were lines of authority in the law, and then authority structures in the individual families. The three principles that had been present in the Garden of Eden would remain: authority, responsibility, and accountability.

Parents, for example, were placed in authority over children to teach them about God and to lead them in His ways: "And these words which I command you today shall be in your heart. You shall teach them diligently to your children, and shall talk of them when you sit in your house, when you walk by the way, when you lie down, and when you rise up" (Deut. 6:6–7). They were to be God's representatives of authority in the children's lives so that the children could later be turned over to the direct fatherhood of God and His authority.

Children were to internalize the things they learned into an obedient heart and be prepared to follow their heavenly Father in the same way as their earthly father: "Honor your father and your mother, as the LORD your God has commanded you, that your days may be long, and that it may be well with you in the land which the LORD your God is giving you" (Deut 5:16). There was to be an identification through obedience with the statutes and ways of God as the children were nurtured and raised in the things of the Lord. This was to ensure wisdom and tribal relations that would allow them to do well for the rest of their lives. If they learned the right way to live, and could get along with the extended relatives, they would have a pretty good road ahead of them.

The role of authority started with the rulership of God being delegated to man to rule for Him. It began with Adam, went to Moses and the patriarchs, and extended through the different judges and kings until the prophets told of the coming of Christ, at which time there was a fulfillment of the real King and the One to whom all authority is given. He would then set up His own kingdom and be its authority.

Then, as He established that authority, everything would be in subjection to Him. From that position of authority, He would submit to the Father, and *God's ultimate authority would be reestablished*. Paul describes this pattern:

> For as in Adam all die, even so in Christ all shall be made alive. But each one in his own order: Christ the firstfruits, afterward those who are Christ's at His coming. Then comes the end, when He delivers the kingdom to God the Father, when He puts an end to all rule and all authority and power. For He must reign till He has put all His enemies under His feet. The last enemy that will be destroyed is death. For "He has put all things under His feet." But when He says, "all things are put under Him," it is evident that He who put all things under Him is excepted. Now when all things are made subject to Him, then the Son Himself will also be subject to Him who put all things under Him, that God may be all in all (1 Cor. 15:22–28).

This is the plan of redemption. Christ would get back what God lost by taking authority, and then give it back to God, submitting to His authority. His ability to be authoritative would enable Him to recapture what was lost and give it back to God, who gave Him the authority to do that. What an awesome plan! That is what Jesus does with us, that is, He does the same thing with us that God did with Him. He gives us authority in Him to take back what was lost and to reclaim it, then give it back to Him so that He can give it back to the Father. In a real way, God is allowing us to take part in the war to regain what was lost, and to do that we must do two things Jesus does.

The first is to submit to authority and learn obedience, as Jesus did: "In the days of His flesh, when He had offered up prayers and supplications, with vehement cries and tears to Him who was able to save Him from death, and was heard because of His godly fear, though He was a Son, yet He learned obedience from the things which He suffered" (Heb. 5:7–8). We must learn first from parents, then from the Lord, to obey, so that we are perfected through discipline. "And having been perfected, He became the author of eternal salvation to all who obey Him" (Heb. 5:9). We must submit to the authority of God in Christ and internalize His likeness as we are perfected.

Second, as we submit to Him, we must do the other thing He did. We must take authority over what is delegated to us and redeem what has been lost, so we can give it back to Him. We must take the role of authoritative ruler in the domains of our lives and follow His example in order to be agents of redemption. Then, we will reign forever with Him as joint heirs of what is inherited under His domain.

Jesus took authority over situations, and He asks us to do the same. They are too numerous to list, but let's look at a few so that we understand just how much authority we have been commanded to take.

Power

Jesus proved His authority by exercising power over certain situations, and He had dominion over them:

> Then they were all amazed, so that they questioned among themselves, saying, "What is this? What new doctrine is this? For with authority He commands even the unclean spirits, and they obey Him" (Mark 1:27).

> But He said to them, "Why are you fearful, O you of little faith?" Then He arose and rebuked the winds and the sea, and there was a great calm. So the men marveled, saying, "Who can this be, that even the winds and the sea obey Him?" (Matt. 8:26–27).

Expertise

Expertise, or the development of His talents and abilities, involves authority in an area of knowledge or skill: "And so it was, when Jesus had ended these sayings, that the people were astonished at His teaching, for He taught them as one having authority, and not as the scribes" (Matt. 7:28–29).

Office

Office concerns the delegated authority given to someone, in this case Jesus from the Father: "For as the Father has life in Himself, so He has granted the Son to have life in Himself, and has given Him authority to execute judgment also, because He is the Son of Man" (John 5:26–27).

Influence

Through exercising His gifts and person, Jesus gained influence with people: "And they were all amazed, so that they debated among themselves, saying, 'What is this? A new teaching with authority! He commands even the unclean spirits, and they obey Him.' And immediately the news about Him went out everywhere into all the surrounding district of Galilee" (Mark 1:27–28 NASB). He did not do that for narcissistic reasons, however. People who are respected for their skills, knowledge, and talents have earned influence and can use it for good.

Submission

Jesus teaches that an integral part of being an authority like Him is to be able to give up rights and serve others: "You know that the rulers of the Gentiles lord it over them, and those who are great exercise authority over them. Yet it shall not be so among you; but whoever desires to become great among you, let him be your servant. And whoever desires to be first among you, let him be your slave—just as the Son of Man did not come to be served, but to serve, and to give His life a ransom for many" (Matt. 20:25–28).

This is what He did to submit to the Cross and to submit to God the Father. We are to model that submission, an aspect of authority resolution: "Let this mind be in you which was also in Christ Jesus, who, being in the form of God, did not consider it robbery to be equal with God, but made Himself of no reputation, taking the form of a bondservant, and coming in the likeness of men. And being found in appearance as a man, He humbled Himself and became obedient to the point of death, even the death of the cross" (Phil. 2:5–8).

Becoming an authority is something Jesus did by exercising power, officiating, having expertise, gaining and using influence, and submitting to higher authority. As we develop these personality traits, numerous problems disappear. Although the task is difficult, it is God's will for us to become image bearers; therefore, we can depend upon Him to perform it.

We are to grow up and become an authority in terms of power, officiate the roles that He has given us, develop expertise, use earned influence, and be able to submit to others. When we do that, we begin to get amazed at the ways that things like depression, guilt, anxiety, sexual problems, and the like are affected. More about that later.

We must remember, however, that "we do not have a High Priest who cannot sympathize with our weaknesses, but was in all points tempted as we are, yet without sin" (Heb. 4:15). Jesus had to go through the process of growing up just as we do: "Therefore, in all things He had to be made like His brethren, that He might be a merciful and faithful High Priest in things pertaining to God, to make propitiation for the sins of the people" (Heb. 2:17).

In other words, Jesus was a person like us; He just didn't make mistakes! Therefore, He can be a sympathetic model who was tempted in all of the problems of growing up, but made it nevertheless. He "continued in subjection to them; and His mother treasured all these things in her heart. And Jesus kept increasing in wisdom and stature, and in favor with God and men" (Luke 2:51–52 NASB).

Since Jesus went through a growing-up process, He can lead you through one, no matter how old you are. He can help you to become an authority over your life. Let's see how that happens.

A Developmental Perspective

If we think of becoming an adult authority as a task that has to do with power and expertise, it is easy to see why it is so difficult. When we are born, we have very little of either. All of the power and the expertise is in other people, and we correctly perceive ourselves as very much smaller than they.

As we continue to grow, however, and we increase in wisdom and stature, as the Bible says, we gain more ability and expertise to do things. We primarily do that through internalization and identification, as we internalize aspects of our parents and identify with them as role models. Through this identification process with our authority figures, we learn to take on their roles, and then become like them. This path to adulthood lasts about eighteen years or so.

In the beginning stages, the main internalization is in the nature of love. We learn that big persons are loving, which builds a bond allowing us to internalize later aspects of them. If that goes well, we receive limits from parents and, with somewhat of a struggle, learn that limits really are good; we reach some sort of acceptance about having limits placed on us.

Gradually, we develop more and more expertise, and the process of delegation should be taking place as well. Parents are to respect our budding abilities and give us tasks to do the same way that God did with Adam. If we do those well, more and bigger ones are given us, and we become more capable of handling more responsibility. The expertise, delegation, power, and accountability are all working together and increasing. At first the child is allowed to ride his bike down the street; at age sixteen he may be allowed to drive the car to a neighboring city. "He who is faithful in what is least is faithful also in much" (Luke 16:10). There is a progressive realization of increasing power and responsibility.

As we approach ages four to six, more specific identifications take place, such as sex-role typing and sexuality development. The little boy identifies with the father as a man, and the little girl identifies with the mother as a woman. In turn, they both identify with that parent's relationship with the opposite sex, and he wants a "girl just like the girl that married dear old dad" or vice versa for the girl. This is just one more step in the identification process that paves the way for later adult functioning.

Around this same time, we internalize the standards of our parents, and performance becomes very important. Parental approval is the only way out of guilt at this time, so we repress rebellious feelings and competitive feelings toward the authority, even though these feelings are increasing. The guilt of wanting to usurp the same sex parent is too strong to battle, so we identify with the competition and become like that parent.

Then, as we get a bit older, mastery of tasks and work roles become significant. Between ages seven and twelve or so, our increased industriousness helps us develop all sorts of skills. Play is like a job as we learn the ways of the world. This is the age of learning to be a member of the "work force" of play, and childhood chums are very important.

Some parenting variables can aid or hurt identification with authority. Let's examine them.

Power

The first variable would be power. The child is going to need power to carry out his adult responsibilities later, and this power comes from identifying with the authority early in life. If that power is gentle, warm, loving, and firm, a sense of personal power will be taken in as a good thing. If there are extremes in the model, there is trouble.

No power is learned from a passive model. Jesus has called us to be able to stand, but if there is no picture of what a "standing" adult looks like, how can the child learn that? He begins to feel as strong as the adult, and that is a pretty weak view of power. (This sort of power is inherent in the personality of the parent. It is not the attributed power of the office of parent. I will mention that later. In this instance it concerns whether the child feels as if he is with a passive person, a domineering person, or a healthy person with a good sense of personal power.) On the other hand, if power is used harshly and cruelly, the child gets into a hate relationship with power and cannot internalize it without conflict.

The New Testament presents two clear passages on this dynamic: "Children, obey your parents in the Lord, for this is right. 'Honor your father and mother,' which is the first commandment with a promise: 'that it may be well with you and you may live long on the earth.' And you, fathers, do not provoke your children to wrath, but bring them up in the training and admonition of the Lord" (Eph. 6:1–4); and "Children, obey your parents in all things, for this is well pleasing to the Lord. Fathers, do not provoke your children, lest they become discouraged" (Col. 3:20–21). The child is to obey, which is the process of identification, and the parent is not to inspire wrath or make the child lose heart or become discouraged. A child cannot identify with someone he hates. But the child desperately needs the functions of authority in his soul for later life. If he is in conflict with authority, he will have a difficult time submitting to the authority of God later and also developing his own.

Ralph was twenty-eight when he came in for counseling. He had been fired from almost every job he had had and, consequently, was getting nowhere in his career. He always managed to get into some sort of conflict with the boss and then was asked to leave. He had talent, although he had difficulty following through on his work.

"Why does this happen?" I asked him.

"Well, those guys always order me around like I'm a nobody. I can't stand to be talked to like that. So, I decide that I'll show them, and then I do."

"Problem is, though, it always costs you your job. Is it worth it?" I wondered aloud, almost anticipating his answer.

"Every time," he said definitively. "I'll never bow down to them that way. Nobody will ever do that to me again."

"Do what?" I asked.

Ralph was visibly shaken with anger. As we talked further, he described years and years of suffering angry abuse from his authoritarian father. Hating all authority figures with a passion, he had not been able to take in the function of submitting to them and acting authoritatively with his own life. He was still an angry little boy in a power struggle with his father.

Through a lot of work, he was able to get to a new place with his authority problem. He had to deal with a lot of anger toward his father and find some new relationships with older people to help mentor him, but God did that for him as he submitted himself to change. As a result, he became a pretty good authority himself and took charge of his life.

Mike had the opposite reaction to an exasperating father. He had always succumbed and had an almost total rejection of his own sense of power. He would just fold his cards whenever any male figure told him what to do. He allowed his life to drift by, and well into his thirties he was afraid of everything. He was plagued by feelings of insecurity and confusion. Truly, he had lost heart.

He went into a group of powerful men, who were also supportive. For about a year, he avoided any competitive conflict with the other men, but gradually he began to challenge them. He found out that he was capable of more battle than he thought, and that he would not be crushed as he had been when he was a child.

He even took them up on some challenges in sports activities, and competition became fun again. He was not as afraid of winning as he had been in the past, and he found that there were men whose egos could stand it.

Those feelings carried over into the work world, and he gradually tried new risks and jobs. Through the mentoring and challenging of those other authority figures, he overcame his fear of male authority. But his passive solution was just like Ralph's aggressive one. Neither one had been able to get adult authority roles in order because the original figures had disobeyed God's command, one by provoking anger and the other by causing discouragement.

Expertise

The second variable worth mentioning is that of expertise. We have seen that we are to become people of some sort of expertise. The Bible is full of examples of how we are to develop our talents and gifts. In the growing-up process, there should be ample opportunity for children to learn more and more expertise, and the parents should support that effort. In addition, the parents need to be models of expertise for children to get a picture of the value of work and industriousness. They can identify with those positively, and learn that "a desire accomplished is sweet to the soul." There are few things sadder than children who cannot be proud of the expertise and skills of their parents. They have a real need to look up to their models to be good at various things. It helps them to strive for excellence as well as to have a vicarious sense of self-esteem and the early forms of "worship" of someone other than themselves.

Expertise is also developed as the individual strengths and talents of children are recognized and built up by the parents. I remember one young man describing how he would spend hours and hours practicing a sport, only to have his father say nothing. Also, when he would want to try a new project, his father would discredit the idea. Later, in early adulthood, when he was in a position of having to go out into the world, he suffered major depression at the thought. It totally overwhelmed him because he had no image of an encouraging parent figure to cheer him on and believe in him. His expertise had not been built up.

As children develop an ability, the opportunity needs to accompany it. This does not have to be elaborate, just adequate enough to allow children to get a sense of being good at trying and learning. Parents should reward effort by providing children the resources to develop to the next level. For example, a boy learning to play baseball doesn't need the best baseball bat in the store, but it would help to have some sort of bat available when he is ready. The same concept applies to books or lessons or whatever. If children learn that they can learn, the rest of life is a cinch. They have a basic belief in their ability to develop expertise in the area they encounter, and that is an authoritative position.

Correction

Another variable is the nature of correction by the authority. We learned earlier that the relationship of the ideal to the real needs to be loving and accepting and at the same time prodding onward. Good parenting follows this guideline, just as God does with us. If one is treated harshly for failure, a fear develops toward trying anything. We all have known people who are paralyzed by fear of failure, and often that comes from a harsh authority figure's reprimand for a mistake, whether big or small.

This picture is quite different from Scripture's depiction of God's attitude toward us as we learn. Hebrews 5:14 indicates that we learn through practice, and therefore God works with us as we are learning and gaining experience: "But solid food is for the mature, who because of practice have their senses trained to discern good and evil" (NASB). Correction of children needs to be understanding and patient as they practice new skills so that they learn to love trying new things without fear.

The book of Hebrews describes an authority who is very loving toward that process of maturity:

> For we do not have a High Priest who cannot sympathize with our weaknesses, but was in all points tempted as we are, yet without sin. Let us therefore come boldly to the throne of grace, that we may obtain mercy and find grace to help in time of need (Heb. 4:15–16).

> For every high priest taken from among men is appointed for men in things pertaining to God, that he may offer both gifts and sacrifices for sins. He can have compassion on those who are ignorant and going astray, since he himself is also subject to weakness (5:1–2).

If this is a parent's attitude, learning expertise is a joyful experience.

Office

Parents need to hold an office that has authority to enforce consequences. This parental role affects the child's ability to identify with authority and to see his actions as having real power as they bring about consequences.

We have seen that in the story of Adam and Eve, God held an office as their authority. In addition, He gave them the office of steward. When their behavior was out of line, He showed the power of His office to enforce the consequences of their behavior. This instilled a basic view of the authority of God in the universe for eons to come. Human beings and the heavenly hosts learned that when He said something, He meant it.

People raised in situations where authority has no power do not learn to respect authority nor do they learn to identify with it. According to researchers, models are followed who have these characteristics: they must be warm and loving; they must have some similarity to the person following them; they must be a coping model, not a perfect one; and they must have perceived power.

Children in the developmental process need parent figures who are authoritative and have power in the *office of parent*. The respect that is gained enables children to follow them out of a healthy "fear" like the fear of the Lord, based in love. Loving power is the best sort of power to identify with, and some of that has to come not only from the person, but from the office of parent. The office being respected gives children the basis for later respecting the law, governing authorities (Rom 13:1), church authorities, the IRS, and so forth. Not only should the office of parent be identified with power, it should command respect.

Children coming from such backgrounds develop the ability to execute whatever role they have later with authority. It may be a job, a role as a homemaker, church leader, or company president. They have a model in their heads of what it means to take a role or office and execute it with authority.

Adolescence: A Normal Psychosis

If all of these processes go well, the stage is set for a healthy twelve-year-old to go crazy. That craziness is called adolescence, and it is the beginning of the undoing of the yoke of slavery called child-hood. It is the beginning of stepping into an equal role with the adult world, and like every other overthrow of government, there is usually a rebellion.

The Scripture puts the role of childhood under parents' authority in the light of slavery because one does not yet legally own his or her life. Paul compares it to being under the law:

> Now I say that the heir, as long as he is a child, does not differ at all from a slave, though he is master of all, *but is under guardians and stewards until the time appointed by the father. Even so we, when we were children, were in bondage under the elements of the world.* But when the fullness of the time had come, God sent forth His Son, born of a woman, born under the law, to redeem those who were under the law, that we might receive the adoption as sons (Gal. 4:1-5, emphasis added).

From that position of bondage, there is a rebellion until the child recognizes his freedom as an adult and then can reidentify with that role. And that, friends, can be a stormy process. During adolescence, a little person is becoming a big person and trying to take the power over his life, but he is not quite there. It is a nether land of adulthood, with all of the equipment of adulthood. The child, or near adult, has one foot in each camp, and he is in the process of overthrowing authority and becoming his own person.

Adolescence is a time of questioning authorities and choosing things for oneself. In a real sense, all parental *control* has vanished, and all that is left is parental *influence*. The parents can try to influence the child through the relationship—if they have built a sound one over the years. They can have a great influence in this time period but will have little control. By this time, the child is big enough and mobile enough to do pretty much what he wants to do. Parents can only enforce limits and consequences; it is very difficult to control an adult.

In this wonderful time of life, all sorts of things prepare one for adulthood proper. One experiences power that is different from earlier times. There is real mobility to get around and to get work that pays more than baby-sitting. Therefore, there is the buying power of money as well as the intellectual power to figure out the world and deal with it. The common cry is, "Let me do it. You always treat me like a child." The adolescent is testing his power to run his life.

Also, there is a shift in terms of the office that is respected. Parents lose a lot of respect at this time, and that is a good thing. The adolescent listens to authority figures outside the home and learns that Mom and Dad are not the only ones who know anything. Youth leaders, teachers, and coaches become valuable sources of influence, and their influence is even greater if they differ from parents! Heeding others' advice gives the child more of a feeling of *independence from parents, which is the chief task of adolescence.*

In addition, the peer group becomes the main attachment. As adolescents move into adulthood, they need the support of community and friends, in addition to that of their parents. This move is healthy for adolescents. By establishing strong peer relationships, they will have the ability to create support networks for the rest of their lives. I have seen many people in their early thirties, for example, who have never emotionally left home. As a result, when they try to separate from parents, they do not have the skills to build real support networks, and their move to adulthood does not work. They are stuck as children because they cannot depend on friends instead of parents.

Adolescents recognize more of their real skills and talents so that authority can be taken in that area. They pursue many activities and get the idea of whether or not they like sports, academia, social concerns, or the arts. They aren't ready to pick a career, but they begin to discover their basic interests and talents. They often run into problems with parents, for their interests may not be what the parents want "for them." Parents need to lose this horrible conflict or they will lose worse in the end. Things begin to be more and more the child's choice by this time. Children's choices need to be respected if they do not like certain sorts of activities.

As they realize the bents God has given them, they begin to pursue things outside of home to nurture those talents. Sports teams, school clubs, service organizations, church groups, and explorer groups are invaluable for the teen to learn more about the world. Work should become more important, and the teens should earn money in some substantial way. They also need the freedom to decide how they will spend most of their wages. If a parent remembers that adolescence is a boot camp for adulthood, the parent approaches situations by asking, "What will help them to prepare for when they will not be living here and have me around?'' That will take a lot of the power struggle out of them.

Then there is the issue of sexuality. The teen years are a wonderful time of learning about the opposite sex and how to relate in a more intimate way. They discover their bodies and experience new feelings. They learn emotionally to risk romantic attachment in a way that is much deeper than the puppy love of earlier times. They throw off the repression of the last decade of their lives, and they become factories of impulses that they have difficulty controlling as well as difficulty understanding why control is such a good idea to begin with.

They need sound guidance from parents and other authority figures that upholds the value of sex and gives proper guidelines and limits without being repressive. This is a difficult thing for most parents to do, because of the fear of the teen's sexuality. On the one hand, they do not want to destroy teen's view of sex; on the other hand, they do not want to avoid appropriate limits. Good youth leaders are very helpful here.

And in a related issue, there is the struggle with values. Teens for the first time are in a position to question what parents have taught them to be true, and they need to do this. They need to question the things that Mom and Dad believe and to come up with their own reasons for faith and other values. If their faith does not become their own, they will lose it later or become Pharisees. Exposure to good youth groups and leaders is so important, for it allows opportunity to take doubts and questions to someone other than parents. Their friends will give them all sorts of answers, so they need to have solid youth leaders and peers to relate to and go through the "valley of the shadow of death of the childhood faith" with. The Bible provides many examples of people who go through that questioning period (the prodigal, and the two sons in the vineyard, for example).

They overthrow parental standards and select their own standards and values for life. Don't get me wrong; parents are significant in this process. But teens need freedom to think and choose, to question and doubt, especially later in adolescence and early adulthood. In these times, other adults are very important in their lives.

If the process goes well, the persons who come out the other end can be called adults. They are responsible for themselves, leaving home and establishing lives of their own with their talents, direction, purpose, power, office, influence, and expertise. That is the process of adulthood and authority, and one can see why it is not an easy one.

By this time, however, they need only to be able to have a good beginning in those areas of personal power, expertise, influence, office, and healthy submission. It cannot be complete yet, just started down the right road. If the good seeds are planted for those things, as well as some good experiences in those areas, they are prepared to dive into adulthood with all of its trials and victories; each of them is ready to become an authority. They have begun to think for themselves, stand on their own two feet, disagree with authority figures, and have their own opinions. They have the tools to be released from parents to the authority of God and the brotherhood of man.

The main issue here is that they feel adequate enough in those areas to basically come out from under the one-down position to adults that they have had all their lives. They are beginning to feel more of an eye-to-eye equality with other adults and *are no longer looking to other adults to perform parental functions for them.* If they have really reached adulthood, they do not expect other adults to be performing such parental functions as thinking for them, telling them how to live or what to believe. They do not ask friends to be parents for them and run their lives. They do not seek the approval of others for self-esteem and validation or release of guilt feelings. They look to others for advice and input, but they are responsible for their own lives. That is adulthood.

The Theology of Being Released
from Parental Authority

It is essential to make the connection between this step of maturity and the spiritual implications involved. When we are talking of the adolescent passage, we are talking about the overthrow of legalistic structures that interfere with one's relationship with God. It is the overthrow of the authority of parents as godlike figures so that God can be our parent. In short, it is *adoption*. Paul equates these parental structures with the law, as we saw above. Let's look again at this perspective that will help us to understand many spiritual problems people have.

Now I say that the heir, as long as he is a child, does not differ at all from a slave, though he is master of all, but is under guardians and stewards until the time appointed by the father. Even so we, when we were children, were in bondage under the elements of the world. But when the fullness of the time had come, God sent forth His Son, born of a woman, born under the law, to redeem those who were under the law, that we might receive the adoption as sons. And because you are sons, God has sent forth the Spirit of His Son into your hearts, crying, "Abba! Father!" Therefore you are no longer a slave but a son, and if a son, then an heir of God through Christ (Gal. 4:1-7).

Paul compares being under the law to being under the slavery of childhood to "elements of the world." These elements referred to elsewhere as the rules of religion, are said to be worthless in creating real maturity:

If you died with Christ from the basic principles of the world, why, as though living in the world, do you subject yourselves to regulations—"Do not touch, do not taste, do not handle," which all concern things which perish with the using—according to the commandments and doctrines of men? These things indeed have an appearance of wisdom in self-imposed religion, false humility, and neglect of the body, but are of no value against the indulgence of flesh (Col. 2:20-23).

Basically, Paul says that we are to be freed from elementary principles, or rules of behavior, and adopted as sons of God. This freedom of parental structures leads people to a love relationship with God and an obedience to His principles of love. Also involved is a move from a rule-based way of thinking to a love-based way of thinking, which enables them to work according to *principles* instead of rules. But if people have never questioned the authority of earthly parents and parental substitutes, the givers of the first law, they cannot question the authority of the law itself and *reject its ability to save them!* That is why authority-bound people like the Pharisees are always so legalistic. They are always trying to be "good enough" to be accepted by their legalistic consciences.

Paul has a relevant comment on this point: "But before faith came, we were kept under guard by the law, kept for the faith which would afterward be revealed. Therefore the law was our tutor to bring us to Christ, that we might be justified by faith. But after faith has come, we are no longer under a tutor" (Gal. 3:23-25). We have to come out from under the law, for its tutorship is over. We are to be adopted by our new parent, God Himself! Like Paul, we must reject the notion that through obedience to parental structures we can save ourselves: "Therefore by the deeds of the law no flesh will be justified in His sight" (Rom. 3:20). This puts one into a direct relationship to God as a parent, and out of the slavery of the legal mentality: "Therefore you are no longer a slave but a son, and if a son, then an heir of God through Christ" (Gal. 4:7). This is a calling to the freedom of bond-servanthood with God, as opposed to a childhood system of rules: "But now after you have known God, or rather are known by God, how is it that you turn again to the weak and beggarly elements to which you desire to be in bondage?" (Gal. 4:9). We have to move past the system of rules and parental governing of behavior to reach a place of freedom and obedience to the Spirit.

Paul speaks of the nature of this freedom: "For you, brethren, have been called to liberty; only do not use liberty as an opportunity for the flesh, but through love serve one another. For all the law is fulfilled in one word, even in this: 'You shall love your neighbor as yourself'" (Gal. 5:13-14). He echoes Jesus' statements to the Pharisees, the authority-bound people of His time. Jesus called them to get out from under their parental-based rules and elementary ways of seeing and move toward love. They had never gone through the adolescent phase of questioning their elders and fathers and coming up with their own beliefs.

In this example, Jesus points out that their questioning of Him and judgment of His disciples came from their fusion with their parental figures and parental structures, called tradition. They were not free enough from them to see truth:

> For the Pharisees and all the Jews do not eat unless they wash their hands in a special way, holding the tradition of the elder. When they come from the marketplace, they do not eat unless they wash. And there are many other things which they have received and hold, like the washing of cups, pitchers, copper vessels, and couches. Then the Pharisees and the scribes asked Him, "Why do Your disciples not walk according to the tradition of the elders, but eat bread with unwashed hands?" He answered and said to them, "Well did Isaiah prophesy of you hypocrites, as it is written, 'This people honors Me with their lips, but their heart is far from Me,

and in vain they worship Me, teaching as doctrines the command-ments of men.' For laying aside the commandment of God, you hold the tradition of men" (Mark 7:3-8).

Then the scribes and Pharisees who were from Jerusalem came to Jesus, saying, "Why do Your disciples transgress the tradition of the elders? For they do not wash their hands when they eat bread." He answered and said to them, "Why do you also transgress the commandment of God because of your tradition?" (Matt. 15:1-3).

He tells them that they thought it was more important to them to please parent figures than to please God. Again, another fusion with the ways of their fathers:

Woe to you! For you build the tombs of the prophets, and your fathers killed them. In fact, you bear witness that you approve the deeds of your fathers; for they indeed killed them, and you build their tombs" (Luke 11:47, 48).

Here Jesus says that to approve the evil deeds of our parents and parent figures is to become like them. He calls us to question our fusion with authority, leave that allegiance, and give our allegiance to Jesus: "Do not think that I came to bring peace on the earth. . . . For I have come to 'Set a man against his father, a daughter against her mother, and a daughter-in-law against her mother-in-law'; and 'a man's enemies will be those of his own household.' He who loves father or mother more than Me is not worthy of Me. And he who loves son or daughter more than Me is not worthy of Me" (Matt. 10:34-37). Allegiance to Him must be stronger than the earthly parent-child relationship, for our parental relationship must be to God.

"Then another of His disciples said to Him, 'Lord, let me first go and bury my father.' But Jesus said to him, 'Follow Me; and let the dead bury their own dead'" (Matt. 8:21, 22). Here Jesus is saying again that there must be a separation from the allegiance to parent figures, and an allegiance to Him. Again:

"And another also said, 'Lord, I will follow You, but let me first go and bid them farewell who are at my house.' But Jesus said to him, 'No one, having put his hand to the plow, and looking back, is fit for the kingdom of God" (Luke 9:61, 62). Jesus commands a total break with the allegiance of the place from which he had come.

The Scriptures provide a few glimpses of Jesus' interaction with Mary when He began to assert His life and purpose. Up until a certain age, it is certain that He was under parental authority, as was commanded in the law. But in adulthood, things began to change. One example occurred at the beginning of the adolescent period, at age twelve. Joseph and Mary discovered that He had separated from them to go to the temple, and He said, "Why did you seek Me? Did you not know that I must be about My Father's business?" (Luke 2:49). Later, He delineated His timing to be obedient to God instead of to Mary. "Woman, what does your concern have to do with Me? My hour has not yet come" (John 2:4). Jesus was growing up and transferring His parental allegiance, just as we all must do.

In these examples, Jesus pointed out a couple of things. First there is to be a coming out from under the authority of parents and parental structures and a going toward an allegiance to Him, and second, when that happens, there is a shift in thinking from rules to principles.

On one Sabbath Jesus and His disciples, being hungry, picked some grain and ate it. But the Pharisees strongly objected, declaiming that it wasn't lawful to pick grain on a Sabbath. Jesus responded by citing the example of David, who entered the house of God and ate the consecrated bread, which was not lawful for him to eat. And He added, "Have you not read in the law that on the Sabbath the priests in the temple profane the Sabbath, and are blameless? Yet I say to you that in this place there is One greater than the temple. But if you had known what this means, 'I desire mercy and not sacrifice,' you would not have condemned the guiltless. For the Son of Man is Lord even of the Sabbath" (Matt. 12:1–8).

When Jesus says that the Son of Man is Lord of the Sabbath, He is saying that He is *higher than the rules themselves* and that the rules were made to serve His agenda of love. This reflects a shift from a rule-based thinking of black and white to a principle-based thinking of grays that must be interpreted in light of love. Our obedience to Him must supersede our obedience to traditions of our parental figures.

Rigid, pharisaical people who cannot handle ambiguity cannot tolerate this teaching. If they do not have a strict rule to apply to a situation, they are lost and will invent one, as did the Pharisees of Jesus' time. The Bible tells us to love, and if we have to do something that upsets a "tradition of the elders" in order to love, so be it. The Pharisees' theology wasn't big enough to allow for the need of the person, be it hunger or healing (Matt. 12:10–12). A theology that will not allow people to help someone who is hurting is not big enough to hold the love of God. They "condemn the guiltless" (v. 7).

I am reminded of the man I mentioned earlier who told me that if the only way an autistic child could be helped was through the intervention of therapy, it must be God's will for that child to suffer! He said that therapy has no place in the Scriptures, and if that were what the child needed, it must be God's will for the child to stay cut off from love and relationship! I actually heard that with my own ears from a spiritual leader. His theology was not big enough for love to fit in. He was not free to heal on the Sabbath. That is the case for many hurting people who need help—their spiritual leaders will not permit it unless it fits into their "theology," which is usually some "tradition of the elders." They are condemning the innocent, for they don't know what it means that God desires "mercy and not sacrifice" (Matt. 12:7).

When someone separates from legalistic elements of the world, changes take place inside, both in reasoning ability and in the ability to love. The actual thought processes change from rigid, concrete to symbolic, which permits one to understand the mysteries of God and relate to Him on a love-based relationship, growing into wisdom to apply His truth instead of hiding behind strict formulas. The gospel becomes more of a relationship between God and man than a system of rules designed to keep people in control.

The ways that people think about situations begin to change, and reasoning begins to see things in the light of love. Paul, in the great love chapter, asserts the following: "When I was a child, I spoke as a child, I understood as a child, I thought as a child; but when I became a man, I put away childish things. For now we see in a mirror, dimly, but then face to face. Now I know in part, but then I shall know just as I also am known. And now abide faith, hope, love, these three; but the greatest of these is love" (1 Cor. 13:11–13).

This step always happens when someone begins to reason as an adult, not as a black-and-white, "elemental" child. Mystery and ambiguity become more acceptable (we see "dimly"; I know "in part"), and love becomes most important. People who have not gone through the adolescent passage of coming out from under parental rules do not think of seeing dimly or partially. They think they have the "absolute" answer for everything, which explains why many thinking people are turned off to what they perceive as evangelicalism. They hear a bunch of "know it all's" who cannot tolerate mystery and are very low on love.

When we go through this step, we cling much more closely to God our Father, for we need His direction through the fog. We are not so sure of everything, and our theology does not have every answer for every situation. We need a relationship with Him instead of just a system of rules. We reach a point of going through our own Gethsemane, trying to submit to the will of God in the midst of the pain (Luke 22:42). The book of Hebrews notes, "In the days of His flesh, when He had offered up prayers and supplications, with vehement cries and tears to Him who was able to save Him from death, and was heard because of His godly fear" (5:7). That is not exactly a simple theological answer to pain; it is a relationship with God in the midst of pain. That is a vast difference, and those who need things in neat little packages cannot tolerate such a faith.

People who make this transition let go of the elements of the world and attain a real adopted relationship with God the Father. As a result, their reasoning changes to principle thinking instead of rule thinking; their theology changes to one of the "greatest of these is love"; and their faith changes from an ethical system to one of a relationship with God. That is why the step of rejecting the tradition of men and looking inside to find the real, impulsive adolescent self at times resembles utter chaos, but it is the only way to a real relationship of needing a Father. When we let go of the elemental structures that "keep things in check," then we find ourselves "poor in spirit" (Matt. 5:3) and in need of a Father. That is what being adopted is all about.

Recall the parable Jesus told about the two sons and the vineyard (Matt. 21:28–31). The one who had openly resisted and knew the nature of his sin and need could feel remorse and come into a relationship with God. But the one who passively complied with the father on the outside had not yet faced his rebellious heart. He was still a passive-agressive child who did not yet own his life, and therefore could not give it to God. People who know their sinfulness because they are not being "nice guys" and hiding from parent figures can come to a remorseful repentance and accept the fatherhood of God. When this happens, they move out of the "elements of the world," out of pharisaism, out of the slavery of childhood, out of the slavery of the law of sin and death, and into a real relationship with God through the adoption of sons through Jesus Christ. That is redemption and the spiritual adolescent passage. We must become aware of the rebellion that is underneath the outward compliance, confess it, and be welcomed home by the gracious Father.

That sort of courage of coming out from under the parental bondage allowed the spiritual greats to accomplish their stands. John the Baptist stood against the parent figures of the day. Think of trying to call the religious leaders a "brood of vipers" (Matt. 3:7) if you needed approval from parent figures! Or think of the stand Martin Luther made against the authority structure of his time that said we could not have a direct relationship with God without intermediary interpretation. What an awesome individuated stance against the "parental voices" he made!

We must feel equal to other adults to do the things that God asks us to do. We must own our lives and not need parental approval so that we can walk "not as pleasing men, but God who tests our hearts" (1 Thess. 2:4). Or, as Paul said,

> But with me it is a very small thing that I should be judged by you or by a human court. In fact, I do not even judge myself. For I know of nothing against myself, yet I am not justified by this: but He who judges me is the Lord. Therefore judge nothing before the time, until the Lord comes, who will both bring to light the hidden things of darkness and reveal the counsels of the hearts. Then each one's praise will come from God (1 Cor. 4:3–5).

Certainly, his office as an apostle was a bit different, but there is a principle here. We need to be able to fear God and not man.

Symptoms of Inability to Achieve Adulthood

Whenever we try to live adulthood from the one-down child position, there are signs of this disturbance. These symptoms reveal an inability to achieve adulthood.

Inordinate Needs for Approval

People who suffer from some sort of authority struggle often cannot function independently of approval from others. They constantly

SYMPTOMS OF INABILITY TO ACHIEVE ADULTHOOD

Anxiety attacks
Black-and-white thinking
Competitiveness
Compulsive behaviors, sexual addiction,
    and substance abuse
Dependency of functioning
Depression
Fear of disapproval
Fear of failure
Feelings of inferiority
Feelings of superiority
Guilt
Hate for authority figures
Idealization of authority
Idealization of childhood
Impulse problems and overinhibition
Inordinate needs for approval
Judgmentalism
Loss of power
Need for "permission"
No equal differences
Outbursts of rage and passive-aggressive
    behavior
Parenting others
Sexual struggles
"You can't do that" syndrome

strive to gain the approval of a "significant other," such as their boss, their spouse, their friend, their pastor, or their coworker.

This need is different from validation. That need is normal; a job done well should be commended and appropriately recognized for what it is. The kind of approval that is problematic has to do with the way the person feels about himself or the work itself. There is some sort of waiting to know if "I am good" or if the work is good until the "authority" figure pronounces it. If the figure pronounces it good, the entire self-image changes. Obviously the other's opinion carries too much weight and has taken on the role of judge and jury for the person instead of being another opinion.

Fear of Disapproval

Fear of disapproval goes along with the need for approval. Often people experience the need in terms of fear. They are inordinately anxious around an authority figure, and oftentimes anxiety can interfere with the ability to do the job well. Every time there is some sort of evaluation, the fear is activated, or there is a constant fear of being evaluated, even when there is not one planned.

One young graduate student would have panic attacks near the end of every semester. Everything would be going well until there were about three weeks left, at which time he would go into a state of tension that would increase to panic proportions. He would lose sight of the tasks at hand and focus on whether or not his professors would like his papers.

His history revealed a perfectionist father who criticized his work harshly. As a result, he had always feared his father and had never challenged his attitudes. He had remained a submissive little boy well into his twenties. Therefore, because he had never come out from under his father's rule, adult authority figures still had the role of judge in his life. They had the power to render him approved or disapproved, and exam time provided a platform for that dynamic to happen.

Gradually, as he challenged the professors, though, he learned that they weren't so powerful after all, and he eventually felt as if he were their equal. As a fruit of this battle, he could enter an evaluation without problematic anxiety. He had gone through a "rite of passage" of becoming equal with his father figures. He was a peer, and he no longer feared being judged.

Guilt

Guilt always has as a component the loss of parental approval. Therefore, someone who struggles with guilt still feels "under" the parental voice. The internal parent has not been dethroned so that it cannot punish from a lofty position.

The interesting thing about guilt is that it keeps the focus off the consequences. An adult conscience lives according to reality consequences, not guilt. An adult who gets a traffic ticket, for example, feels something about the money for the fine and maybe sadness over a violation of a value (if it is one). However, a person in the child position would feel guilt more than the reality of the consequences.

This is the same sort of battle when people feel pressure by credit card balances, bills, deadlines, assignments, and tasks. The demand itself is perceived like a parent; there is pressure to comply or one is "bad." A comply-resist dynamic is set into motion that ends up in a guilt-procrastination battle.

Sexual Struggles

People who feel one down to authority more than likely have some sexual difficulty. The reason is simple: they have not gone through the adolescent passage of disagreeing with parents and therefore overcoming guilt and repression. Sexuality is still a no-no to them because psychologically they are children who "shouldn't think about such things." In reality they are adults, but inside they feel like they are still under their parents' authority. And so psychologically, they are children. It follows, then, that children don't have sex, so there is some sort of interference in sexual functioning. This problem can manifest itself as inhibition (which is usually fear of parental criticism), problems with orgasm, guilt, loss of desire, or performance anxiety.

When people consider themselves adults on an equal basis with other adults, they believe their bodies are their own to give away to their spouses and enjoy as they please. Then there can be a mutual giving and receiving to one another.

After Sally got married, she had a complete loss of sexual desire. It had been something that had intrigued her before marriage, but as soon as the wedding came, the desire disappeared. After months of trying, she came into therapy to resolve her sexual dysfunction.

As she began to unravel the problem, it became clear that she was still "Daddy's little girl." He was overinvolved in the relationship with her and her husband, and she was still functioning as his daughter, not as a wife. She also wanted to please him as best she could. In a real sense, she had not left home.

Since she had not come out from under his authority, she was still a child inside—and children do not have sex. Also, since her main attachment was to her father, not her husband, any sexual wishes would have been too incestuous for her to handle. Consequently, her entire sexuality was repressed.

She had to let go of the relationship with her father and her wish to please him. She even wrote him a letter resigning as the one who was responsible to make him happy. As she moved through this process, she went from being a repressed little girl to a sexual woman. Because she let go of her parent, her adolescent function of sexuality was able to emerge. She began to enjoy sex and was more and more uninhibited with her husband.

Fear of Failure

People still within a parent's domain fear failure because of the disapproval of the "elemental" conscience (Gal. 4:3; Col. 2:20). They internally feel that they can be judged because of their actions. In biblical terms, they haven't been released "from under the law" (Gal. 3:23 NASB).

When they realize their standing in grace "in Christ," the dynamic of being under some sort of judge and approval standard is broken (Gal. 5:1). Therefore, they are free to practice without fear of failure and to learn without guilt and anxiety.

Need for "Permission"

Many struggle with an inordinate need for permission to do almost anything. They invariably feel that someone has to be asked, or clearance has to be received, before they can do whatever it is. They often ask, "Can I say something?" when it does not apply. They are speaking from an internal state of bondage under a parental authority.

They are hesitant to test the limits of any system or organization to find out just what is OK and what isn't. Therefore, they virtually live in a box that is much smaller than the system they belong to. Their bosses are often bothered by the amount of supervision and direction they need to make decisions because of their fear of "getting into trouble."

"You Can't Do That" Syndrome

This symptom of authority-bound people stifles creativity. Someone will come up with a new and creative way of doing something, and the authority-bound type will say, "You can't do that," or "It'll never work." It seems almost as if they have a prison cell around any creativity or anything new. They are pessimistic about trying things, preferring the "tried and true."

In reality, this stance is an overidentification with the limiting and punitive parent, always giving restrictions and rules. They have not thrown off the parent's restrictions and found their own. They are sort of like robots who do whatever their parents said, even at age forty.

Inventors and entrepreneurs hate this sort of person. They refer to people with authority problems as "tunnel-visioned" or "myopic." Everyone who has ever started a new business has heard discouraging messages from these scared observers.

Feelings of Inferiority

The term *inferiority* means "less than" or "lower than." It is easy to see, then, how people who have felt very put down or held down by authority or authority structures feel this. Often their parents have not treated them with respect as people in their own right, and they believe that personhood is reserved for "big people." They invariably look up to others. They tend to think that someone else is always better in some way. There is little feeling of equality.

Martin's life was marked by feelings of inferiority. He felt one down to many people he had contact with. A successful businessman, he had done well when he was in the servant position as a subcontractor in business transactions to the "big cheese contractor." He tried hard to please the person he was working for and, as a result, was rewarded.

At the same time, however, he suffered panic attacks when he interacted with those figures. He vacillated between fearing their disapproval of his ideas and being terrified that they would think he was too smart and then resent him. He was in a bind that made his work life a wreck.

Competitiveness

Since getting to an equal stance with others means some sort of competing with parents for the role of "boss," people who have never established equality with parents have some unresolved competitive issues that often get acted out, especially with people of the same sex.

Our earliest forms of competition come from competing with same-sex parents, and if this is not resolved into some healthy identification, then competitive struggles can linger for a long time. It is easy to see in competitive people that they are always trying to usurp the one-up person, or are trying to jockey to one-up positions themselves.

They cannot stand for anyone to win "over" them, for they think they are in a one-down position. Instead of a realization of "I lost the game," the inner message turns into "I am an inferior person." Therefore, they must win to avoid being inferior to anyone. They are often trying to still feel equal to Mom or Dad.

Loss of Power

Some individuals repeatedly give away power in relationships or feel that they lose power. To them, a relationship is not two people mutually submitting to each other's preferences in love; instead, they give all power to the other person and then obey that person like a parent. They seem to see being "in charge" as a hot potato that needs to be passed along as quickly as possible.

On the other hand, they can actually lose power to controlling and domineering people. They think what a pastor with a "strong personality" thinks. They buy the kind of Bible a spiritual leader has. They give the adult functions of life to this authority figure to a ridiculous extent. Half of the problem is that too many people are willing to play God in other people's lives. Many spiritual leaders think that their job is to parent such "children" and keep them in check instead of lead them into maturity under the lordship of Christ.

In the Christian world many people do not think for themselves; they do not question teaching or doctrine. Something is "right" because "so-and-so" says it is. If that person is a big name leader, it must be right. That was the problem Martin Luther rebelled against; he argued for the priesthood of all believers. He agreed with the Bible that all people could have a relationship with God and could listen to teachers and decide what they believed instead of being told what to believe: "But the anointing which you have received from Him abides in you, and you do not need that anyone teach you; but as the same anointing teaches you concerning all things, and is true and is not a lie, and just as it has taught you, you will abide in Him" (1 John 2:27). There is a reliance on the Holy Spirit and the Word for the persons to interpret the interpreters and thus decide for themselves what they believe. They can use other teachers to do this, but they have the final decision as to their beliefs.

No Equal Differences

People who live in a one-up and one-down world rarely consider differences to be acceptable. If someone believes something different or thinks something different, someone is "wrong." There is no such thing as a difference of opinion or an "agreement to disagree."

There is also a tendency to see other differences of taste as right or wrong. If a friend gets a certain kind of car or moves her kids to a certain school, there is an internal questioning: "Do I have the right car?" or "Should I move my kids as well?" These people experience difference as a threat; someone must be doing the wrong thing. This can happen with very small things such as what sale to go to or what clothes to buy or what sports equipment is "better." There is always a tendency to think of what is "better" between the two instead of "you like that one, and I like this one." That is the way two equal adults experience their differences.

These pharisaical minds have such a stringent list of what is "right doctrine" that the real doctrine of "love your neighbor as yourself" is missed. They are so concerned with determining how others are "wrong" that they can't love them. The Pharisees did this over and over again; they saw others as "less than" them, and therefore, bad.

Black-and-White Thinking

This problem is similar to the one above. When individuals can see the world only in black and white, right or wrong, they are stuck in a preadult way of thinking. They are thinking like an eleven-year-old. They are unable to think in terms of gray; there are no tough moral dilemmas. Everything is simple: "If the rule says it, do it."

Jesus repeatedly ran into this sort of thinking with the Pharisees, and He tried to call them past that rigidity into the adult position of love. I wish we all had a nickel for every time He heard "Is it lawful for . . . ?" They were so preoccupied with the rules and right and wrong that they could not get to wisdom, truth, and love. There was much more of a concern for being right than for being loving. They were concerned with rules; He was concerned with love.

People who are stuck here adhere to the "basic principles of the world," as Paul mentioned in Colossians 2:20–23. Those rules, such as "do not touch, do not taste, do not handle," have an "appearance of wisdom in self-imposed religion," but are worthless to bring about maturity. This is always an authority problem because someone is under the authority of man-made rules instead of God-made love. That is why the adolescent passage of "breaking the rules" is so important, as long as they are not destructive behaviors, such as license.

Judgmentalism

Judgmentalism is a fusion with the parental, legal position and a looking down on everyone else. It is a resistance to identify with the acting-out adolescent inside, and a judgment of it.

Jesus spoke to judgmental people who would not identify themselves as sinners, and therefore could not be forgiven, could not become loving. Instead they acted as if they were perfect and "above" sin: "Woe to you, scribes and Pharisees, hypocrites! For you are like whitewashed tombs which indeed appear beautiful outwardly, but inside are full of dead men's bones and all uncleanness. Even so you also outwardly appear righteous to men, but inwardly you are full of hypocrisy and lawlessness" (Matt. 23:27–28).

Anytime we look down on someone else, we have put ourselves "in Moses' seat" (Matt. 23:2) above everyone else and have not identified with the sinner within. The essence of the adolescent passage, the confession of the sinner within, gets us to a humble position under God instead of a proud position with men.

Anxiety Attacks

Both generalized and specific anxiety can be related to authority problems because there is a fear of disapproval externally as well as internally. Anxiety at this level is basically a signal that something dangerous is about to emerge into consciousness. There is a fear of disapproval from the parental conscience.

Sam came into therapy because of anxiety attacks. As we talked about them specifically, they seemed to emerge whenever he was dealing with some parent figure. Discussing a negotiation with a "father figure" in the law firm, he would be overwhelmed by anxiety.

He had self-diagnosed this as fear of authority, but in reality it was a fear of his strengths. He was afraid of his feelings of equality emerging and thus threatening the internal demand of his conscience to stay one down to father figures. In reality, each negotiation was bringing him closer to a realization of his strength, which threatened the internal parent.

He gave himself permission to grow up and challenge those parent figures, and his internal demand changed to one of permission to have equality and aggression. His anxiety went away, and his ability to close cases enormously increased. In a few years, because he had gotten rid of his fears of challenging authority figures, his income quadrupled, and his anxiety was gone. His was a fear of being equal, not of an inability to be equal. Most of this sort of anxiety comes from a fear of strength and equality instead of an inability to have strength. People are afraid of challenging the internal parent.

Impulse Problems and Overinhibition

Both license and inhibition are problems of authority at times. Some people can be so angry at authority that they completely split off any rules or standards and live lawlessly. These persons have little impulse control and do whatever they wish. These out-of-control adolescent adults have done away with authority, even God's.

On the other hand are legalists who are so bound up with guilt that they cannot even be aware of impulses; they feel inhibited to get in touch with themselves. They seem to be very shy, and they embarrass easily. That is why their friends often say to them "let your hair down sometimes"—or, in Solomon's words, "why should you destroy yourself?" (Eccles. 7:16). They don't feel free to enjoy life or their feelings.

Feelings of Superiority

Obviously, superiority is the opposite of inferiority. Some people always find a way to see themselves as better than everyone else. It can look like narcissism, or idealism, but it is really one-upsmanship. Proverbs 30:21–22 declares, "For three things the earth is perturbed, Yes, for four it cannot bear up: For a servant when he reigns. . . ." Someone who has been dominated by authority plays the superior role in a brutal way. Some people, because of their own struggle with authority, dominate others to get revenge.

Parenting Others

This symptom of thinking that one knows what others "should" do is the inability to realize one's limitations of knowledge of others' situations as well as their responsibility and adulthood to deal with them. Counselors and teachers who directly tell others what to do make persons dependent on them and do not foster their maturity, only slavery. These counselors invariably resort to justifying their omnipotence by aligning themselves with the authority of Scripture, but oftentimes they use the law as the Pharisees did to place themselves in Moses' seat. They pay little attention to the "weightier matters of the law: justice and mercy and faith" (Matt. 23:23). These people like to dominate those "under" them.

They are not like good parents; they do not allow others to go through process and time and learn to develop into mature people. They speak little of process and growth and instead demand obedience to them, thus keeping the counselee or parishioner in subjection.

You can almost spot "parenting people" by the overuse of "you should." Others often speak of feeling "crummy" or "guilty" or "convicted" after being with them. But the conviction is the type that makes individuals feel like prisoners instead of being the true conviction of God, which is tender and graceful.

Hate for Authority Figures

Sometimes people do not identify with the authority position; they resist it, either actively or passively. These adults are perpetual teenagers, never coming to an identification with the adult position and always taking adolescent cracks at leaders of any type.

The passive ones constantly criticize people in authority, and they seem to feel superior to their superiors. They undermine the decisions and wisdom of authorities and speak of them behind their backs. They are cynics who find the bad in every leader or pastor.

The active ones are the haters of authority that the Bible mentions.

They openly resist any authority figure and generally rebel against authority of any kind, including God's.

The two sons in the vineyard parable (Matt. 21:28–32) give some idea of these two positions. However, only the one who was aware of his rebellion could repent and own it.

Depression

This depression is usually of the "bad me," self-critical kind. It involves the guilt and "badness" of being under the criticism of the internal parent, and there is not yet a full realization of the freedom from parental structures. When individuals get in touch with the anger at the critical parent and use this anger in a constructive way to form their adulthood and separate through the adolescent passage, their one-down depression goes away, and they find all sorts of creativity in its place.

Compulsive Behaviors, Sexual Addiction, and Substance Abuse

Because of the loss of freedom in authority problems, many suffer compulsive behaviors. The feelings created by being in the one-down position drive some to find relief in food, drugs, alcohol, and sex. These are only symptoms of being children in pain, in bondage to the law.

Outbursts of Rage and Passive-Aggressive Behavior

We were not created to be in bondage to parent figures as adults, so a lot of anger often appears. This anger usually can go undetected for a while, but it will come out in some way, either through passive-aggressive behavior, such as procrastination, or through outbursts of rage. The anger is only a symptom of the underlying problem of being a slave in bondage.

Dependency of Functioning

This symptom is similar to giving power to others, but I emphasize its active aspect. Some people who actively avoid taking responsibility for themselves find someone to parent them in ways that they need to do for themselves. They give executive power of their lives to others, but their dependency does away with self-respect and creates a lot of rage and resentment at the "parent" figures keeping them as children.

It is not unusual for someone to marry out of this need, but then resent the partner for treating him or her as a child. There is usually a rebellion of some sort in the marriage, and the person acts out either actively or passively to get an equal standing with the spouse. Sometimes the person obtains a divorce to get autonomy from the "parent spouse," virtually acting out the adolescent rebellion toward the spouse and taking down a household in the process. Parents must allow their children to become adults before they get into situations where "finding themselves" has too great a cost to everyone concerned.

Idealization of Authority

The perception of someone in authority as perfect obviously presupposes a one-down position. People who identified with authority would realize that the authority figure is just like them, with warts and all. Idealized authority figures are not expected to have weaknesses and faults as well as strengths, even though the Scriptures tell us they will. It is always good to remind people of the sins of David, Paul, Moses, and Peter to show them that being an adult is not as scary as they think. In other words, they don't have to be perfect to pull it off. It is really only the stepping up to a different kind of childhood, that of being God's child (Gal. 4:4–5).

Idealization of Childhood

Because of the conflicts with the adult authority position, some people idealize childhood and see it as the only life worth living. They think that adulthood is something of drudgery and responsibility, and it is seen as boring. There are several reasons why this happens, but the end result is the same. There is an avoidance of assuming the authority position and, in some sense, a devaluation of it.

Barriers to Achieving Adulthood

In the same way that other tasks can be adversely affected because of convictions about ourselves, God, and others, so can the task of becoming an authority. These need to be challenged and risked in new relationships other than the ones that they developed in. These beliefs are so common that I will list only a few.

Distortions in Our View of Ourselves

"I am bad if they don't approve of me. That proves it."

"I am less than others."

"I must please others to be liked."

"I am bad if I disagree."

"My opinions are not as good as others'."

"I have no right to my opinions."

"I must get permission from others to . . ."

"I am bad if I fail."

"Sexual feelings are bad."

"My plans will never succeed."

"I should defer to their beliefs, even though I disagree."

"I need someone else to manage my life. I am not _____ enough."

"If I differ in some way, I am wrong."

"I think they should . . ."

"I shouldn't let myself feel . . ."

"I am better than they are."

"My group is the right group."

"We really have the best theology."

"Our ministry is the only *real* one."

"I know what's best for them."

"I could never teach him or her anything."

"Adulthood is out of my grasp."

Distortions in Our View of Others

"They are all disapproving and critical."

"They are better than I am."

"They will like me better if I am compliant."

"They think that I am wrong or bad for disagreeing."

"Their opinions are always right."

"They will think I am bad for failing."

"They have no weaknesses."

"They never fail like I do."

"Their beliefs are better than mine."

"They know what's best for me."

"They never feel . . ."

"They know everything."

"They are never this afraid or mad or sad or . . ."
"They will hate me for standing up to them."

Distortions in Our View of God

"God wants me to be nice to everyone."
"God wants me to always defer to authorities, never questioning."
"God does not want me to run my own life. He wants my 'leaders' to do that."
"God disapproves of me when I fail, just as my parents disapproved."
"God does not like me to be aggressive."
"God does not like me to disagree with the pastor."
"God does not allow me freedom to choose some of my own values. They are all prescribed in the Bible. There are no gray areas."
"God thinks others are more (or less) important than I am."
"God wants me to adhere to a bunch of rules."
"God likes discipline and sacrifice more than compassion, love, and relationship."

Distortions in Our View of Life

Then there are some distortions about the way that life works. Here are some examples:
"Competition is bad; someone always gets hurt."
"Disagreement is bad; someone always gets hurt."
"Conflict is bad; someone always loses."
"There is no such thing as a 'win-win' relationship."
"People pleasers are liked better than people who say what they think."
"Everything has a 'right answer,' especially since we have the Bible."
"There is a right and wrong way of seeing everything. Perspective makes no difference."
"Flexibility is license and lawlessness."
"Sexuality is evil."
" 'It' will never work."
These barriers are heartfelt convictions about God, self, and others and have been learned through experience. If they are felt, there is

probably some way in which they have been true in the family of origin; others are just a part of the preadult mind.

Skills Needed to
Achieve Adulthood

Barriers can be overcome only with work, risk, prayer, relationship, and practice. Let's look now at some skills needed in the areas of authority.

SKILLS NEEDED
TO ACHIEVE ADULTHOOD

Acknowledge talents and pursue them
Appreciate mystery and the unknown
Become a "Pharisee buster"
Deal with your sexuality
Disagree with authority figures
Discipline yourself
Gain authority over evil
Gain equality with the same-sex parent
Look for times with parent figures
*   where you can practice*
Love people who are different
Make your own decisions
Practice
Recognize the privileges of adulthood
Reevaluate beliefs
Submit to others out of freedom
View parents and authority figures realistically
Walk in good works

Reevaluating Beliefs

This skill involves developing a mind of one's own. The time has passed for "inherited beliefs," and it is time for an adult faith. Individuals determine if they believe something because they really believe it or because someone told them so. It is important to see what is a belief of "tradition" versus what are real heartfelt convictions from God, His Word, and experience. This questioning period could last a while.

Disagree with Authority Figures

Most people disagree with what they hear authority figures say and teach, but they are afraid to let themselves be aware of how strongly they disagree. Further, they are afraid to state their disagreements. If you are in a group where you are not free to have a different opinion on gray issues, the group borders on being a cult. Be very careful. These would be issues that have to do with Christian freedom, or doctrines not agreed upon by different *orthodox* groups.

Make sure that you have freedom of thought and do not make yourself "bad" for your opinions. No one is right about everything, and we all go through periods of reshaping what we think on topics. Speak them forth, and listen to the criticism. It may help you shape your views, or you can help shape others'. Critique others' thoughts as well. Disagreement is healthy—"iron sharpens iron."

View Parents and Authority Figures Realistically

Parents and other authority figures don't belong on pedestals. Be aware of their strengths and weaknesses as well as the ways that you disagree with what they believe and think. If you agree with someone on everything, you are unaware of some of your thoughts, or you are flattering that person. No two people agree on everything.

One essential aspect of this skill is to confess the sins of our fathers and then forgive them. If we idealize our parents, we are fused with their wrongness, which will make us like them, as were the Pharisees. We must disagree with bad patterns and call them sin; then we can be different from the generations that went before. Think about the spiritual heroes of the Bible and their frailties, as Hebrews points out. They were all humans, as we are.

Make Your Own Decisions

If people in your life tell you what to think, believe, do, or buy, take those functions back. You are an adult who must learn to think and act for yourself. Who cares if someone disapproves of the purchase you made? It is your money, and that is between you and God. If people say buy this or don't buy that, or read this or don't read that, or attend this or don't attend that, they are parenting you.

Giving advice or feedback is good. That isn't what I'm speaking of, for we are called to listen to that. I'm referring to the parenting "shoulds" by which people try to take away others' freedom as redeemed, adopted sons of God and become parents to them all over again. Remember the words of Paul: "But then, indeed, when you did not know God, you served those which by nature are not gods. But now after you have known God, or rather are known by God, how is it that you turn again to the weak and beggarly elements, to which you desire again to be in bondage?" (Gal. 4:8–9).

These legalists or parent figures or pushers of "weak and beggarly elements" are "not gods." Therefore, listen to their opinions, but do not feel compelled to do what they require of you. You have only one God. Listen to Him.

Look for Times with Parent Figures
Where You Can Practice

If you struggle with these issues, there is probably no shortage of parental types in your life. Therefore, you have some great opportunities to practice what you could not do when you were growing up: disagree and don't do what self-appointed human gods tell you to do.

Be aware when someone is parenting you, and take that opportunity to say what you are thinking or to disagree. You don't have to be mean or confrontational. Just say, "Well, I see your point, but I look at it differently. I think . . ." That is normal conversation, even though it may feel disrespectful to you if you have these fears. Learn to be equal with the ones who have assigned themselves as gods in your life or to whom you have given that position.

Deal with Your Sexuality

If you are embarrassed by sex, your parents are still looking down their noses at your sexuality in some way, or at least you perceive it that way. Work on reeducating yourself as to its acceptability, and try to get desensitized to the no-no attitude you have toward it. If you feel ashamed, you are in a preadolescent stage regarding sex.

Become familiar with your body, and cherish it. You may need to talk with someone you trust in order to get over the "hush-hush" feelings about sex that come from childhood. Stop whispering!

In addition, try to become more aware of your sexual feelings. This is a normal adult thing that happens around age thirteen. By repressing them, you keep other sorts of adult functions from developing as well, for you remain under parental authority as a preadolescent. All of these functions affect one another, and as your repression of your opinions lifts, so will repression of sexuality and creativity.

I worked with one woman whose sexual feelings returned by spending a few weeks becoming aware of her opinions in relation to her boss! The repression of her thoughts in relation to a female authority figure repressed other adult functions as well, and they were all recovered. You can't just repress one aspect of yourself; it usually affects many areas.

Gain Equality with the Same-Sex Parent

Most authority problems have something to do with the inability to assume the role held by the same-sex parent. There is either a dislike of the way the parent functioned in the role or a fear of taking over the role. In either case, that is the role we were born to assume: the adult role of our gender. Look at the particular ways that your parent fulfilled the role that you don't like, and choose other models. Consider what your parent did well, and appreciate that. It will help in your transition from child to adult. In addition, think of the ways that you fear usurping your parent's position. Many people fear going through the adolescent passage, for they do not want to dethrone the same-sex parent.

Acknowledge Talents and Pursue Them

Becoming an adult requires owning and recognizing the talents and gifts God has given you. You may be aware of some area in which you are gifted, and God has been telling you to develop it in some way, but you have been keeping that talent hidden.

To develop expertise, we must do something with the talents God has given us: take a course or get a mentor or do some study. But the important thing is developing the talents. If you do not know what your talents are, ask God. He will tell you. Also, get some other people's insight. Often we cannot see our strengths.

Practice

You cannot learn to be an authority and have expertise in any area if you cannot have the freedom to practice and learn. No one ever became an expert in any area without much trial and error. Whether it is homemaking, basketball, business, personal finance, teaching, Bible exegesis, or child rearing, it takes practice to develop a skill. This aspect is vital in realizing independence and adulthood.

Go out there and fail, and then laugh it off and do it again. Learn to value the process more than the result so that you can internalize the substance of the task as much as the product. People who are only results oriented do not feel like experts, nor do they enjoy their talents. It would be a good idea to learn to enjoy them; you will be exercising them for a long time.

Recognize the Privileges of Adulthood

When individuals realize what their child position is costing them in terms of freedom to develop as God intended without approval from other adults, the one-down position starts to look like prison. There is a certain "safety" to remaining in the child position, for others have to think for you; but there is a lot to lose.

Adults have freedom to choose their own talents, values, beliefs, relationship with God, tastes, friends, and church. They also can express God-given aspects of themselves, such as feelings and sexuality without inhibition and fear or need for approval from anyone else. They can be themselves. As Paul says in Galatians 4:1, the child owns everything, but is not free to use it.

Discipline Yourself

Adults discipline themselves. The book of Proverbs offers this advice:

> Go to the ant, you sluggard!
> Consider her ways and be wise,
> Which, having no captain,
> Overseer or ruler,
> Prepares her supplies in the summer,
> And gathers her food in the harvest" (6:6–8).

The key phrase here is "having no captain, overseer or ruler." In other words, the ant is not under another ant's authority, yet takes responsibility for her tasks. She has real power and expertise, and she officiates her office.

Sometimes there is a lack of discipline in the growing-up years, and we need to be accountable to someone else to learn discipline. Get a good friend to help you in this area; agree on something that you are going to be disciplined to do.

Gain Authority Over Evil

The Bible commands us to "resist the devil and he will flee from [us]" (James 4:7). Jesus said that He had given us authority to command the evil spirits. The Word and the power of Jesus' name are enough for you to bind the forces of evil as they present themselves, and if you do not know how to do this, you would do well at some point to learn about spiritual warfare. We are to take dominion over the evil one.

Submit to Others Out of Freedom

Another aspect of becoming an adult is learning to submit to others in love without an authority conflict, including government, spouses, friends, evil people, bosses, and God. When we submit in love, we really display our freedom. If it is in compliance, it is not submission. That is slavery and we shouldn't do that (Rom. 13:1; Eph. 5:21; Matt. 5:39; 1 Pet. 2:18-19; Heb. 13:17; James 4:7).

Submitting to others as God has ordained a role is an identity-affirming thing to do. It is a choice, and that always enhances us, for it is love. If it is done out of freedom, it is very helpful to bring our authority image into completion, and it is a form of worship of God for us to submit to others.

Walk in Good Works

Paul calls our attention to this point: "For we are His workmanship, created in Christ Jesus for good works, which God prepared beforehand that we should walk in them" (Eph. 2:10). In the same way that Adam was created to have dominion and exercise good works in the Garden, you have been created for a purpose.

As you work with God to find your talents and develop them, seek Him for the good works you are to walk in. They don't have to be grandiose. Perhaps you could be a link between Him and a few of your neighbors, using your skills as a homemaker, or you could use your academic skills to develop a relationship with someone in your class. Or you could donate some time in your area of authority to an orphanage or to a needy family. There is no limit as to how big or small it could be. You have some expertise somewhere, and it will help you realize your adulthood to use it in good works. That is why it was created.

On the other hand, you may be in a building time, like Paul. God may have set you aside to heal you and develop you. Give Him time to do this, and do not think you have to save the world too quickly!

Become a "Pharisee Buster"

We all have remnants of the legalistic way of thinking and remaining under the tutor of parental approval. Try to pinpoint the ways that you still operate under the old system of gaining approval in order to be OK. Look for legalistic ways that have crept into your faith and ways that you are being "made for the Sabbath." Release all of the ways that you are trying to earn approval; they can only eat away at your soul.

Appreciate Mystery and the Unknown

People with authority problems cannot tolerate mystery and the unknown. They require an answer to everything, and everything has to be wrapped up in a neat little package. Jesus kept trying to knock the Pharisees out of this rigidity.

God is in many ways "unfathomable" (Rom. 11:33-34 NASB). He is so awesome that the more we know Him, the more we realize that we don't know, and that is where worship begins. We worship His very transcendence, and it will help to appreciate the things that you cannot figure out about Him and let them be. That is why we call Him God. If you can know everything about Him, He is no longer God—you are. And that is the most serious authority problem of all. Worship His mystery. Get out of the "elemental" black-and-white, "we have all the answers" mentality that keeps God in a box. He is much greater than that.

Love People Who Are Different

This love is integral to getting into the brotherhood of man and away from sibling rivalry. People often perceive that other groups are not as good because they are still trying to be the "better child." When you can appreciate all kinds of people, you have stopped the childhood battle of being the better person and have begun to assume an equal stance with adult siblings.

An Inventory of Progress
Toward Achieving Adulthood

By now you know the purpose of taking an inventory: to redeem the past, evaluate the present, and be different in the immediate future, thus making the distant future a lot different. Let's look at those areas in terms of adulthood authority.

The Past

Your attitudes about authority came from somewhere. You must recognize where you got them so that you can actively disagree with their negative aspects and forgive the injury. This process will help you get out of conflict with the adult role so that you can assume it. You can't assume a role you hate.

1. Who were good authority figures for me in the past, and what did I appreciate about them? What kind of modeling was good that I want to cherish and keep?

2. What were some negative aspects of authority figures that I disagreed with and would like to be different from? Why did I not like these attributes, and what feelings did they bring on for me?

3. What are the strengths and weaknesses of my parents? Of my other early authority figures?

4. How did they injure me? Have I forgiven them? Why not?

5. What authority figures did I falsely comply with after I was old enough not to do that? Why?

6. What was my adolescence like? Have I entered adolescence yet? Why have I resisted becoming an adult, and who helped me resist by playing God in my life?

7. What legalists have I succumbed to? What elemental things? Why?

8. Can I think of detrimental situations where I have ended up because I let some parent figure run my life for me? What are they?

9. What talents have I omitted from developing in the past? Why?

10. Where have I fused with the ideas of someone else without thinking for myself?

11. *With whom in my life have I been afraid to disagree?*

12. *Have I come into my own sexual identity since adolescence? Am I still repressed?*

The Present

Take a prayerful inventory of the present and ask God to show you what situations are currently hurting you and keeping you from growing up.

1. *With whom do I feel one down right now? In what areas? Why? Is it a good one down as in mentoring, or is it a bad one down as in personhood?*

2. *With whom am I trying to be one up? Why? Do I realize that I am playing God in their lives?*

3. *Who am I trying to please? Why? Is it worth it? Has that pattern ever helped me?*

4. *What talents and expertise am I not developing at present because of some fear? What am I doing about the fear? Am I getting help? Am I stepping out in faith to develop that expertise and allow God to make me into an adult?*

5. *What role or office am I resisting identifying with because of conflict? Why?*

6. *What authority roles in my life am I failing to submit to lovingly (boss, police, board of elders, God, IRS)? Do I realize how destructive that is?*

7. *Which individuals am I fusing with presently in terms of their thoughts and opinions and not stating my own? With whom am I afraid to disagree?*

8. *In what situations do I hide from my sexual feelings or thoughts? Why? Who is the parent figure there?*

9. *Is there a "spiritual" group that I act "nice" around and then have another group of more adolescent friends? Why am I trying to please this "spiritual" group and then passively rebelling on the side? Is that practice keeping me a child? Which one of the people am I most afraid to be judged by? Why?*

10. *What are some doubts and questions I have about God or my theology that I am afraid to face and research on my own? What is keeping me from finding out what I believe?*

11. *What current spiritual leaders do I disagree with? Am I afraid to state my thoughts?*

12. How is my spouse functioning as a parent figure in the negative sense of the term? What about my close friends?

The Future

Carefully consider these questions pertaining to your future.

1. *What authority figure do I need to disagree with? When?*
2. *What person will I stop hiding from? When?*
3. *What ideas will I stop being afraid to voice and think about? When?*
4. *Who will I show my real thoughts to? When?*
5. *How will I get in touch with my adult sexual role? When?*
6. *What plans will I make to find and develop my expertise and be a good steward of my gifts? When?*
7. *What role will I do better at assuming authority over? When?*
8. *What person I have dominated will I apologize to? When?*
9. *Who will I stop "obeying" that I have no business obeying? How?*
10. *What sibling will I stop treating like a parent (real sibling or brother-sister in the Lord)?*
11. *What will I do the next time I hear "you should"?*
12. *What am I going to do about my lack of discipline?*

Conclusion

In looking at the problem of starting out as a little person in a big person's world and getting to be a big person, we can see what a difficult task it is. Let's review a few things.

First, realize that you were created to be an authority. You are to be God's representative in a domain. You are to have power, expertise, a role or office, influence in your group, and an ability to submit. These are all good and necessary things.

Second, recognize that there is a developmental process to achieving those things. If you missed out on some ingredients, as we all did, you need to do some work. Some good models and friends can help you develop those aspects within. Your own talents are an important aspect of the unique identity God has given you. Develop them.

Third, the chief barrier is remaining one down to other adults as if you were a child and they are parents. God has said that they are your siblings under His parenthood. This stance is founded on adherence to the law of sin and death, or the elemental ways of the world called legalism. It has to do with pleasing authority figures and remaining in bondage to parental structures, and these need to be given up to be a disciple.

Fourth, you must go through a spiritual adolescence. You must question those structures and believe and think your own thoughts, along with getting input and knowledge from others. You must stop hiding from parent figures and trying to comply with their views of what you should think, feel, and be. Question them and disagree. Disagreement is good for both of you.

Fifth, as you can accept responsibility for your life, acknowledge the role of submission to God's authority and the roles of authority that He has established in your life. This is healthy and good. Stop fighting them, for they are important structures in your life if you have chosen to submit out of freedom.

This process is basically one of becoming a "big person." God lost a lot when we decided to sell our birthright in the Garden. He had given us the role of being His authoritative representatives on earth, and we were to exercise our gifts and strengths, enjoying this role of being adults. Instead, we blew it, and He lost His creation for which we were to be stewards.

But He had a plan, and that was to have a new Adam get it back for Him. God gave Him all power and authority under heaven and earth, and He is in the process of regaining what was lost. In that process, He has granted His authority to us to fight that battle. We are to take responsibility for redeeming the time, getting into grace and truth, and growing up into the representatives that God originally started with. He has promised that if we cooperate, He will redeem the image within us that we were created with. As this happens, by our taking authority over our lives, we can be His representatives in our particular role or domain, exhibiting power, expertise, influence, role, and submission. In that pursuit, there is real fulfillment.

Allow Him to redeem in your talents what was lost. When we become men and women who are submitted to Him as He submitted to the Father, God's plan of redemption will not be defeated, and He will win back what was lost. We are a team, and we will win. Now, get out there and play ball!

Sara

In the beginning of the book, we learned about Sara. She felt symptoms of anxiety related to performance, domination by older peers, fears of disapproval from others, sexual unresponsiveness, among others. Her life was being run by everyone but her because of a one-up, one-down dynamic of people pleasing.

As she and I examined her life, most every important relationship had this quality to it. A look at her history helped her understand what had gone wrong and what needed to happen.

Sara had come from a home with very strict principles and performance-oriented parents. Her mother was what she called a "strong personality" and generally had some idea how Sara "should" do something; she even dictated what Sara should be doing. Then Sara would try to do things the way her mother wanted, only to be criticized. Her mother had not allowed her to find out what sorts of things she liked to do and to practice them at her own pace. She had not seen failure as a normal part of achieving expertise, and she would be critical of Sara when she would not do things perfectly. She generally withheld all approval from Sara, looking only at what was wrong with what Sara had done.

When Sara hit adolescence and started to find further interests and friends, her mother found fault at every turn. It seemed that the dynamic got stronger through the teen years, and her mother pressed her hard to perform in school and clubs. She wanted Sara to do the things that she approved of and did not want her to pursue interests that didn't conform to her standards.

Sara's father was somewhat distant. He did not help much in buffeting her mother's performance standards, nor did he give much approval of his own. He would criticize her if he felt she was not living up to her social protocol or achievement standard. In short, she had little room to grow.

When she became a Christian in college, she joined a rigid group. She had been well trained by that time to comply, so she did whatever the spiritual leaders asked. She was caught in a performance trap, still trying to please the parent figures and at the same time not expressing her own thoughts, opinions, and wishes that would have been disapproved of. She complied with those brothers and sisters as she had done with her parents.

When she got married, her compliance continued. She did everything possible to please her perfectionist husband. She almost always did what he wanted, unless she could find a good excuse, and pleasing him was the order of the day. In her church, she tried to do everything right.

It is easy to see her problem in light of the developmental process we have discussed in this book. She had not been allowed to pursue her own talents, opinions, and thoughts, and instead was on a performance trip. At the same time, she had never disagreed openly with her mother, and therefore was still in a preadolescent position to her. Still a child in relationship with other adults as well, she had never assumed adulthood.

When she began to understand this, she went to work on these issues. She found a couple of supportive friends who understood her needs, and they formed a regular group to meet and have mutual support. There was no parenting done by any of them, only feedback and support.

Since her parents lived nearby, she started to change in relation to her mother on their visits. Instead of trying to satisfy her mother's wishes for raising her kids, she would say things like, "I understand that you would do it that way, but I think I'll do this instead." For months, her mother could not handle this "disobedient" thirty-year-old, but over time she had to realize that Sara was not going to live to please her anymore, and she would have to deal with it.

In other settings as well, Sara began to express her opinions and thoughts. In a couples' Bible study she voiced her opinions about the material, even when they were different from the leader's. She chose clothes that she liked, which were different from her spiritual leader's tastes, and she elected to do things for her children that some of the perfectionistic women around her disapproved of. They filled her ear with the "shoulds," but she disagreed with what they said and did what she thought was best for her. Slowly, she began to fear their power less and less, and she could see that they were just humans like her. Even though they gave directions forcefully, she did not have to order her life as they wished.

She also worked on the internal parent in her head that drove her to perfection. She answered back to it and learned that she could survive the anxiety that "disobedience" brought on. Slowly, it began to dissipate.

As she looked at who she really was in light of the talents that God had given her, she took risks to develop them. She worked on her fear of failure mainly by changing her view of the perfection of her "parent figures." When she did not project so much power onto them, it was easier for her to allow herself to be human and to fail while learning.

In this process, also, she became aware of some anger that she had been denying toward the parent figures who had controlled her. She stopped blaming herself for their criticism and allowed herself to see the truth of their prideful stance toward her. She needed to see that truth so that she could stop bowing down to their self-proclaimed authority in her life. And her anger went away as a result.

She gained an awareness of her equality with other women, which affected her sexual relationship with her husband. She was more direct with him about what she liked and didn't like; she allowed herself to be less inhibited, worrying less about his disapproval. By getting some power back in the relationship with him, she forced him to become less demanding, for she put up with it less. Consequently, she turned into a much more sexual wife.

This process took quite a bit of time, prayer, and work on her part, but she won. God grew a real adult out of a thirty-year-old "little girl." She had to go through a stormy adolescence to get there, but it was worth it. She now has a feeling of being in charge of her life, no longer a little person in an adult's world, asking permission for everything. She enjoys the rights and privileges of adulthood, as she and God worked out her salvation with fear and trembling.

ing. Purpose comes from direction and truth, which form boundaries. Satisfaction comes from having the less than perfect be "good enough" in the light of God's ideal, and fulfillment comes from the adult ability to exercise talents.

And last, "the greatest of these is love" (1 Cor. 13:13). What I have written about is a model that can help us become functioning human beings. But, if that is the final goal, we have sold ourselves short. We were made to love, and the fully functioning person is one who takes his bonded, separate, forgiving, adult self into a world and denies that self for the sake of others. We have seen how this does not mean being without a person inside; it means having such a full one that it can be imparted to others.

Work on your ability to attach to others so you can have your empty heart filled. Work on setting your boundaries so you can own your own life. Work on confessing and receiving forgiveness so you can develop your real personhood. Work on assuming adulthood so you can be an authority. Then, go out and give it to others.

Remember, "Greater love has no one than this, than to lay down one's life for his friends" (John 15:13). God bless you.

HENRY CLOUD, PH.D.
Newport Beach, 1989

For more information regarding materials, tapes, seminars, or speaking engagements, write:

Dr. Henry Cloud
260 Newport Center Drive, #450
Newport Beach, CA 92660

If interested in the treatments programs of the Minirth-Meier Clinic West, call:

1-800-877-HOPE

or write to the above address.

Conclusion

I began this book with the story of four struggling Christians who had visible struggles with the issues of bonding, boundaries, good and bad, and authority. It is hoped that by now those issues have become clearer and that some other things have become clear as well. Let me comment on a few of those.

First, in terms of understanding the four issues above, there are no clear cut lines of struggle. We all struggle in all four. The Fall has affected every aspect of our being, and to some degree we will all be able to see the four issues in our lives. I think that our sanctification has a lot to do with resolving these issues in God's way.

Second, there is no such thing as either an emotional problem or a spiritual problem. We all have problems in broken relationship with God, others, and ourselves. Because of this brokenness, we develop symptoms that are felt on an emotional level and lived out in our spiritual lives. For that reason, we need a spiritual solution that involves our emotions, and any spiritual solution must be one of Love. This means that relationship reconciliation is at the base of all healing.

In the final analysis, therefore, this is a book about relationship, and the issues that must be resolved in order for us to have real relationship with God, others, and ourselves. Any solution short of a relational one is a solution short of love.

Third, our symptoms are not the problem. For years Christians have focused on the symptoms and not the issues. As a result, healing has been superficial. We must learn to use our symptoms as signs that lead us to issues. Issues can be resolved; symptoms cannot. If we resolve the issues, the symptom will no longer have a reason to be.

Fourth, meaning, purpose, satisfaction, and fulfillment are fruits of these issues. Meaning comes from love, which flows out of bond-